Do My Heart Good

Do My Heart Good

My Odyssey Through Country Music, Medicine, and History

CLEVE FRANCIS

UNIVERSITY OF ILLINOIS PRESS
Urbana, Chicago, and Springfield

CMF PRESS
NASHVILLE, TENNESSEE

To hear music by Cleve Francis, visit
countrymusichalloffame.org/CleveFrancis

Published by the University of Illinois Press
and the Country Music Foundation Press
Manufactured in the United States of America
1 2 3 4 5 C P 5 4 3 2 1
∞ This book is printed on acid-free paper.

Cataloging data available from the Library of Congress

ISBN 9780252059995 (hardcover)
ISBN 9780252089848 (paperback)
ISBN 9780252049415 (ebook)

The manufacturer's authorized representative in the EU for product safety is Mare Nostrum Group B.V., Mauritskade 21D, 1091 GC Amsterdam, The Netherlands. Email: gpsr@mare-nostrum.co.uk

Dedication

To Mary Bower Francis
March 18, 1929–April 26, 2022

Mama,

When I was a child, I spoke as a child, and I didn't know how to thank you for being my mother. I didn't know how much you gave up in your own life to give your children the life that you wanted for them. I didn't know how much you struggled, how much you cried. I didn't know how you could make us laugh even when we had nothing, how you made us understand that if we were poor in dollars we were rich in dreams. I didn't know the way your sweet smile would remain embedded in my heart. I didn't know how much you were teaching me, how you bestowed moral lessons that I would take along for the rest of my life—faith in God and hope for humankind, how you would manage to instill in me both a strong, healthy ego and at the same time a sense of humility, how the truths you embraced would make me the man I am, how you taught me the virtues of gratitude, grace, dignity, and forgiveness. I didn't know that because of your example I would dedicate my life to helping others. I didn't know why memories of that cold Christmas Eve when I was twelve would stay with me long afterward, with you bending down to kiss my cheek as the voices of the church choir floated across the congregation. I didn't know how the memory of your face, your laughter, and your presence would be mine to have and to hold forever.

Sometimes I feel as though I didn't know anything back then. Except for one thing—I always knew that you loved me and I loved you. I still do. I miss you every day.

Love,
Your son

Contents

Foreword

> Every man lives in two realms: the internal and the external. The internal is that realm of spiritual ends expressed in art, literature, morals, and religion. The external is that complex of devices, techniques, mechanisms, and instrumentalities by means of which we live.
>
> —Rev. Martin Luther King Jr.,
> Nobel Peace Prize Lecture, 1964

I met Cleve Francis in the early 1990s, when he was living in Nashville. I was the director of the Country Music Hall of Fame and Museum; Cleve was a hardworking entertainer, signed to a major record label, building a music career in a tough, competitive setting. It was an exciting time in Music City. George Strait, Randy Travis, and Patty Loveless were established acts; Alan Jackson and Martina McBride were getting started. Garth Brooks had just redefined what it meant to be a country star. Even in such company Cleve stood out. He was different: a grownup, nearing fifty, a physician, and Black.

Cleve was born in small-town Louisiana, just as World War II was winding down in Europe and Japan. Jennings was a poor, segregated community, a living embodiment of the Jim Crow South. For Cleve and his family, Jennings was mostly about limits—constraints that shaped behavior and chilled ambition, but the town managed to provide a measure of security and stability. Aided by support from his mother, who embraced hard work in school, joy in music, and the church, and by finding solace in isolation and self-reflection, young Cleve figured out how to navigate Jennings.

Once clear of Jennings, Cleve progressed through undergraduate study at Southern University, then grad school at the mostly white College of William & Mary, and finally the Medical College of Virginia. In every setting, Cleve surveyed the landscape, discovered mentors, and embraced opportunity. He was adept at managing his dealt hand: which cards to play, which to throw away, when to leave the game. And, hovering above the social framework of Jennings, Baton Rouge, Williamsburg, and Richmond were the evolving realities of the American experience—the civil rights movement, the Vietnam War, and the changing character of the popular arts.

For a Black kid coming from an impoverished, segregated town in southern Louisiana, a successful emergence into a thriving medical practice in Virginia would be story enough. But that's just part of Cleve's journey. His lifelong love of the guitar, singing, songwriting, and music itself presented a second identity—one that forged friendships and provided an ambitious Black artist and scholar with a point of entry into society wherever he lived. In time, his music helped pay the bills and became almost a second career. Combining elements of gospel, R&B, folk, and country music into a unique repertory and performance style, Cleve created a music niche that appealed to a growing live-performance audience. By 1988, when he had established a thriving practice in cardiology, Cleve had become a featured regular at the Birchmere Music Hall, a popular and prestigious performance space near Washington, DC.

And then something almost miraculous happened. Cleve was presented with a startling, once-in-a-lifetime opportunity by Jimmy Bowen, a hard-charging country music executive based in Nashville. Was Cleve willing to put everything he had worked for aside to become a country music recording artist for a major record label? Cleve Francis was faced with one of life's fork-in-the-road opportunities.

Cleve decided to take the risk. He had grappled with racism and with the challenges of building a medical practice while sustaining a respectable sideline as a popular entertainer. But Nashville was something different and—though he had no idea at the time—more intractable. He was going to find that the allure of country stardom was tempered by the hard-edged reality of a Nashville music establishment built to keep anyone perceived as an outsider at bay.

Over several decades, Nashville had established itself as the preeminent center of country music. Dubbed "Music City" in the mid-1950s, the city had solidified its position by crafting an alliance among business interests. Its music executives forged a Nashville-centric "Iron Triangle" that linked major record labels, music publishers, and radio stations from coast to coast. The system worked like this: Nashville-based companies signed performers and songwriters, financed record production, and promoted new releases to country radio stations. With luck, a new release would be programmed by dozens, even hundreds, of stations. Radio hits meant popularity and robust sales of CDs. And it meant revenue for the Nashville industry.

Lurking within Music City's friendly, aw-shucks exterior, however, was a power structure determined to thwart intrusion from outside Nashville. In the twentieth-century country music ecosystem, full-time country music radio stations were the enforcers who maintained the dominance of Nashville product. At any given time, a station might play a couple dozen records, and those records were picked for one reason: to make sure listeners didn't twist the dial to other programming and—crucially—to other advertisements. That meant programming records that felt comfortable, familiar. It was a system that didn't welcome outsiders, that didn't honor *difference*. But in 1992, when Cleve Francis arrived in Nashville, he *was* different—new, talented, and Black. With the help of his Liberty Records team, he hit the recording studio, went out on the road, and sought country stardom. Though some Nashville gatekeepers (particularly television) embraced him, radio was not welcoming, and, as Cleve recounts here, stardom without radio hits was an uphill struggle.

★ ★ ★

For Cleve Francis, his embrace of a multidimensional existence meant disciplined action directed to helping others, to nurturing family, faith, and home, and to spreading feelings and ideas through music and music making. Cleve didn't become the country star he hoped to be, but his major-label career was notable. He made a difference and put a crack in the rigid, inflexible façade of Nashville's music establishment, letting in new light. Today things are different. Spotify, Amazon, and other music streaming services have dismantled the defining power of country radio. The country music success of Black artists like Rhiannon Giddens, Kane Brown, the War and Treaty, and Darius Rucker has signaled something unimaginable a half century ago—the possibility of a full reintegration of country music. Viewed from our vantage point in the twenty-first century, Cleve's book tells an important story. It's a good one.

Bill Ivey
Nashville, Tennessee
May 2025

Author's Note

I am an unapologetic pack rat. I have kept journals, diaries, and random jottings all my life, along with newspaper clippings, letters, notebooks, and song lyrics typed carefully or scribbled down on napkins. This book was largely written from that material. A heartfelt thanks goes to my wife, Hardeep Francis, for helping to organize the archives. If you come across an exchange of dialogue from forty years ago, and think, "How could he possibly remember that?"—well, you would be right, I probably wouldn't be able to, not word for word, anyway. But the archives tell all, reveal all, document all. This is the way it happened.

Do My Heart Good

CHAPTER 1

On the Road Again

IN THE SPRING OF 1993, the band and I were rolling smoothly through the night in the heart of America, traveling by tour bus south on Interstate 165. We had just left Owensboro, Kentucky for the trip back to Nashville. Owensboro is a small city, home to the Bluegrass Hall of Fame. The town stands at the state line of Indiana, on a stretch of the Ohio River where the banks are made of yellow sand.

Earlier in the evening, I had sung my songs in front of a good-sized audience at the Owensboro fairgrounds. Though we also performed shows in the light of day, I really enjoyed night performances more. Gazing into an audience wrapped in darkness tended to focus my mind by reducing all distractions. An expanse remained in front of me, filled with silence, singing, whistling, applause. There's no better feeling in the world. Performing is like mountain climbing. Everyone wants to *have* climbed the mountain, but only a few people actually enjoy the tough hard climb. Everybody wants to be a star. How many people want to put in the necessary work?

I love the American countryside, and I especially love driving through it at night, when folks have mostly finished up their business and the land turns sleepy and peaceful. From my vantage point on the tour bus, I felt as though I were looking at the country from the outside in, removed from it and at the same time part of it, just watching America go by. I am a son of the South, so I knew this landscape well, these large tracts of farmland punctuated by small towns.

Owensboro to Bowling Green, via Masonville, Hartford, Beaver Dam. Morgantown, Sugar Grove, Hadley. Traveling the highway in the dark, I would see the lights of some sort of human settlement, a tiny foothold of civilization, slowly rising ahead of us along the interstate. A few lit-up buildings emerged from the shadows. Then we passed the town and it slid away into the dark, receding behind us.

On tour I usually didn't go to bed until after midnight. Instead I sat right behind the driver and watched the highway roll out, touched by a little white-line fever.

In my own mind, I thought of the bus drivers as vampires. They slept during the day, their vampire-coffins being motel rooms with all the shades drawn. They only came out after the sun had set, at night and in the dark. Then they appeared, pale and bloodless, possessing all the refreshed energy they would need to drive the giant carriage to our next destination. I wondered who they fed upon.

Generally, we had a new bus driver for every tour and only occasionally had a driver who had taken us out before. They were usually conservative politically and definitely not starstruck, the "glamour" of show business being totally lost on them. Tour bus driving was simply a job, getting us to the shows and back safely.

As they drove, the drivers mainly ignored their passengers, speaking via citizens band radio to other bus drivers, truckers, and even to the police. This was the early 1990s, still the era of the "10–4 good buddy" CB, and the crosstalk formed the static-heavy soundtrack for the drive. I remembered C. W. McCall's massive #1 hit "Convoy," from back in 1975.

That night on I-165 the driver's name was Danny Morel. He and I listened to the long-haul truckers shoot the breeze back and forth on the CB. The freight haulers in the big rigs loved to ridicule the state troopers, who would sweep in with flashing blue-and-red bubble lights atop their black-and-whites, setting up rolling roadblocks, slowing everyone down. Danny put in his two cents' worth, too, adding to the conversation on the citizens band.

"Hey, Smokey," he said into the CB handset, "once you get out of the way, us all can keep on going and get where we're headed."

After a blast of static, the state police answered. "We need you to mind your own business, you hear?"

The band members were quiet in the bunks behind the bus's lounge area. I could hear the dialogue from an Arnold Schwarzenegger movie a few of the guys were watching on the VCR (more antique technology). Beneath all of it came the constant hum of vulcanized tires on the road, sounding like some sort of Middle Eastern drone instrument.

Some of the music venues provided hotel-like accommodations for the acts as part of the package—showers, dressing rooms, and such. Or the bus driver would drop off the equipment, drive the band back to a hotel or motel to rest, and then take us back to the venue for the show. From there we would ride the bus back to Nashville or on to the next tour stop.

Three or four firms cornered the band tour bus business out of Nashville. There had to be fifty-one flavors of vehicles used for the purpose, from actual school buses to nightliners and executive coaches, all the way up to deluxe monsters that came equipped with hot tubs. On the other end of the spectrum in those days was a notorious rattletrap nicknamed "the Brown Bear" for its faded paint job. The Brown Bear's manual transmission made for a herky-jerky ride that every so often would jolt you out of your beauty sleep.

This string of concerts in the spring of 1993 represented my first music tour, and we hired a beautiful ride, a fifty-foot silver behemoth with pink-and-red swirly graphics on the sides. Rumor had it that my labelmate Garth Brooks used the $600-a-day sleeper on his first tour.

"Did you know there's another Nashville?" Danny the driver's voice came out of the dark. I couldn't be certain he was speaking to me. "A little village in Michigan. On a map Grand Rapids, Lansing, and Kalamazoo form a sort of a triangle. Nashville, Michigan is right in the middle of that triangle. Never been there myself."

"We are headed to the one in Tennessee, though, right?" I asked, just to make sure.

Danny laughed a "yeah," a raspy nicotine sound. I thought how these tour bus drivers must have a whole American atlas right there in their heads. Immediately behind us was the bus's lounge area, the main hangout for card-playing, movie-watching, and tall-tale telling. Then came the sleeping area, six bunks on each side of the aisle for a total of twelve. Finally, all the way back, was the so-called state room in my rolling home, aka the master bedroom.

For the members of the band, I was the Act, capital "A." It was my show, the Cleve Francis magical mystery tour. They naturally ceded the state room to me. The space had a very comfortable bed-couch, windows on each side, a television, a personal closet, a sound system, and a door that separated it from the main cabin. I set myself up back there but was surprised at how isolated I felt.

"How come nobody ever comes back and visits?" I asked Tony Hamrick, the gentle giant who served as road manager for the tour.

"Well, that's your personal room, Cleve," he said.

"I know that, and I appreciate it, but the door's always open. No need to stand on ceremony."

He glanced around at the band members, who were listening in on the exchange while pretending not to. "You're going to find out the truth sooner or later, I guess, so I might as well tell you now."

"Tell me what?" I ventured a joke. "You know how Black folks have a thing about being put in the back of the bus."

Tony laughed. "Truth is, the ass-end of the bus is where diesel fumes sometimes come up," he said. "Nobody likes sleeping back there."

I laughed, he laughed again, and the members of the band all laughed. After that, I moved my kit into one of the front bunks, reserving the state room for songwriting, guitar rehearsal, and poker—plus my private dressing room whenever I needed one.

Tony Hamrick's friendship and support was one of the great gifts country music gave me. Anyone familiar with the music business understands there's a whole platoon of hardworking folks in addition to the ones the audience sees onstage. The band is just the visible tip of the iceberg. Mostly unseen are the roadies, sound guys, publicity teams, A&R execs ("artists and repertoire," the talent scouts and song finders, who are a crucial element of a record label)—a whole crowd, right down to Danny the driver.

Standing six-foot-four at 240 pounds with a bushy red beard, Hamrick had worked security for years before becoming a tour manager. Tony's gentle presence took a huge weight off my shoulders, as he handled the million details of being on the road with a band. He set up rehearsals, got everybody on and off the bus, and made sure no one was left behind (we only lost one guy, one time, and had to go back and pick him up).

Most importantly, Tony ensured everybody got paid the thirty-five-dollar per diem for food and incidentals as well as their weekly paychecks. He was a workhorse who had been in the music business for a long time, running tours with the group Alabama and other bands.

Hamrick made for an impressive presence both physically and through his open, sunny personality. He was the big reason the random collection of souls on that bus had melded into one big family after only a few weeks together. He functioned as my road warrior and bodyguard, but most of all he was my friend. With his honeyed Georgia drawl, he always called me "Bud," which made me feel more a part of the group and recalled my childhood nickname of Butch.

Prior to this first tour I had never traveled much. I was twenty-two years old before I ever set foot outside my native state of Louisiana. For a couple of decades after that, I kept my head down and concentrated on completing my education. Then I became a doctor and opened my own cardiology practice. Back home in Alexandria, I lived only ten minutes from my office, but in the music business, the "office" could be anywhere in the country.

During a tour of radio stations the previous year, I had visited most of the major cities in the country, mainly flying in with the promotion team to places like Seattle, San Antonio, St. Louis, and Philadelphia.

"Boots-on-the-ground" tour bus travel had a different feel from air travel. It was as if I were making a house call on the real America. Because I had not yet received sufficient play on country radio, I wasn't being invited to appear at major venues in major markets, performing at stadiums or concert halls. We stayed mainly on the rural circuit: small clubs, state and county fairs, and outdoor summer festivals. I was a common man out to meet the common people.

At heart I remained a small-town country kid. Tour travel still managed to tickle me with fresh experiences, new horizons, and new worlds. Our route once took us through the busy hive of Chicago during rush hour. I enjoyed the sensation of emerging from the frantic tempo of the city's Loop, moving past the fringe suburbs and into the Illinois prairie, witnessing the quiet serenity of the countryside unfold.

I beheld some of the greatest sunrises and sunsets of my life, unobstructed by the tall buildings of civilization. After a show in Chesapeake, Virginia, I watched the sun rise over the Atlantic Ocean, bright yellow against a crystal-clear blue sky, with a pinprick of light called Venus fading in the heavens. Crossing Texas by bus I marveled at Western skies that featured towering pink-orange-purple cumulus clouds shaped like ten-gallon hats. I didn't know Texas was so big.

But while on tour, the naive excitement in my core battled with another pit-of-the-stomach emotion that I tried my best to keep tamped down.

Fear.

The music business was always a roll of the dice. I could easily visualize the bones coming up snake eyes. Folks asked me all the time, "Aren't you afraid?" In reply I'd smile and joke, pretending my knees were trembling, but I knew what they were talking about. Fear shadows show business like a phantom—flop sweat, stage fright, performance anxiety, whatever you want to call it.

Yes, I was fearful, though I never experienced the kind of paralyzing dread that stops performers in their tracks. I heard the stories of even big stars who suffered from it: Rihanna, Adele, Barbra Streisand, Eddie Van Halen. Laurence Olivier used to panic-vomit before going on stage.

My fears weren't exactly on that level. But all transitions are hard, and I was moving from a secure home environment into an unknown alien one. This time I wasn't just singing to my friends in my local club—the Birchmere Music Hall, just a few miles from where I lived, so familiar to me that it fit like a comfortable suit of clothes. On tour I'd be out there in front of crowds of complete strangers. The stage is no place for introverts.

Although I might have been a bit out of practice from working as a doctor for the past thirteen years, I tried to remain confident about my performance skills. I had kept my hand in with music, but medicine always took the lion's share of my time. At forty-six years old, I couldn't match the energy of some younger performers—no sprinting across the stage, no busting guitars, no combining singing with Olympic gymnastics. We had no Jumbotron to track my movements or intercut fan reactions.

The bred-in-the-bones paranoia of a Black man in America also figured into my vague sense of nervousness. The band and I would mainly be touring in the Deep South. I came out of that same territory. I knew all too well that if you peeled back the polite social veneer of the South it could expose all sorts of lurking demons.

I was the only Black act in venues where few Black acts had appeared. Like the Starship *Enterprise*, my mission was "to boldly go where no [Black] man has gone before." Would there be hecklers? Threats of violence? Would the country music community see me not as a real musician but as a carpetbagger? Finally, would I be shutting the door on my medical career for good?

Any level of failure on my part would have a ripple effect on the security of the entire Francis family. My mother, my sisters, and my nephews looked to me as their primary means of support.

I had other worries. I was afraid of my fear, too, afraid to confess my anxieties to others, even to Tony or the band members. I knew displaying brash confidence led the way to success, and I was afraid my fear would bleed past the façade and wreck everything. At times I felt as though I was just bluffing to make it through.

"You've got to be sincere," the comedian George Burns used to say. "If you can fake that, you've got it made."

On this tour I sang country, and I sincerely loved the music, and most of all I loved its love of story. Country music represented the last refuge of story in American popular culture. At times it seemed every other kind of music had abandoned story, from rock to rap to pop. Country delivered narratives to which everyone on the planet could relate: songs of work, songs of the road, songs of cutting loose, songs of heroes and heroines, songs of light and darkness.

Story was what drew folks to country music, people of all ages, all cultures, all races, religions, and communities. In what other genre of music could you find three generations of the same family in the audience at the same show? Tell a good story around the campfire and you'll find people coming out of the darkness to sit down and listen. "The universe is made of stories, not of atoms," said poet Muriel Rukeyser.

An hour or so out of Owensboro we made the junction at Bowling Green onto Interstate 65, heading southwest for the final run back to Nashville. The now-familiar sequence of small-town light bubbles rose up and faded in the night. Drake, Gold City, Franklin. We crossed from Kentucky into Tennessee at Mitchellville. Cross Plains, New Deal, White House.

Tour bus travel resembles travel by train, or maybe it's only a country music tour bus that feels that way. I had Johnny Cash's "Hey Porter" running through my mind. ("Hey porter! Hey porter! Would you tell me the time? How much longer will it be till we cross that Mason Dixon Line?") But stuck in my head most of all was the Steve Goodman train song I used to play in my shows, "The City of New Orleans," with its refrain, "Good morning, America, how are you? Don't you know me? I'm your native son!"

We were a long way from morning. But it wouldn't be the first time that America by night turned a traveler on the lost highway philosophical. Gazing out at the darkness, I could not help but ask how in the world I had landed there, hurtling through the South with Tony the majordomo, Danny the driver, and a band of seven kickass musicians.

We were headed toward the last stop on this leg of the tour, my most important show yet, appearing at Nashville's celebrated Fan Fair, where I would play for the largest audience I had ever faced, some 25,000 souls. Now known as CMA Fest, the annual June event featured a curious mix of huge crowds and face-to-face, personal interactions between fans and artists. Folks came to Fan Fair not just to listen to their favorite acts, but to reach out and touch them.

I had traveled a long road since my humble beginnings as a singer, many miles and many years. What was I doing here? How had it come to this? I felt a constant impulse to pinch myself and see if I was dreaming.

A false sunrise rose on the horizon ahead of us. I heard somewhere that every big city has its own nighttime light spectrum signature, a function of its kind of street illumination. Los Angeles is bronze, New York City is white-yellow, Chicago is green. What I was seeing up ahead was the indigo-tinged reflective glow of Nashville, shining on the underbellies of the clouds.

CHAPTER 2

Two Hearts Are Better Than One

ONLY A YEAR BEFORE that bus ride from Kentucky to Nashville with the band, I had no dreams whatsoever of going on the road with my music, just like I had no dreams of flying to the moon. Instead, I was comfortably established as the head of a medical practice in Virginia known as Mount Vernon Cardiology Associates, a successful enterprise that I founded and had directed for over a decade. That was my life, and it was a comfortable one. I took home a solid six-figure income. I loved medicine and thrived on helping people.

But medicine was never all that I had going on inside of me. From a very young age, music had been central to my existence. I still played locally around the Washington, DC area, singing my own songs and accompanying myself on guitar. People who knew me as a doctor called my music a hobby, a sideline, or even a side hustle. I knew it for what it was, a passion. I did music for music's sake.

I was happy enough with my low-key place in what Leonard Cohen called the "Tower of Song," or what I always thought of as "the singing tree." I was never one of those hopefuls who haunted Nashville's Music Row, knocking on doors, seeking the Big Break. I enjoyed my work as a physician very much, but it required intense focus and a great deal of time. I didn't have a master plan for a career as a singer-songwriter, and hadn't done the year-in, year-out hard work it takes to crack the entertainment industry.

What I did do, somewhat as a fling, was dig into my savings to bankroll a music video for a tune called "Love Light." Written by Glen Castleberry and Bill Graham, the song had a previous life as the B-side of Glen Campbell's hit "Rhinestone Cowboy." The cut had a lot more magic than I had realized at first, featuring a catchy, lifting beat, a country gospel sound, and a hook as sharp as a fishing barb. It all added up to a tune natural for a sing-along, and singing it always made for a good time.

'Cause the love light
Has to shine bright
Sending a strong beam
Into the cold night
And touch your soul right
Down where it's lonely
And gets warmed only
By the truest love light

Lo and behold, that humble, personally financed video ended up in heavy rotation on CMT, Country Music Television. The hugely popular syndicated channel reached over seventy million viewers. Through the wonders of cable TV, I was regularly beaming my love light into three-quarters of American households. The video rose to #9 on the CMT charts, with millions of views.

The wide distribution of "Love Light" surely represented a surprising and encouraging development. But was it encouraging enough to make me drop everything and head to Nashville? I didn't think so. I've been a risk taker all my life, but I also carefully calculated the odds before I jumped into anything new. When you take a leap, be sure to check for a landing first.

CMT played the "Love Light" video so often that I was beginning to get recognized on the street. *Okay*, I thought to myself, *that's all well and good, but I'm not going to give up my practice to do this.*

No way.

I prided myself on living a "multidimensional existence." That's really how I phrased it in my own mind. For most of my life I had embraced this concept. I've always existed in different dimensions, and the easy transfer between music and medicine made it possible for me to access a fairly constant stream of rewards. Using both sides of the brain—the creative part and the scientific part—enhanced the experience of both.

With a multidimensional existence, the possibilities were endless. I'd met people I would never have met if I had restricted my world to music or medicine alone. I had expanded my opportunities far beyond where I would have been if I had limited myself to a single dimension. I fell asleep at night looking forward to the next day.

Many of my colleagues were single-lane people, in that they focused on medicine to the exclusion of almost everything else. They were very good at what they did. Of course, they had families and some of them also loved golf, but medicine was always dominant. They tended to look curiously at my involvement in music. I witnessed them struggling to explain it to themselves as "just a hobby" of mine.

In the medical profession, a single-lane concentration is natural and vital, simply because there is so much to know. The knowledge base in medicine constantly evolves and grows. Learning is a lifelong pursuit. I certainly appreciated the truth of that, and it always bothered me that people might think I was in some way a dilettante or that I was somehow not taking the practice of medicine seriously. I read the judgment in the eyes of colleagues: How can you divide your time between these two interests? Which is your true calling?

Among my Black friends who were not in the medical profession the judgment was equally strong. Many of them looked upon me with some suspicion. A person of color does not often have the opportunity to attain the level of education I had achieved. What, you're not satisfied? You want more? Stay in your lane!

I understood these sentiments. I often had difficulty justifying this multidimensional approach to myself. I eventually resolved the dilemma by thinking in terms of rooms in a house. I had two rooms in mine, one where my primary focus was medicine, and one where music was in the fore. The two rooms were adjacent and open to each other and to some degree complementary.

The context of each room dictated my behavior. *Be true to the room you're in*, I told myself. When I was with a patient or if I was in the ER, I was always fully present. When I was onstage, I had a laser focus on making contact with the audience and submerging myself into the character of the song I was performing.

The tension involved in leading a multidimensional existence would crop up again and again in my life, and in a sense this memoir is an attempt to address this question: Was I my stage name, Cleve Francis, or was I Dr. Cleveland Francis? In the end I hope the truth is made evident. I was able to balance these two identities without any degradation in either one.

Back in 1992, a foot in both worlds seemed to work fine for me. My recent signing with Capitol Records Nashville meant I had achieved the impossible dream of landing a record contract with a major label. But I still had not made the decision as to when to stop practicing cardiology and do music full time. I'd make it happen sooner or later, I told myself. What was the rush? Cardiology had been very, very good to me. I was the multidimensional superman. I could manage both gigs for a while, couldn't I?

Or so I thought.

Then one night I got called to the emergency room where a patient of mine had presented with chest pains. I knew Buddy well and had met numerous members of his family. Right from our first meeting, the Black physician and white patient hit it off like brothers. A thin, mustachioed gent with a gentle demeanor, Buddy had come to me with the simple goal of living long enough to see his grandchildren grow up.

I lived only ten minutes from the hospital, and that night I made the trip in six. I examined my patient, looked at his EKG, and confirmed that yes, he was indeed having a heart attack. I proceeded to outline his treatment.

Buddy's internist, who had called me in to see him that night, asked if I had heard a murmur when I examined him. The internist told me that he thought he had detected one.

"Did you hear anything?" he asked.

A heart murmur, like something out of Edgar Allen Poe's story of the telltale heart, can be a dead giveaway. The sound arises from blood crossing a heart valve. Murmurs can be feathery, slight, right next door to silence. The many subtle variations can indicate both normal and abnormal functioning of the heart, depending on the setting in which they occur. As his longtime cardiologist, I knew Buddy had no history of having a cardiac murmur.

"Well, I didn't hear anything," I told the internist. But I returned to Buddy's room to check a second time.

This was in the days before medical clot busters or coronary stents, expandable metallic tubes inserted into clogged arteries to assure the smooth flow of blood. Back then, the patient had to be treated medically, not surgically. I was looking at spending the rest of the night at the hospital with Buddy.

The sounds, murmurs, rushes, and echoes of blood coursing through the chambers of the heart were the language of cardiology. I had been trained in that language and had been a student of it all my professional life.

Auscultation, listening to the heart, is something of a lost art today. When I came up through med school, the field had not yet been inundated with sophisticated technology such as sonograms and digital listening devices. During my training I was taught by the old masters, practiced in the art of examining the sounds of the heart to assist in a diagnosis.

The sounds of the heart are a scientific audioscape, certainly. But also, if you step back and think about it, as I sometimes did, a mystical one, too. Each beat propels blood to and from the organ. I was listening to the sound of life itself. Echoes of ancient oceans, eons of evolution, the flow of time and humankind and all the mysteries of existence.

When a cardiologist performs auscultation, the exterior world has to be shut out. My concentration had to be at its peak.

A heartbeat takes around zero-point-eight seconds. In that time I had to know to divide the cardiac cycle into the systolic (pumping) and the diastolic (filling) phases. On top of that, both phases had to be divided into early, mid, and late. In order to make a diagnosis and determine their significance, a cardiologist gauges the murmur's pitch (high, low, coarse) and intensity (on a scale of one to six).

I was back at Buddy's bedside just to make sure. I put the stethoscope to my patient's chest once again.

There. There it was, in the aortic area, high pitched and in the early diastolic phase. Faint enough, almost ghostly, but a sign of serious, life-threatening trouble. What I heard was a new murmur in the area of the aortic valve. This vital anatomical feature allows oxygenated blood to be pumped to the body, then shuts to prevent the blood just pumped from leaking back.

The aortic valve represents one of the wonders of the human body, with three leaflets that open and close precisely with each heartbeat. The sound I detected indicated that the precision process had been disrupted. The leaflets were being pulled apart and could not close. The trouble lay in an aortic root that anchored the valve. Normally, the aortic root remains within a finite, healthy dimension. But Buddy's was now expanding.

A dissecting aortic aneurysm is one of the true cardiac emergencies in our field. A tear occurs in the lining of the aorta, the body's main artery carrying blood away from the heart, causing it to split, or dissect. If the blood bursts through the outside aortic wall, the result will be deadly.

Technically, my patient was indeed experiencing a heart attack, but contrary to popular belief, not all heart attacks are equal. This one was caused by the blood supply being diverted away from the coronary artery. When the heart valves cannot close, when the leaflets of the aortic valve cannot function correctly, blood previously pumped leaks back into the left chamber of the heart.

It is imperative that an aortic dissection be correctly diagnosed and surgically addressed immediately. Otherwise, the patient faces the possibility of almost certain death.

We went into crisis mode. I sent Buddy in for a chest CT scan to verify the condition. Since we had no tertiary care unit at the hospital, I ordered up an emergency medical helicopter transport to transfer him to Inova Fairfax Hospital. That tertiary facility was some twenty-five miles away, but it was a trip of anywhere from half an hour to forty-five minutes in the jam-packed Beltway traffic. The air transport was quite literally a flight for life—a flight to save Buddy's life and allow him to see his grandkids grow up.

As the helicopter lifted off, I stood there in the harsh glare of the emergency room lights, struck by a blinding flash of the obvious. *Okay, this is it,* I said to myself. That multidimensional life that I thought was so fine? Maybe it wasn't just the ultimate thing after all. The practice of lifesaving cardiology could ill afford distractions.

I had been playing that game for months, ever since the "Love Light" video blew up and Capitol Records executive Jimmy Bowen gave me a call. In two weeks, I would be taking a break from medicine to run off to Nashville. My leap into a music career had developed quickly. Suddenly I had media events in New York City. There were press interviews lined up.

In New York for an appearance on *The Today Show* with Katie Couric and Bryant Gumbel, I assured the cohosts that I could balance music and medicine. But I had bumped up against a world of doubt. Gumbel introduced me (with an eyeroll) as "a doctor . . . who'd rather sing." He made it sound like the most outlandish thing in the world.

Katie Couric said her cohost Gumbel had questions for me. "Why did you put yourself through the anguish of medical school? Why didn't you decide earlier that this was something you wanted to pursue and then you wouldn't have had to go to school that long?"

She was confronting me and my double bind right there in front of a national TV audience. "This wasn't a decision I could make back then," I responded. "Maybe if a record company had offered me a music contract when I was twenty-five, I might have gone in another direction."

That's what came out of my mouth on camera, but what I wanted to say to Katie was something different: "Good lord, woman, stop asking me questions I can't answer and let me perform my song!"

Which I did, debuting my new single, "You Do My Heart Good." The title could refer to cardiology or country music, either way.

Most of my life I was happy to have twin passions. Socially, it served as a great hook. People found it interesting that I was passionate about two disciplines at once. But what they observed from the outside was a different story from what was going on in my head and my heart. Though I was managing both music and medicine, I was careful to prioritize my commitment. During my education, medical training came first. Later on, in my cardiology practice, patients were always my priority.

So music took a back seat. I never pursued it as a career. I was a doctor first, keeping my passion for music firmly in place. I needed to focus to gain and maintain the trust of patients who put their lives in my care.

"Hey, Doc, are you thinking about song lyrics right now?"

No one ever asked me that, and I never wanted even the faintest suspicion to cross the minds of my patients. As a physician, I owed them my full attention to their health. When I was singing, I wasn't thinking about medicine, but I was still a doctor. My professional obligations determined where and when I sang.

Then the "Love Light" video broke through. I had had some success in music before, but this was something else. More than simply springing on me unawares, the development totally sideswiped me. I've heard that intelligence is the relative inability to be surprised, but signing a deal with a major record label in Nashville was like winning the lottery. There's no way anyone could plan for such an unlikely occurrence.

Never before had such a stark choice been presented to me. Suddenly I was traveling all over the country, showing up in magazine spreads and on major network TV shows. The situation represented a dream come true for a lot of folks, but for me it was a "be careful what you wish for" scenario.

I had been juggling music and medicine like a circus performer. Then out of nowhere music had morphed into a monster. Singing had been a ball that I managed to keep in the air with a little art and effort. Suddenly the ball turned into a chainsaw. From being a sideshow performer, I was abruptly shoved into the center ring of the circus.

I had been a doctor who did music. Now I had become an entertainer who also happened to be a doctor. In a life-and-death situation, this was not a viable position. I had lied to Katie Couric. There could be no such thing as an even split.

Music is not normally life and death. But medicine certainly is. In fact, life and death is essentially the classic aspect of medicine. With Buddy's case, I had just been reminded once again—as if I needed reminding—that the specialty of cardiology can feature not just death, but instant death.

My mother, Mary Francis, had just called me that afternoon. Here was my first and biggest fan, the woman who had purchased my first guitar for me when I was nine. She had witnessed my musical trajectory rise higher and go further than we had ever imagined.

I was chattering on to her about Nashville and concerts and the "Love Light" video. She stopped me to dispense a dose of her tough-love wisdom.

"You just can't let music take away everything you've built in your life as a doctor," she said. Warning me against the dangers of multidimensional multitasking, in other words. She might as well have been quoting Matthew 6:24, which in the King James Version reads this way: "No one can serve two masters, for either he will hate the one and love the other, or else he will be loyal to the one and despise the other."

Apart from the Bible there are all sorts of conventional sayings about this situation, pithy little reminders folks like to print out and tack up on their office cubicle walls. "To do two things at once is to do neither." "The shorter way to do many things is to do only one thing at a time." "To make good use of your time, you've got to know what's most important and then give it all you've got." "Don't make the same decision twice."

That kind of thing.

The rhythmic beat of the flight-for-life helicopter blades broke the night silence. The emergency aircraft lifted Buddy to a cardiac surgery operating room at another hospital twenty-five miles away. I stood alone in the foyer of the ER, the faint hum and crackle of the fluorescent lights above me the only sound that broke the silence. Outside, the fresh air signaled the beginning of spring.

A voice came over the hospital loudspeaker. "Dr. Cleveland Francis, you must change your life." Well, no, that didn't happen. I was just imagining things. But I knew I had to make a decision.

CHAPTER 3

Under the Jennings Dome

A GIGANTIC WILLOW TREE stood in our backyard when I was growing up in Louisiana. It was a weeping willow, a species that I've learned is also called a Babylon willow. We had southern live oak, cypress, magnolia, pine, fig, pecan, and Chinaberry trees, too, but that lonely weeping willow was all mine. Swaying in the swing of wind, its thin green branches dropped gracefully from the tree like a fringe.

As a child I sat for hours hidden under the tree, daydreaming with my back against the textured bark of its base, or striding back and forth play-acting in the emerald circle of shade—all the time not twenty yards from our house. Because of the curtain of leaves, my parents and sisters would not even realize I was there. I could hear their nearby voices, the clatter of dishes, the creaking of the floorboards, and the slam of the screen door. But I was unseeable. I was there and not there all at the same time.

Invisibility was my superpower. The sensation brought me a childlike thrill of satisfaction and superiority. I knew where I was, but the world didn't. At least I thought so. Later on, my mother, Mary Francis, told me she used to watch me from the kitchen window, seeing right through the delicate screen of willow leaves as if her superpower was laser sight (all mothers have this superpower).

She was amazed at just how long I could remain there. The weeping willow cast its spell. I often entered into a dream state, having several little stories going on at once, acting out scenes and playing all the characters in dramas of my own invention. I performed the roles of warriors on both sides of my pretend battles. I alternated Comanche and calvary, the American soldier and the German, patriot and redcoat.

As a kid I was called by the nickname of Butch, and Butch didn't play the same games as his sisters. He was on his own. I was a solitary boy who liked to dream big, and the weeping willow enclave allowed me the freedom to do so.

The right to refuge ought to be listed among the basic universal human rights. Every person on the face of the planet needs a safe personal space, a place of protection. It's such a fundamental necessity, like food, water, and shelter, that I wonder why it's not spoken of more often. I remember the great actor Charles Laughton playing Quasimodo in *The Hunchback of Notre Dame*, calling out "Sanctuary! Sanctuary!" over and over.

That's the cry of the human soul.

My refuge served me well. When I turned nine years old and got my first guitar, that backyard sanctuary became my practice space. "Woodshedding" is slang in music for working hard on learning an instrument or a song. The term comes from beginner musicians heading out to the woodshed or some similar place, where no one would bother them and they would bother no one, because nobody was present to hear the false notes they struck. The willow tree served as my woodshed.

That first guitar of mine, a highly varnished, blue-and-white Sears Roebuck model, was hard-won. It didn't come to me right away. From the music I heard on the radio, I became fascinated with the guitar at an early age. The miracle of actually possessing one seemed unlikely to the point of being outright impossible. Other boys in the neighborhood owned guitars, like my friends Jerome Vincent and Charles Cook. But my folks could not afford to buy me one. So I contrived to make my own.

For a body I used one of my father's King Edward cigar boxes. A circle cut into the cardboard of the front functioned as a sound hole. A one-by-two length of wooden slat became a fretless but serviceable neck.

Because of the soupy Southern heat, and because the neighborhood mosquito population was numerous, ferocious, and bloodthirsty, houses in Jennings had to have screens on every window and door. So there was always a lot of screening material around, rolls of it available for making replacements or repairs. Carefully, thread by thread, I took apart a length of the metal mesh window screen and used those thin wires as the strings on my homemade guitar.

Such an ungainly monstrosity did not exactly sound like a Martin dreadnought, a Gibson Country Gentleman, or even an Arthur Godfrey plastic ukulele strung with fishing line. In fact, the King Edward Cigar Box Special didn't sound like anything known to humankind. I was plucking that thing all day long. Small mammals fled. Birds fell from the sky. My dog Jack covered his ears.

I once heard someone claim that there are no sane grade-school band teachers. The poor afflicted souls suffer day after day, listening to the fingernails-on-a-chalkboard fumbling of children learning to play an instrument. The closest I got to music with that cig-box guitar resembled the sound of a cat being strangled. I couldn't tune strings that came from a porch screen door. I couldn't manage a chord to save my life.

But Mary Francis was nothing if not a game woman, God bless her. If my mother had people come over to the house, she would call me up to sing while I stood there and strangled the cat. She would actually *feature* me.

Later on in life I marveled at the woman's fortitude. "That guitar I made when I was a kid, how did it sound?" I once asked her.

"Sounded all right," she said, keeping a perfectly straight face. "Just all right."

I suspect the family purchase of my first commercially made guitar might have been born out of my mama's frustration from hearing me play the King Edward Special. In an attempt to preserve her sanity, she started putting quarters in a jar up in the cupboard.

"Don't touch this money," she told my father and sisters. "That's for Butch's guitar."

Through the year the amount gradually grew, quarter by quarter, slow as the drip of Chinese water torture. I tried to refrain from peeking into the cupboard every minute of the day to check on the progress. A quarter went a long way in those days. Mama had to buy bread and milk for a family of six kids. But to save quarters outside of the tight household budget, just for the gift of music? That is love to an extraordinary degree.

Finally, Mary Francis had enough in the cupboard jar to go over to Sears Roebuck and make a down payment on a twenty-five-dollar guitar. The purchase process took longer than just the down payment and the ordering, since my mom also had to pay the balance before we could actually take possession. ("Buy guitars or mandolins on easy terms!" read the Sears catalog copy. "See page 1282!")

When the day of glory dawned at last, I remember going to the department store to pick up the guitar. I could hardly contain myself. Goodbye, King Edward Special, hello Silvertone 1220—Silvertone being the Sears brand name for the company's line of guitars.

Everybody has to start somewhere. B. B. King received a Stella acoustic when he was twelve years old. As was the case with me, it was a gift from his mother. Eddie Van Halen's first guitar was a fifty-dollar Lafayette, also purchased from Sears. Thirteen-year-old Eric Clapton received a West German Hoyer acoustic from his grandparents. A cheap, beat-up five-dollar acoustic came to fifteen-year-old Jimi Hendrix from his father.

Of course, I'm not in the same league as any of those guitar gods. The point I want to make is that we always hold dear the milestones in our lives. We usually remember our first day of school, our first car, our first lovemaking—and for boys in times past, it used to be their first pair of long pants. Who first put a paintbrush in Vincent van Gogh's hand? I bet he remembered. If you love music, your first guitar is going to rest in your memory like a blessing, like a kiss, like manna from heaven, as though there was a before and an after and nothing has ever been the same since.

Oh, how beautiful that instrument was! I didn't care that the damn thing was bigger than me. It was mine! The strong chemical tang of the epoxy finish overpowered my sense of smell, mixing with the odor of glue and the faint scent of wood sap that wafted from the laminated spruce body.

Here was heaven.

★ ★ ★

On Sunday, April 22, 1945, in the spring heat of the South and the darkness of predawn, before the neighborhood roosters would signal sunrise, a sixteen-year-old unmarried Louisiana girl named Mary Bower gave birth to her first child, a son. That would be me, though of course I have no memory of this most important development in my life.

In the state of Louisiana in that era, abortion did not exist as an option. Birth control and sex education remained nonexistent. The community certainly had no problem having children. Large families predominated, averaging six to eight children. The largest family in our neighborhood boasted twenty-five children. Even babies born out of wedlock, though somewhat stigmatized, were not put up for adoption but rather accepted within the brood.

I came into the world in the back room of my grandmother Ella Breaux's house, delivered by a midwife named Helen "Mammie" Mouton. My birth featured part of the placental sac called a caul, a membrane that can cover the head and face of a newborn at birth. In Louisiana as well as elsewhere, a common belief held that being born with a caul carried a mystical significance. It meant that I would grow up with the ability to see ghosts.

If I could have focused my infant eyes, I might have seen a few ghosts right there in Ella Breaux's back room.

The issue of my last name had yet to be determined. My mother had become pregnant by a local teenager by the name of Lloyd James, who was on furlough from the U.S. Navy and immediately headed back into military service. My paternity represented a particularly thorny problem, since she had promised another local boy that she would marry him.

Cleveland Francis Sr. was always called "Pete," a nickname he picked up early in life. In her youth, Mary Bower had been adopted by Pete's grandmother. She and Pete had grown up "sweet" on each other, as my mother later phrased it.

With Pete Francis gone on deployment in the army, sixteen-year-old Mary had a one-night fling at a party with Lloyd James during his navy furlough. According to my mother, when it became known that she was pregnant Lloyd James said he wanted to marry her. She refused, because she had promised that she would marry Pete. Ella Breaux also favored Mary marrying her grandson and was against her marrying the James boy. But Lloyd James was a ghost that lingered around my birth.

Mary, Pete, and Lloyd. Got it all straight? Are we on solid ground now? What a tangled web we weave. The Jennings community frowned on women who bore children out of wedlock. The local guardians of morality referred to the mothers as "whores," and the children as "bastards." Life in small-town, 1940s Louisiana could be doubly difficult for both. Mary Francis watched as Pete's father, Andrew Francis, took one look at me as a newborn and pronounced an immediate judgment.

"This baby is not a Francis," he said, and stalked out of the room.

When Mary and Pete Francis married on November 16, 1945, I was seven months old. I grew up calling Pete Francis "Daddy" and not knowing I was another man's son.

Ignorance is bliss, and during the first years of my life I was blissfully unaware of my true parentage. I also didn't have a grasp of the segregated town environment or the caste system I had been born into. We were poor, but everyone around us was poor, too.

Let me paint a picture of poverty in the Deep South of the late 1940s. The original Francis house at 300 Pearl Street in Jennings had four small rooms, no front porch, and no indoor plumbing. We used an outdoor toilet that had to be moved every six months to be placed over a new hole. My sister Fayester and I carried the "slop jar" and emptied it into the outhouse pit every morning.

Being poor meant unceasing rounds of daily, weekly, and yearly chores. Our water supply came from a faucet in the yard, from which we filled galvanized steel buckets, a gallon at a time. Kerosene powered the kitchen stove and the home's heater.

Enormous, well-established raspberry and blackberry bushes produced fruit by the basket every year. Whatever else it might be said to be, the Deep South is a cornucopia. Out of the yard, the harvest went straight into delicious berry pies.

Yardbirds and guinea hens roamed the property. When we had meat we ate Cajun jambalaya, fried chicken, smoked ham, andouille sausages, and chicken gumbo. If I could bottle the scent of Mama's cooking, you would line up and buy it by the case.

For bathing, we used a three-foot aluminum tub that had to be filled with hot water from tea kettles on the stove. As the oldest I got "first water," and my five sisters would bathe after me. The tub would then be emptied and refilled so my parents could bathe. We did this every other day. The same tub also served for washing laundry, which we hung out to dry on cotton-rope lines strung across the yard.

My parents slept in the bedroom in the front of the house. My sisters slept on mattresses in the back, next to the kitchen and my room. We did not have air conditioning the entire time I was growing up. And I'm not sure we always had electricity, since I can remember using kerosene lamps for studying.

At some point in my childhood, though, I know we got connected to the power grid, because a particularly annoying roommate came to live with me. I called it the Fat Black Bat, an enormous ventilation fan Pete Francis installed in a window of my room. The thing ran as loud as a swamp boat engine.

I didn't curse but I was tempted to learn a few choice words to address the F. B. B. directly. I even yelled at it a few times, but it gave no sign of listening. When I went down on my knees and recited my prayers every night before bed, the Fat Black Bat clattered away, so noisy I was convinced the Almighty would not be able hear my devotions.

But magically, with the passage of time, the sound faded into the background. Familiarity brought indifference. I was like the city apartment dwellers who no longer notice the thunder of the subway trains rushing by their windows. I was able to fall asleep peacefully despite—or maybe because of—the racket of the fan.

Happiness came naturally to me, a small kid, slight in stature, knocking around the green fields and single-story wood-framed houses of the neighborhood. I had a strong sense of home. Pearl Street ran directly off the town's main north-south highway, Route 26, leading down to Lake Arthur. The pavement petered out just before our house, not with a clear line but with jagged shreds of asphalt, as if city funding dried up and quit the scene. After that the street went on for a quarter mile as a single-lane dirt dogleg, turning into a muddy trough when it rained.

My world dead-ended where Pearl Street did. My mother's mother lived next door, next to an irrigation canal we simply called "the Big Ditch." The slimy, Jello-like standing water bred giant bayou mosquitoes, but was also full of frogs, turtles, and salamanders, which we hunted with childhood enthusiasm. The town dump also lay nearby, which the neighborhood kids saw not as an eyesore but a place of adventure and opportunity.

In summer, barefoot and shirtless was the only way to dress. Finding shelter in the shade of trees was another essential strategy, but one that had its own dangers. Snakes cooled off in the shade just like humans. Nested wasps, digger wasps, and cicada killers could sting like the scourges of Jesus.

A few houses down on Pearl Street stood a tumbledown shack, home to my running buddy of my grade school years, London White. He acted as Huck Finn to my Tom Sawyer. What can you say about a childhood friend of the heart, so close to you back then, but whose path would diverge from yours in later years until you became unrecognizable to one another? I keep London in memory as the fearless, rambunctious, tough-as-nails little kid he was in his youth.

The main horror of our common childhoods, beyond being bitten by a snake, was the sting of a wasp. Yellow jackets were mean and aggressive. Many times we didn't even realize we were near a large nest until it was too late. Wasp stingers felt like knives embedded under the skin and driven deep into the tissue beneath. The wound itched viciously for days.

"Do you think any folks ever got killed by a wasp?" I asked London, rubbing a recent bite of mine that had swelled to the size of one of those buboes you get from the Black Plague.

"You have it all wrong, Butch," he said. He could take on an authoritative tone like a college professor. "Don't you know a wasp won't sting if you hold your breath?"

I wasn't certain about the wisdom of this, but London for sure sounded sure. If it were true, it would represent a significant breakthrough in my childhood world. A few friends and I poked around the neighborhood and finally located a giant wasp nest. We immediately went to London's house to give him a chance to prove his theory.

When we ushered him over to the testing ground, he approached the hive with a boldness and confidence I admired. The rest of us kept a safe distance. In the Southern heat the quiet hum of the nest gave me the shivers.

"I'm going to take a deep breath and hold it," London announced. "Because that's how you do it, ya see?"

In silent anticipation we watched as a yellow jacket the size of key fob landed on the brave boy's bare arm. The insect crawled back and forth, exploring, not stinging. "See! See!" London forced the words from between closed lips so as not to disturb the little guy.

"That wasp looks sort of surprised," I said to my buddies. "Maybe London has stumbled onto something."

They nodded in solemn agreement.

The yellow jacket rose effortlessly like a miniature helicopter, transferring itself from arm to face. A split second elapsed, and then the wasp struck.

London screamed, emptying his lungs as though they had been a pair of balloons popped by the insect's stinger.

"Ay-ay-ay!" he yowled, slapping himself in the face. Other wasps joined in the attack.

We ran. The whole crew abandoned the scene and the poor victim, laughing like maniacs as we sprinted away.

Lesson learned. There's a thin line between theory and reality, and it measures about the length of a wasp's barbed stinger. At least for the remainder of the summer, all the kids of the neighborhood stuck to our proven practice of avoiding the deadly yellows altogether.

★ ★ ★

Located ninety miles west of Baton Rouge, Jennings is the county seat of Jefferson Davis Parish. They have parishes in Louisiana, instead of counties or boroughs, a heritage of the state's French and Spanish Catholic past. Our parish was named for the president of the Confederate States of America. I would grow up to attend Jefferson Davis High School. Such was the state of ignorance in which I was held, that throughout my youth I never understood who Jefferson Davis was or what he represented. I never asked. I was never taught.

In *Under the Dome*, one of his science fiction novels, Stephen King imagines a town that wakes up one morning encased in a transparent, unsmashable dome. The townspeople, unable to interact with the outside world, are left to their own devices. Typical in Stephen Kingland, it doesn't end well. The situation twists off into terror.

A strictly segregated dome of ignorance, fear, and predictability enclosed my hometown. The dome fit so snugly, and was held in place so neatly and completely, that it might as well have been some enormous bell jar. Most of the time I didn't notice the dome was there. I and everyone else who lived under it existed in a state of perpetual suffocation, and we never realized it.

A dome, a Ku Klux Klan hood, a blanket, a quilt, a cloak—it doesn't matter what you call the covering. What I'm trying to get at is that the Louisiana hometown of my youth represented a closed system, a tightly controlled zone organized by unwritten laws. With rigid social protocols firmly in place, the system laid out the boundaries of my life, my mother's life, and the lives of everyone I knew.

Do this, don't do that. Go here, don't go there. Allowed, not allowed. Rules so assumed they became inborn.

Who put the dome in place? I know that I didn't do it. I was only a child, born in 1945, a postwar baby. I could never have had a hand in creating anything covering an entire town. Who could ever have devised such a strange monstrosity?

Here's the odd thing—growing up, I sort of liked it. If I thought about it at all, which I didn't, I would have probably thought about the dome in terms of comfort and safety. I lived beneath it, grew up beneath it, and at some level I enjoyed the sense of stability, certainty, and sameness.

Yes, there was fear mixed up somewhere in the arrangement, but that element could be mistaken simply as fear of change. It's nice like this, isn't it? A place for everything, and everyone knowing their place. What if someone ripped the dome away? Then what? Chaos. Violence. Better to leave the thing in place. That way, at least, we know how to go about our days and ways in some semblance of peace and quiet. Here's three cheers for peace and quiet.

Thinking back on my hometown, I always remember the thick enveloping summer warmth against my skin, and take in the rich, slightly sour smell of earth. I recall a green so overpowering that it seemed not a color but a state of being, the green of the American South, so deep it could hurt the eye. During light rain showers, the patter of drops on our tin roof lulled me to sleep. Heavy thunderstorms were of a different order, sounding like a cannonade, as though someone poured a giant bucket of water on the roof. Claps of thunder shook the entire frame of the house.

But heat, not storms or rain, was the real dominant force of nature. The physical aspect of the Jennings dome was the Southern heat, closing down over the town, enfolding us in its grip, relentless, stifling, throttling all thought and action. The phrase "ninety degrees in the shade" is no exaggeration. August afternoons brought not a single breath of breeze to stir the air.

The area featured a pancake-flat landscape, with the surrounding countryside planted in rice, corn, and sugarcane. Jennings could definitely be classified as rural, but some of the deep pockets of the surrounding countryside were "Rural" with a capital *R*. The man who founded the town in the 1880s came from up north, in Iowa. He said he wanted to find "a place where there are no winters and no mortgages." Well, one out of two isn't bad.

Formerly the homeland of the Choctaw tribe, Jennings developed first as an agricultural outpost, then a railroad town, then, briefly, an oil town, aka "the Cradle of Louisiana Oil." The petroleum rush in Louisiana began on September 21, 1901, when a well in Jennings Field brought in the state's first gusher, seven thousand barrels a day. Though the oil boom was long gone by the time I came on the scene, here and there the pumps still worked the landscape like a species of mechanical dinosaurs. I grew up with the faint smell of petroleum wafting in the air.

The town's Carnegie Library, founded in 1889, was the oldest established library in the state of Louisiana. Colored folks were not allowed inside except to clean and empty the trash. Sidney Briscoe, a biology teacher at Jefferson Davis High and a mentor of mine, had the audacity to enter and try to check out a book. The authorities not only threw him out on his head, but they arrested him, too.

As I grew up and started to read, that town library turned into a symbol for me. I'd walk past on the opposite side of the street, as if the structure emitted radioactive rays. We could go to restaurants if we used the back door, and we had our own schools and churches, but the library was off limits to the Black population of Jennings. We couldn't enter, couldn't even shelter ourselves in the big building's generous shade.

The situation burned me, the first hint I ever got of segregation's sting. What are they hiding in there? Why do they feel the need to shut me out? I imagined enticing worlds hidden inside, Scheherazade realms, vital evidence, keys to the universe. The vision wasn't far wrong. I delight to imagine the day when a copy of this book will rest on a shelf of the Jennings library, a fortress of knowledge closed to me as a child.

Strict racial separation was also the rule at the town's movie palace, the Strand. Black patrons sat in the balcony. No one cleaned or tidied there. The bathrooms were urine-soaked and foul.

To the east of Jennings lay Têche country. The word Têche means "snake" in the Creole language, a reference to the twisty watercourses and wetlands that mark the landscape. This is the area of Louisiana that was settled and populated by *Les Acadiens*, or Cajuns, French Canadians who in the middle of the eighteenth century were evicted from their homes up north and deported to the wild bayous and marshy lowlands of a foreign country. This was the Great Upheaval, the Great Expulsion. The Acadians called it *Le Grand Dérangement*.

The turmoil of the French and Indian War triggered the forced removal of the Acadians, sent packing by the military might of the British Empire. This wholescale ejection of people from their homes can be compared with the internment of 120,000 native Japanese Americans during World War II. Or the ghettoization of Jewish people in Nazi Germany. Or the Cherokee Trail of Tears. Or the twelve million enslaved Africans transported to the New World over the course of four centuries.

Jennings encompassed ten square miles, laid out in an almost perfect square. The tracks of the Southern Pacific railroad line cut through the town diagonally, a splice so perfect it might have been done by a straight razor. The rail line broke Jennings into halves, the northeast triangle and the southwest one. There was a right side of the tracks and a wrong side. A horrible phrase, when you think about it, "the wrong side of the tracks." As if anyone living there somehow became a wrong human being.

Wrong side or right side, the dome that lay over Jennings was invisible. Someone once told me a joke about two young fish who meet an older fish swimming by. "Morning," says the old guy. "How's the water?" The young fish just nod and swim on, and one asks the other, "What the hell is water?"

That's how it was in Jennings. If you'd asked about the dome covering the town, folks would have looked at you quizzically. What dome?

★ ★ ★

As a schoolboy at James Ward Sr. Elementary School, my small stature led me to avoid any sort of physical altercation. I wasn't always successful. I was a tiny kid who was bullied all over the place. I did more running away from my adversaries than putting up my dukes. I didn't like to fight. I figured I got enough of that at home, with my nemesis daddy, Pete Francis, who never held back his hand or spared the rod.

The progressive idea of kindergarten had not yet filtered down to rural Louisiana, so the first day of first grade was my first time at James Ward. Mary Francis walked me to school, saw me into the classroom, and sat me down at my desk. She petted my head. "You be a good boy, Butch," she said, and then turned around and left. I was having none of that. I followed her out, trailing her the half mile back to Pearl Street.

When Mary Francis got home, she was still a little teary-eyed. It's always an emotional milestone for parents, putting a firstborn child in school for the first time.

"My baby looked so pitiful and alone over there," she told a neighbor.

The neighbor nodded. "Uh-huh, well, I don't know what you did, Mary, but your baby boy, he's standing right behind you."

Whirling around, Mary Francis exclaimed, "No, no, baby! You've got to stay in school!"

She brought me back, and this time I stayed. But my trials weren't over.

For some strange reason, Mary Francis had sent me to school dressed in white shorts, white shirt, white shoes and socks, with a bow tie and suspenders. I looked like nerdy Steve Urkel from the nineties TV series *Family Matters*. In that outfit, I resembled a walking invitation to bullies. I should have had a "come beat me up" sign pinned to my back.

My classmates thought I was hilarious. As soon as we got out of school, they threw me to the ground and dragged me back and forth across the lawn like a rag doll. My pretty, first-day-of-school costume looked like I was acting in the "before" sequence of a laundry detergent commercial.

After that, I had to get up and run home. My clothes were grass-stain green. My mother was fascinated. "I never could imagine a boy getting his clothes so dirty!" she marveled. My father had a different reaction. He was upset with me because I had run from my tormentors instead of staying to fight.

But as it turned out, I quickly fell in love with school. James Ward Elementary became just as much of a refuge as my backyard willow tree. I might have encountered bullying there, but at least I didn't have to face Pete Francis. Right from the start, I grasped the most vital lesson of all: I learned how to study. I became a good student.

My mother had an interesting rule. We could not come home without books. We didn't have lockers in elementary school, but most kids just left their textbooks behind on their desks.

I returned from school one day and Mary Francis confronted me. "Where are your books?"

"Oh, I'm all caught up," I said, confident and smug.

Mary Francis could throw a look that would have you questioning your right to exist. "Do you know everything in those books?" she demanded.

"No," I admitted, caught in her stare like a deer in headlights.

"Do you know everything there is to know?"

I was tongue-tied.

"No, you don't know everything, do you? I want to see you bringing your books home every single day."

Going and coming, my sisters and I had to lug our textbooks back and forth from school. My mother reviewed all report cards at the dinner table as soon as they came in. Any grade below B had to be explained and often prompted her to visit the school for a discussion with the teacher. Occasionally, I'd show up with a D in conduct for playing around or talking with my friends in class. Taking away access to my guitar was always a possible punishment.

While Black boys had the military as an escape hatch from the dome, no such option existed for Black girls. Mary Francis had given birth to five daughters. She possessed a steely-eyed determination to educate my sisters and give them a fighting chance in the world.

My mother could be extremely strict with her children, especially her girls. She monitored their social life closely, as well as their dress and overall behavior. In a small rural town, the Louisiana heat, good music, a little alcohol, and a smooth-talking rounder could change everything. She had seen it happen over and over, to herself and many others.

An unplanned pregnancy meant educational pursuits would immediately come to a halt. The smooth trajectory of life would take a screeching hairpin turn. She stood watch not only for her daughters, but for her children's children, my mother's future grandchildren.

Mary Francis was something else. She was a wise woman. For somebody who didn't have much education herself, she was ahead of her time. She took a look around and understood where she was, where we all were—under the dome in Jennings. I don't think she had any particular magical insight. She just figured something out that had escaped the notice of a lot of other folks who were in similar circumstances.

Those textbooks I was lugging home were hand-me-downs from segregated white schools on the other side of town. They came to us with ripped-out pages, stains and scribbles all over them. It didn't matter. I inhaled the knowledge contained there and looked around for more.

Whenever our old beater of a car wasn't working, my mother walked three miles to work in the morning, three back in the evening. She crossed from the wrong side of the tracks to the right side. She wore her maid's outfit, an apron and an old-fashioned woman's cap of thin white fabric, perched on her head like a crown.

A maid's uniform on a woman, like a workman's overalls on a man, indicated that a wrong-side-of-the-tracks person had ventured into the other side for an acceptable reason—to perform menial labor. Persons of color straying out of their place and not wearing a recognizable, appropriate outfit did so at their own peril.

If school wasn't in session, I went along with my mother, enlisted for work in the yard of the house she was cleaning. One day we were on our way home, crossing the boundary railroad tracks to the southwestern sector. I must have been around eleven or twelve years old, so it was 1956 or '57. I asked her a question.

"Mom, why are we colored?"

Mary Francis gave me one of those side-of-the-eyes looks. "Why are we colored?" she repeated. "Well, you know, you know," she said, stammering a little. "God made us the color we are."

I had expected a religious answer and I had gotten it. "Look at all this stuff we're passing by," I said. "All these people have got everything. They've got televisions. These kids are in there watching cartoons on Saturday morning. You're cleaning the house. I'm doing the yard work. I mean, why are we colored?"

It had taken eleven or twelve years for me to grow old enough that I could ask the question out loud.

What the hell is water? Why are we Black?

They lynched James Comeaux in Jennings on August 27, 1913. In Jefferson Davis Parish there were five lynchings in the thirty-year span between 1889 and 1918. Statewide, such incidents during the same period numbered 262 Black victims and 43 Caucasians—mostly Italian immigrants.

Some of the dead are anonymous to this day, listed on the rolls simply as "Negro," or "unnamed Negro." Though they lived and died like any of us, a few are known by a single name only, for example, "Cotton" or "Mixy."

Ostensible reasons provided for the lynchings ranged widely. Accusations included murder, rape, theft, and burglary. The entire list of causes paints a portrait of an era: "unknown cause," "race prejudice," "no offense," "slapping a white child," "insulting a white woman," "disobeying ferry regulations," "mistaken identity," "plot to kill whites," "assault on a white man," "bringing suit against a white man," miscegenation, disorderly conduct, and finally, the revealing "political causes."

Such "reasons," of course, were just rationales, just window dressing. The real motive behind the lynching of Black people had nothing to do with justice and not much to do with retribution. These were instances of domestic terrorism. They were part of the effort to maintain the dome and keep a whole sector of the population firmly controlled.

In a sense, this was why I was Black—not in terms of my skin, but in terms of my social position under the dome. Violence sowed fear and enforced the rules, backed by a whole grab bag of stereotypes, prejudices, and biases. That's what made me Black. It certainly wasn't my skin color, since that was a deep, mellow shade of brown, not black on any color wheel known to man. Whites weren't white, either—they were pink, or tan, or, as in that popular sixties rock song by Procol Harum, a whiter shade of pale.

An answer does indeed exist to that long-ago question posed by a preteen youngster to his mother as they crossed over the dividing-line Southern Pacific railroad tracks in Jennings, Louisiana. I didn't understand the answer back then. I asked Mary Francis because I really wanted to know. It would take a series of earthquake social upheavals before I came to any understanding of the reasons why some people considered me second-class, subhuman, or simply "wrong."

I had to grow into the answer on my own. I had to solve the puzzle myself. I had to escape the dome.

★ ★ ★

The people whom Mary Francis served, trekking across the tracks six times a week to clean house, were prominent figures locally. Taking advantage of the Jennings petroleum boom in the early years of the last century, Charles and Marjorie Holston had moved to town from the oil fields of

Oklahoma. The Holston home stood on East Plaquemine Street, down from Main Street and the town's Founders Park.

Charlie Holston employed my father, too. The Francis family had a long history in Jennings, and we were well respected in the Black community. Pete Francis served as a deacon at St. Paul Baptist Church. In Charlie Holston's eyes, though, he was a handyman, doing yard work, light carpentry, and odd jobs.

An undertone of humor lurked beneath Pete and Charlie's relationship. Within the Black community, "Mister Charlie" was a catchall phrase used to refer to white men in general, or the white establishment as a whole. Charlie Holston was indeed "Mister Charlie." We kept our grins over the name well hidden.

As the head of the Francis household, my father benefited from Holston's generosity. The whole family did. Charlie handed down to Pete a steady flow of barely worn Botany 500 suits and like-new brogan shoes. These clothes allowed Pete to appear well dressed among his peers. My sisters received expensive dresses and other nice clothes as gifts from the Holston family. The phrase *noblesse oblige* applied here, but it's not a concept we would ever have articulated out loud, though we felt its truth all the same.

I am trying to imagine the manifold pressures on an adult African American male within the domelike racial pressure cooker that Jennings was in those days. The miracle of it was that there wasn't more rebellion, more insurrection, more disobedience. The lesson of James Comeaux's violent end lingered in the community memory—on both sides of the racial divide. Toe the line and know your place, or what happened to Comeaux might happen to you.

Jim Crow. In case you aren't familiar with the term, it originated with a theater character from the 1800s, courtesy of New York City–born Thomas Rice, known as "the father of minstrelsy." Rice performed in blackface and sang a traditional plantation song of the enslaved, "Jump Jim Crow." The name went on to morph into an apartheid monster, referring to a set of rigid laws, unwritten rules, and discriminatory restrictions.

The story of James Comeaux's murder was from decades in the past, but other lessons from Jim Crow arose closer to home. When I was nine years old, my godfather died in a mysterious automobile accident. One of my daddy's older brothers, Uncle Theophile—it's a Creole name, pronounced "toe-feel"—arrived in Jennings from California. He blew into town in high style, driving a shiny red Cadillac convertible with a blonde, white woman beside him in the passenger's seat.

The Jennings dome being what it was, Uncle Theophile soon found himself on the receiving end of an anonymous phone call. A rough male voice with a Louisiana accent addressed him with the N-word and ordered him to get out of town pronto. Uncle T ignored the warning, maybe forgetting just exactly where he was, or perhaps misremembering his upbringing. Or it could be his time in the Golden State had convinced him he was a man and free to live his life just as he pleased.

Almost everyone in Jennings had relatives who had left and resettled in California, mostly in Los Angeles or San Francisco. Folks thought of California as a modern-day Land of Goshen, a fabled realm of freedom where you could live anywhere you wanted to live, marry who you wanted to marry, and go to schools, beaches, and theaters without restriction. A state of palm trees, orange groves, and golden skies, where Jim Crow did not abide.

The "California Dreamin'" fable left out some necessary information. The undermanned Los Angeles police department functioned as a virtual terror squad for outsiders, immigrants, and people of color, especially Latinos and African Americans, but also Asians and folks from the Caribbean, India, and Italy. Every few decades the pressure built up beneath the LA dome and the town exploded. The Zoot Suit Riots during World War II, the bloody uprising in Watts in the summer of 1965, and the Rodney King beating in 1992 show up the reality of trouble in paradise.

Uncle Theophile and his companion died horribly in that flashy red convertible, decapitated in a Jennings roadway crash a few days after he had received the anonymous warning. An accident? Most of us believed the deaths to be murders, a stark example of the dome clamping down on disturbers of the town's stratified peace.

CHAPTER 4

Cajun Days

IF YOU LIVED in the Black community in a small Southern town in the years after World War II, the church represented the center of the universe. Every aspect of life revolved around Sunday church services. Even in the juke joints and honky-tonks, folks knew on Saturday night that retribution and correction would surely come Sunday morning. The church served as a communal sanctuary just as sure as the weeping willow served as my personal one. There the community could come together, take note of each other, and monitor the children.

Religion ate up our day of rest. Sundays started with eight o'clock Bible school, then regular services began with an hour of meditation and choir music. At eleven o'clock the major service would begin, ending with the delivery of the pastor's weekly sermon. The length of the sermon depended on how strongly the pastor felt the need for his message, which depended on how far the flock had strayed.

At Union Baptist, where we worshipped, Rev. G. C. Chaney brought the hellfire and brimstone. Damnation existed physically, materially, and eternally, so concrete and factual that Rev. Chaney made us taste it. "Satan Is Real," the 1959 song of the Louvin Brothers, would have fit right in, except unsanctioned popular music was not welcomed within the precincts of the tabernacle.

But gospel music surely was embraced at Union Baptist, embraced and welcomed and cherished. The church blessed me with the great gift of song. I joined the choir, but the real singer in the family proved to be the oldest of my sisters, Fayester. She could belt out any tune, bringing the congregation to its feet and shaking the rafters down. The beautiful, layered harmonies that mark a lot of country music flowed directly out of the gospel music that most folks learned to love from attending church.

For me, a fervent young believer, church felt like a time of beauty. The service could go on until one or two in the afternoon. A baptism or religious holiday stretched the day even later. No strict time limit existed, and we could be in church all day. I can still recall the scent that drifted over my Sunday mornings in those days, a combination of linseed oil cleaner, perspiration, and magnolia blossoms, the mixture made dense and thick as incense by the Southern heat.

Everyone dressed in their Sunday best, the men with full suits and the women in colorful wide-brimmed hats with elaborate floral arrangements attached. I remember looking out at the congregation and thinking that the church resembled just how the Garden of Eden must have appeared to Adam and Eve. The scarlet, pink, yellow, and purple blooms atop the heads of the ladies bobbed up and down as they nodded in agreement with the reverend's sermon and moved to the angelic sounds of the choir.

All the children were assembled in the front rows, where we could be watched and easily reprimanded for bringing in unnecessary noise or attempting to eat candy while the service was in progress. Occasionally, if a child became too rowdy, a parent (usually the mother) would swoop in quickly and very quietly. She would drag the offender outside, sometimes by the arm, sometimes by ear, depending on the severity of the misdemeanor.

The whole congregation, me included, waited in suspense until we could hear the loud, satisfying sound—whack! Then the church door would swing open again and the criminal would be escorted back to the front row for seating. The other kids, again me included, could hardly contain ourselves with smothered laughter. Sometimes a chain reaction would occur, and the gigglers themselves would have to be escorted out.

I pretty much behaved myself, minding my p's and q's so carefully that I impressed Rev. Chaney. He asked my mother if he could take me on as an apprentice. I performed various tasks around the sanctuary. We would meet at his home during the summer to discuss Bible verses and stories from the Good Book. We fell into an easy, familial relationship. Rev. Chaney was a straight arrow, and I was a straight arrow on the straight and narrow, so we got along fine.

During this period I channeled a part of myself that I would later name "the Little Preacher." Pipsqueak preacher was more like it. The spirit moved me and with Rev. Chaney's blessing I stood up in front of the congregation and sermonized on this or that Bible passage.

Good lord, how the ladies of First Baptist loved it! I was like their pet dog who pranced on his back feet. Religious as I was, I discovered a secular side to the Little Preacher. I enjoyed the sensation of performance. I became a leader among church youth, alongside a good friend from the church, Douglas Ray Breaux. Like me, Douglas Ray would go on to a career in medicine, becoming a pharmacist and, when he completed medical school, a neurologist.

As part of my apprenticeship, I would accompany Rev. Chaney to Lake Arthur, Louisiana, ten miles south of Jennings. He took the pulpit at another Baptist church there, preaching every other week in the evenings. I had a secret motivation for liking this arrangement. My girlfriend back then, Janice McZeal, lived in Lake Arthur and attended the same church.

While Pete Francis served as deacon across town at St. Paul Baptist Church, the rest of the Francis brood stayed true to Union Baptist. Pete and my mother had five daughters, all but the last girl three years apart in age. We resembled those nested Russian dolls as we sat in the pew, each one a little smaller than the next: Fayester ("Faye"), the oldest, then Barbara, Lois Marie, Nancy Carol, and Elizabeth ("Liz"), the youngest.

As the oldest Francis sibling, I had to set the example and help take care of my younger sisters. Because of my parents' work schedules, our family was structured as a functional, hierarchical unit. The older kids had to be responsible for the younger ones. I bore responsibility for anything that happened on my watch. This meant that I had to keep my sisters safe and make sure they were fed and did whatever chores had been assigned. For most of the day, we were alone.

When I turned nine, my mother sat me down at our dining table, scaring me a little with her sudden formality.

"Cleveland," she began solemnly, not employing my usual "Butch" nickname. "Do you want to join the church?"

I was puzzled. What did she mean? Every Sunday, as far back as I could remember, we were at the Union Baptist Church practically all day. I thought I was already a member. How could I be more joined than I already was?

I asked, "What do I have to do?"

"Well, you must be baptized. Rev. Chaney dips you in water. That signifies death and being brought back to life by the grace of God."

The prospect sounded frightening. Put under water, where? In my mother's time, baptisms were done outdoors in rivers and streams.

"I gotta go in the Big Ditch?" I asked, thinking about the irrigation canal down Pearl Street from our house.

"No, no, honey," she said, smiling. My mother could light up the room with her smile, just like she could freeze up the place with her stare. She told me that the ceremony would be done at the church.

"It's an ancient ritual, Butch, goes back all the way to before John the Baptist. You're telling the Lord you are committing your life to Christianity."

The first step was to declare my intentions of becoming a Christian before the entire church congregation. After I did that, Rev. Chaney set the date for the ceremony—Easter Sunday, one of the most joyful, holiest days in the church calendar.

I arrived to find several other boys and girls who had also agreed to join the church. I had often wondered about the empty space between the pulpit and the large picture of Jesus hanging against the back wall. This area was set aside for christenings and baptisms.

On Easter Sunday morning after the 11:00 a.m. service, the assembled children stood and were formally recognized by the congregation with a chorus of "Mmm-uh-huh-yes!" and "Come to Jesus!" affirmations. We trooped into a back room to change into clothing that we would not mind getting wet. The ceremony began to be charged with a sort of sacred electricity. I felt as though I was having an out-of-body experience.

One by one our names were called. A deacon escorted us to the baptismal font where Rev. Chaney waited. He extended his hand, so familiar to me from our work and our Bible study together. The expression on his face turned serious and intense. He was wearing what looked like rubber fishing waders to protect the suit he was wearing underneath.

I stepped down into the ice-cold water. The six-foot-plus Rev. Chaney towered over me, and the water in the pool came only to his midthigh. He placed his left hand on my head.

"Cleveland Francis Jr., do you accept the Lord Jesus Christ as your personal savior?"

Shivering, I said, "Yes."

"I baptize you in the name of the Father, the Son, and the Holy Ghost."

Rev. Chaney moved his left hand to the middle of my back and placed his right hand over my face. He lowered me under the water then immediately brought me back out.

The choir burst into song. I was escorted out of the pool by another deacon and wrapped in a thin sheet. In the back room I dried myself off, put my clothes back on, and then joined the postbaptism ceremony. I was now a Christian and a member of the Union Baptist Church.

★ ★ ★

To go from the sacred to the profane, as much as the church governed our lives, I don't want to claim that it was all we had going on. While Pete and Mary's constant work obligations did not allow for anything as outlandish as a real vacation, we did manage to carve out time for visiting and celebration.

Hog slaughtering season in the fall might have been a tragic time for pigs, but it was a festive occasion for the Francis family. No telephone lines existed where we were going, but somehow the word filtered from the countryside back to us in Jennings. I remember well a specific trip we took as a family when I was no more than eight or nine. I felt a tingle of excitement when Mary Francis announced plans for the weekend.

"You get your chores done early, Butch, because we're going out to see Grandpa and Grandma come Saturday," she said.

A visit to the sharecropping farm of James ("Jimmy") and Alberta Bobb, my mother's biological father and his wife, meant a journey of ninety miles as well as a trip back in time. No electricity existed there, no indoor plumbing. The world was stranded in an earlier era. Our hometown was no metropolis, but compared to the dense, endless Louisiana countryside surrounding the farm, Jennings might as well have been New York City.

There wasn't any way to inform the grand-folks that we were on our way. We just loaded up the car, left Jack the dog in charge of protecting the Pearl Street house, and set out on the road.

Pete drove, heading north and east of Jennings toward the Atchafalaya River, passing through the fertile Louisiana countryside. Highway 90 ran east in the direction of Lafayette—Interstate 10 would not be completed until 1957. Turning north off the highway, we plunged into the dirt-road country around Opelousas. This was the Atchafalaya Basin, a watery landscape, always vulnerable to hurricanes, marked by swamps, lakes, bayous, creeks, canals, and spillways.

Acadiana. Têche country. My excited sisters and I loved to call out the names of the tiny hamlets we passed as they began to take on more and more of a Cajun flavor. Sadou, Pont des Mouton, Carencro, Grand Couteau. My parents knew the Creole language well, but to the kids the odd pronunciations sounded hilarious.

We could see our grandparents' house long before we approached it, a small black matchbox at the end of a rutted single lane drive. The homestead appeared to be marooned in a vast sea of green, flat fields of corn and soybeans, with well-tended orchards and vegetable gardens closer in. I could pick out members of the family's flock of twelve children, running and jumping around in celebration, seeing the dust cloud rising from our car and anticipating the new company coming to the isolated farm.

My grandmother would immediately set in to killing chickens and putting sweet potatoes into the cast iron oven, preparing to feed the horde. She brought in tomatoes, peas, and cucumbers from her immense vegetable garden. She gave us raw milk straight from the cow.

The whole farm and its surroundings gave off a scent of black-earth wholesomeness, but possessed a sense of mystery, too. You could stand in the fields and actually hear the corn growing, a *Psycho*-like *squee-squee-squee* as the ears rubbed against their husks. The land around the farm appeared dense, like a jungle, as if creatures went abroad out there that hadn't yet been identified by science. I hesitated to stray too far from the yard.

Spooky or not, I loved it there. I got a chance to ride horses. All the rooms were lit by the mellow glow of kerosene lamps. My grandparents got their water for drinking and cooking from a stream out back.

Their house seemed fragile. I would not have wanted to be stranded there in a storm. The place had no glass at all in the windows, just shutters to keep out the rain and screens against the mosquitoes. A giant woodstove stood in the center of the kitchen. For mattresses our humble hosts put down blankets, cushioned by layers of Spanish moss harvested off southern live oaks and bald cypress trees.

In the afternoon during our visit, neighbors started drifting in, other sharecroppers, subsistence farmers, and laborers from the surrounding area. They were all attracted by the prospect of a hog slaughter, which rose almost to the level of a ceremonial event in the neighborhood. My grandfather conducted the hog killing in a manner that probably had remained unchanged since slavery times.

A giant oak tree dominated the yard, and the slaughtering took place around that. Over a blazing woodfire rested a huge, water-filled iron kettle, the kind that in cartoons is used to roast missionaries in Africa. A squeal and a clatter of hooves announced the victim's arrival from the barn, a pink Yorkshire pig fattened to six hundred pounds, a thick ruff of backfat quivering along its spine. The visitors gathered close, and I elbowed my way to the front of the crowd. But no matter how much I was expecting it and knew it was coming, the actual event took me by surprise.

As if through a conjuror's trick, Grampa Bobb produced a .22-caliber long rifle from behind his back. Without any fussing he plugged the hog with a single shot to the back of its skull. The loud snap of the report made me jump. The pig slumped in the dirt.

Then Grampa B suddenly had a slim-bladed hunting knife in his hand (another magic trick!), and he quickly sliced the animal's jugular so the carcass would bleed it out. In quick order—everything happened boom, boom, boom!—he made precision cuts behind both Achilles tendons. Then he and a crew of others hefted the carcass up in the air, hanging the big hog by its back feet on a gaffer's hook swinging from the yard's giant oak.

The blood from the pig's jugular drained into a metal pot, with the congealing liquid to be used later for blood sausage. Dipping into the large kettle with a ladle, Jimmy Bobb splashed the animal's hide with the boiling water, afterward scraping off the loosened hair. The skin would be fried to make cracklings.

My grandparents went whole hog, utilizing every single useable part of the animal. Everything but the oink. The sole exception to the rule might have been bristles scraped from the pig's hide. Some folks used even that, binding the stiff hair together for scrubbers or toothbrushes.

I stared, open-mouthed, as the butchering began. In my memory of that day the knives seemed like light sabers, effortlessly slicing through the heavy hog flesh. The gutting led to an intense, spectacular, tumbling spill of viscera—intestines, kidneys, lungs, the heart, the liver and smaller organs, all bursting forth to reveal the empty rib cavity.

Nothing was wasted, nothing was thrown away. If Jimmy Bobb could have used the oink, he would have. Washed out and cleaned, the intestines went for chitlins, or casings for the famous Louisiana-style Boudin sausages. The animal's brain matter went into something called hog's head cheese. Bones and remnants from the stripped and carved carcass went into the large boiling pot to be rendered into lard.

Visitors around the yard lined up to be given portions of pork meat, all sorts of cuts, hams, chops, ribs, and shanks. Naturally, the Francis family received a generous helping of the choicest cuts.

As something of a joke, Pete fetched out the pig's heart from amid the mess of entrails and handed it to me. I think he was trying to faze me or gross me out somehow. It didn't seem like a friendly act, anyway. But I wouldn't give him the satisfaction of seeing me flinch.

Did having a heart in my hand foreshadow my later life as a doctor? I didn't think about it at the time, but I remember that I did examine the organ like a little scientist. How did it work? How could the gory, heavily veined wad of muscle in my hand possibly pump blood? At that young age, of course I had no idea that I would eventually become a cardiologist and make the study of the heart my life's focus.

As I write this passage, medical researchers at the University of Maryland have already transplanted pig hearts into two terminal cardiac patients who had been waiting for organ donors. Time was running out for them, so the surgeons performed the experimental operations. As the sad old phrase has it, although the operations were a success, the patients died. But they lived for weeks with a "xenotransplantation," as such cross-species procedures are termed. Surgeons have also successfully transplanted pig kidneys.

Hundreds of patients die every year while on heart transplant waiting lists. There are never enough human organs to go around. In the future, the xenotransplantation could well become refined to the degree that patients with pig hearts become a commonplace occurrence.

★ ★ ★

The countryside around my grandparents' farmhouse served as a refuge for me, and I treated it like my own private nature preserve. The lush fields, forests, and bayous hummed with wildlife, floating butterflies and divebombing flies, and of course plagues of mosquitoes, but also black bear, rabbits, and raccoons. In the air above were waterthrushes, tanagers, mockingbirds, grebes, ducks, cowbirds, thrashers, and the occasional hawk. Water was everywhere, and so were spadefoot toads, skinks, chorus frogs, crawfish, and a creature called a slimy salamander that earned its name very well.

The truth is that back then I didn't care much for nature watching. I was after different prey. Every spare opportunity, I grabbed my fishing pole and headed out in search of catfish, bass, crappies, sunfish, and bluegills. I couldn't walk far in any direction from my grandparents' farm before running up against a dark finger of gator-filled bayou.

"You don't bother them and they don't bother you," Grandma Alberta told me, and I was never the bothering-a-gator kind of boy. But I did like pulling in a big old bass and bringing it home in triumph to the family dinner table.

I was in no way an experienced angler. At home, Pete never once took me fishing. We didn't spend father-and-son time in that way. I heard folks in town talk about the wonderful sport to be had in Bayou Plaquemine Brule, a sluggish watercourse a mile east of Jennings that fed directly into Lake Arthur. But I had never made it out there myself. I always loved it when my cousins took me out to the bayous around the farm.

We would start out together and then split up to our chosen spots. I liked the solitary nature of the pursuit, my head filled with dreams and wonder, the afternoon heat stifling all sound. My focus pulled instantly back to the water whenever a fish struck my line. That water was a wonder in itself, heavy and slow-moving, blackened from mud thrown up from the bottom, and green when the surface reflected the Spanish moss and overhanging boughs of the cypress trees.

Gradually, I came to know the best places in the area to fish. My favorite was a pond-like eddy in a small creek that fed into the larger Marron Bayou. I returned to that hole again and again, spending hours on the shore, waiting for a bite. Even though I caught plenty of fish over the course of the afternoons I spent there, what sticks in my memory most vividly was an encounter not with a bass or a catfish but with another human being.

I had thought I was alone, and practically jumped out of my skin when I heard a voice come from behind my back.

"This here is my hole."

I turned to see a white kid around my own age, carrying not a cane pole like we all used, but an actual storebought fishing rod.

"What was that?" I asked, trying to be polite and nonconfrontational.

"I said, this here is my hole. I need you to leave."

I sized him up. From my youngest days I had learned to prefer retreating over fighting, but something about the kid's arrogant attitude rankled me. He was behaving like he owned the place.

"I was here first," I said simply, and turned back to fish.

Next thing I knew, the boy lashed the side of my body with his rod, wielding it like a whip. The sharp blow stung like bejesus, and I stood up. When he came at me again, I grabbed the thin end of his rod. He hung on, and I pulled the kid toward me, finally striking him hard in the chest. He dropped the rod and ran off.

I settled back in to fish, trying not to think too much about what had just happened. I didn't mention the incident to my cousins when they came to get me for dinner. We returned to the farmhouse. Grandma Alberta had food prepared and we were getting ready to eat. Grandfather Jimmy wasn't there, but he came in soon after, a stormy look on his face.

"Butch, I have to know what happened," he demanded.

"What?" I had the sinking feeling that I knew exactly what he was talking about.

"I just got called over to Victor Stoneman's house," Jimmy Bobb said, naming a white neighbor.

I looked down at my plate, shamefaced even though I knew deep down I was not to blame for the incident at the Marron Bayou. My sisters didn't dare to let a change of expression cross their faces.

"Mr. Victor says I got to bring you over there. He told me if I wanted to do it, or if I wanted him to do it, either way you was to get whipped in the yard in front of his son. If you take your punishment, he's going to let what happened pass. He says if I don't bring you over, he'll come over with some of his friends and do it here."

The whole room fell silent. My mother gave me one of her Mary Francis–special looks, Pete Francis stared angrily, and my grandmother stopped serving the food and gave me a dark look, too.

"I was there first," I said, small-voiced.

It didn't matter. I could have been right as rain and it still would not have altered the rules that Jim Crow laid down over our lives. I was a colored kid who had struck a white boy. Nothing else needed to be said. Under the unwritten laws of the dome, Black males—fathers or grandfathers, uncles or brothers—were rendered incapable of protecting their families from harm. The situation led to the further shattering of the family structure for too many.

"Get whatever you have together right now," my grandfather said to Pete and Mary Francis. "Don't ask me any questions. I don't have time to explain to you. I want you to get in the car and drive. Don't look back. Just leave. Now!"

We left food sitting on the table. The eight of us rushed to put our things in the car. We didn't even get a chance to gather the vegetables, watermelons, and other supplies my grandparents had assembled for us. We just went.

I remember the ride well. Darkness began to close in around the dirt roads we had to travel, mule-wagon tracks barely wide enough to allow a vehicle to pass. The light took on a different quality, gloomy and threatening. We were all thinking the same thought: *If we can just make it to the highway*. I kept looking back through the rear window, or peering into the dark ahead, frightened of seeing the headlights of a vehicle, chasing us down or blocking our flight.

You might think I'm overdramatizing here, but at the time the ghost of Emmett Till still hung over the whole South, a fourteen-year-old child tortured and murdered in Mississippi. Klansmen and night riders still ruled the Deep South, and domestic terror was part of our daily lives.

Every Black person in America—and that includes both the North and South—understood that hair-trigger violence was just a misunderstood word or casual mix-up away. Racial segregation was in that way self-enforcing. People of color tended to limit all contact with white people precisely because any encounter could suddenly turn deadly.

Countee Cullen wrote a famous poem, "Incident," wherein a young child tells of a visit to Baltimore. He's taunted with a racial insult. "I saw the whole of Baltimore," the poem concludes, "From May until December/Of all the things that happened there/That's all that I remember." I treasure the memories of Alberta and James Bobb and their wonderful family farm in Cajun country. No bad thought can possibly erase the love I felt for the place. But the incident along the Marron Bayou will remain with me forever.

CHAPTER 5

Who's Your Daddy?

WHEN HE MARRIED HER in 1945, Pete Francis made a host of promises to his new wife, Mary, one of which he never kept.

On the surface, the man I called Daddy came off as soft-spoken and reserved. Inside, he boiled. His anger arose partly from the status of forced subservience in a segregated community. That rage had to spill over somewhere. When Pete looked around for an outlet, his eyes naturally fell on me. I became quite literally Pete's whipping boy.

Apart from resentment over the indignities visited upon him by Jim Crow, another reason lay behind my father's brutish behavior, something I didn't know about until a schoolyard incident when I was ten. An insult-trading clash with a classmate briefly turned physical. My opponent landed a final blow, not with his fists, but with words.

"Yeah, well, your daddy ain't even your daddy!"

What the hell did that mean? I took the taunt as a joke.

A common aspect of Jennings holds true of small towns everywhere. Nothing remains a secret. Somehow, in some unknown telegraphic way, the truth always comes out. In Jennings, everyone knew everyone else's business. Gossip ricocheted around the dome like pistol bullets. Taboo subjects like out-of-wedlock births were typically never discussed out loud in public. But at times a whisper travels faster than a shout.

When I went home that day, I told Mary Francis about it. "A kid said to me today that Daddy isn't my real father."

She was silent for a long beat. Then she sat me down at the kitchen table. I felt the mood turn from joking to serious. A shock wave passed through me.

"What—is that true?" I asked.

"Yeah, it's true," she said, a tiredness in her voice from a secret long held.

She told me the whole story about my dad entering the military during World War II, and her promise to him that they would get married when he returned. Pete came out of the army in late 1944 to find my mother pregnant with another man's child.

"Your real, true daddy wanted to marry me," she said. "But I had promised to marry Pete, so that's how I ended up. Daddy said he would adopt you as his own, treat you like his blood, and everything like that. But he lied."

I must have been the last person under the dome to know the truth. My paternity was a secret that wasn't really secret. But nobody told me, including my mother. When a grade school classmate knows something well enough to throw it in your face, you can be sure that everyone else in town knows, too.

Later on, much later on, when I came home on my first break from college, my mother informed me that my biological father was in town. She arranged for us to meet.

Lloyd James. He stood about six two, while I'm smaller, five seven. He looked like a bigger version of me. In the movies, Austin Powers has his "Mini-Me." Here was my Maxi-Me. We both immediately recognized our resemblance. He turned out to be a mortician, and looking at him, it was as if someone had walked across my grave. I spent the day with him, but it turned out we didn't have all that much to say to each other.

In the aftermath of that meeting, I might have tried out a new name once or twice. "Hello, I'm Butch James." What's your name? "Butch—Butch James." Like "Bond, James Bond."

It wouldn't stick. Father or stepfather, the man who raised me was my daddy, for better or worse. Much of the time with Pete Francis, it was for the worse. I started to think of him as my stepfather.

I'd like to be able to say that with my new knowledge the scales fell from my eyes and I finally understood my daddy. That was not the case. Pete and I remained locked in a battle of wills that lasted until I reached adulthood.

In a way, what Pete didn't do as a father was as hurtful as what he did do. He never offered a kind word. Never gave me a shred of encouragement. Never acted supportive about anything I did. I can never once recall him embracing me.

I can count on three fingers the number of actual fatherly acts he performed. Number one, he took me to the barber for a rite-of-passage first haircut. Number two, at my mom's insistence, he taught me how to tie a tie, demonstrating on a bedpost as a stand-in for his stepson. Number three, when I got to be dating age, he allowed me the use of the old blue-and-white Oldsmobile that sat in the driveway.

That's it. The exceptions that proved the rule. The absence of love, the withholding of a parent's affection, can wither a child's spirit as sure as any beating. I've heard it called "soul murder," and that sounds about right to describe what Pete Francis tried to do to me.

On the scale of mistreatment he offered up, verbal abuse was level one.

"You're nothing, Butch," he'd growl at me out of the blue. "And you know what? You're always gonna be nothing."

The constant refrain echoed forever in my ears.

He railed at me for staying up in the evening to finish school homework. I was guilty of burning lamp oil for nothing.

"Cleveland," my mother gently responded to Daddy, using his full formal name, "let him study."

"These other boys in the neighborhood don't have to do it!" Pete exclaimed. "They don't stay up late! What's he doing?"

The real reason for my effort was lost on him. *What I was doing,* Daddy, was studying my butt off so I could get the hell away from you.

Pete employed other strategies that were simply mean-spirited. I was a frail and easily frightened young child, terribly afraid of the dark. I took seriously the midwife's prediction that a child born with a caul would always see ghosts. Since I was supposed to see them, I looked for them, peering in the dark so intently that my imagination conjured them up.

The Louisiana night fell hard in Jennings, and because we had no streetlight nearby, the inky darkness in our yard was complete. I had to bring our water into the house from an outdoor faucet, fifteen yards away from our front door. Daddy knew my fear. Whether we actually needed water or not, he delighted in sending me out to get it at night.

One of my most vivid first memories is of carrying a dented metal bucket into the darkness of the yard. The walk to the faucet was the longest trip I could have imagined. No moon. Critters rustled in the undergrowth. I was so little that the bucket banged against the ground, and I banged it all the harder to scare away whatever ghost was about to get me. I quickly filled the bucket from the faucet and lugged it back to the house.

Pete waited, a shadowy form framed in the doorway. "Not enough," he said, gauging the amount in the bucket, lacking an inch from the top.

He kicked over the water onto the ground. "Get back out there," he said.

Again I ventured out into the dark yard, shivering with a small child's fear. I tried to fill the bucket to the rim, but some spilled on the trek back to the house.

The same result. My father judged my effort and found it wanting. The water dumped out, the task repeated. I was Sisyphus pushing a boulder.

Pete must have enjoyed toying with me that first time, since the back-and-forth trip to the faucet became a feature of my young life. There were instances when Daddy would repeat the routine nine or ten times. Fill, lug, spill, fill, lug, spill, until I was exhausted and wanted to scream. He employed similar practices with other chores, ordering me to sweep the floor, for example, then finding the smallest speck of dust to make me do it all over again.

Over the years I tried to do things that would make him happy, but I never seemed to succeed. "Get to your room!" he'd shout. The punishment meant getting on my knees and putting my face up against a corner, like those poor kids in the horror movie *The Blair Witch Project*.

Such petty meanness represented level two of Pete's abuse.

Level three was the physical beatings I took from him. Corporal punishment of children was almost universal in Southern culture. Small-town fathers of the day came down very hard on their children, especially their sons. Pete's brand of harsh physical punishment had a deeper, rawer aspect to it. Blows rained down on me from fists, belts, and lengths of lumber. I knew it was wrong. He knew it, too, and I knew he knew, because he carefully hid the beatings from the rest of the family.

My sisters never knew what was going on, and neither did my mother. Pete Francis's fury betrayed an underlying disdain for me as his illegitimate son. I stood before him as a living, breathing reminder of disrespect to his manhood.

Though he was raised a Christian, Pete believed in witchcraft. His father, Andrew, was known for being adept at casting and lifting curses and spells. People would travel from as far away as Texas to have Andrew ward off the effects of an evil eye. My father carried on the tradition. Somewhere on his person you could always find a rabbit's foot filled with salt.

"If that charm was such a lucky thing, why'd the rabbit lose it?" Mary Francis quite sensibly asked.

One of the worst beatings I took from Pete came because of his superstitious nature. I had left one of my sneakers in the street in front of our house.

"Butch! Don't you realize?" he screamed, laying into me. "Some damned swamp witch'll take that shoe of yours and put the whole family under a curse!"

Insanely jealous of my mother, Pete would accuse her of infidelity with any man who as much as spoke to or looked at her. He would start arguments regardless of the time of day, but mostly between midnight and 6:00 a.m. My sisters and I huddled fearfully in the next room as the two went after each other. The argument sounded loud and furious, my father shouting abuse and my mother fighting back. The shouts, snarls, and curses still echo in my mind. To this day, I can't stand profanity.

My father had his own vulnerabilities, and in our battle of wills I would seek them out and exploit them. He hated the sight of human blood. That phobia made him extra careful when he beat me, but it also allowed me a chance to checkmate him. I once had a cut on my foot, which I fussed with intentionally and repeatedly, making it bleed. Pete stared at the oozing blood and appeared sickened by it.

"Get back into the house," he said, his voice choked.

Every person will carry unresolved issues to the grave. For Pete and me, though we made stabs at reconciliation, we were unable to make things right. No doubt he wondered why I was unable to understand his pain and embarrassment because of my out-of-wedlock birth. The girl he always thought he would marry had become pregnant with another man's child. She then gave birth to a male—a double insult for a man who seemed only able to father girls.

Even though Pete Francis begged my mother to marry him anyway and swore he'd adopt and raise me as his own son, it turned out he was emotionally unable to keep the promise.

His hatred for me grew as I grew older. I mirrored his hate, harboring vivid homicidal fantasies. I killed my father over and over in before-sleep visions, developing intricate scenarios that would result in his death.

On a sweltering afternoon in August when I was ten years old, those waking dreams turned into reality.

Summer was always beating season for Daddy. I dreaded the end of the school year because it meant I'd be home all day long. My mother was away working. I would be gone, too, unless Daddy ordered me to stay within the confines of the yard.

Within his reach.

Over the weeks of that summer, I had developed a slow-burn conviction. It was going to be him or me. Pete or Butch. Father or son. This wasn't revenge for the beatings, it was self-preservation, purely a matter of survival.

That afternoon my sisters were elsewhere. I don't know where they had gone, but if they had been home none of this would have happened. It was just me and Pete in the house. I had just received the whipping of my life. He mocked my tears and pushed me outdoors, but told me to remain in the yard.

Get out but stay close, because I just might have some business with you again real soon.

I heard him cursing and crashing around inside the kitchen. I couldn't figure any other way out. I had to kill him.

I'm going to end this, I said to myself.

It was as though I'd entered a trance. I filled a paint can with a mix of kerosene and oil, punched a hole in the top, and for a wick fed a length of twine through the hole. Like every other structure in the neighborhood, our house sat up on concrete blocks, with a crawl space underneath. I crept under the house and placed my homemade firebomb beneath the kitchen, right under where Pete was, and right under the kerosene can for the stove.

I trailed the fuse out to the shed, far enough away from the bomb that I wouldn't blow myself up. I actually lit the match. I stood there holding the flame in one hand, the kerosene-soaked twine in the other.

A foot-and-a-half separated fuse and flame. But then the full weight of my religious belief kicked in. It was as though the Lord whispered in my ear, "Vengeance is mine." It wasn't my job to even the score with Pete Francis. The Ten Commandments had been burned into my soul, including the sixth, "Thou shall not kill."

The trance broke. I suffered a case of the dry heaves. I quickly went back under the house to retrieve the unexploded firebomb. Returning to the shed, I fell on my knees and prayed. For myself, for my sisters and mother, and even a brief plea for the strength to forgive Daddy.

Mixed in with the sacred was the self-serving and practical. I knew that nothing good would come to me from this act. In those days fathers were beating on their kids all over the neighborhood, all over town, all over the country. My friend London White was beaten almost daily. It was something going on day and night. Most folks considered it *normal*, even healthy. Nobody would sympathize with me, nobody would understand my frame of mind. How could you let yourself get that angry? But I had reached the point where I just couldn't take it anymore.

I was always more of a science guy than a literature guy, but I recall a lesson on Shakespeare's *Hamlet* when I was a senior in high school. The class discussion centered on why Hamlet hesitated to act, why it took so long for him to kill the man who had killed his father. Batting the question back and forth, we finally settled on an explanation. Murder is a very big deal, such a momentous act that of course anyone with half a soul will hold off, waver, and delay.

I felt miserable, but I also felt that two paths had diverged right at that moment. If I had put match to fuse on that hot August afternoon in 1955, I might be getting out of the penitentiary right around now. Instead, I chose the path of putting up with whatever abuse the old man dished out.

Someday, some way, in some unimaginable time to come, I would have to get out from under Daddy's boot. Retreating to my weeping willow sanctuary, I nursed my wounds and my hopes for the future. Years later, I wrote a song that arose from how I was feeling at that watershed moment.

> *Now just because you follow me beneath that tree*
> Don't let me deceive you
> Because all those problems you had before you came
> They're not going to leave you
> But sitting down thinking for a while
> Just might relieve you
> So follow me and you will see
> There's peace beneath the willow tree

CHAPTER 6

Jennings to Baton Rouge

I GRADUATED FROM Jeff Davis High in the spring of 1963. I was the salutatorian of my small class of forty-five, representing the last folks standing of the nearly one hundred of us who had started high school together four years earlier. I had served as the president of the science club, editor of the school's newsletter, and president of the student body.

The summer after I graduated high school the heat of Jennings turned it up a notch, from sweltering to scorching. June felt like August.

During the day I behaved as if nothing had happened, as if a high school diploma represented no big milestone, as if 1963 would provide no turning point in my life. I went about my usual summer routine, picking up a little yard work from Charlie Holston. But every night when I should have been sleeping my mind raced like crazy, keeping me awake.

My diploma testified to the fact that I had graduated from Jefferson Davis High, "a state-accredited Negro secondary school." Uh-huh. I wondered how far a piece of paper like that was going to take me.

In geography class the Sargasso Sea had always fascinated me. A thick swamp of seaweed in the middle of the Atlantic Ocean, the Sargasso ate sailors alive. Ships became becalmed and lost. Columbus got bogged down there. The cartoon character Johnny Quest, required Saturday night viewing for the Francis family, often went to the Sargasso Sea in the course of his adventures.

I felt as if I were stuck in my own personal Sargasso. I drifted through my days, blocked and frustrated. At night I lay in bed and prayed. I had to find a way to escape the dome. But nothing presented itself. No path forward appeared.

Early on during my senior year in high school, I had told Mary Francis of my hopes and dreams for the future. “Mama, I want to go to college.”

“Butch, you know we don’t have money for that,” she had responded, traces of embarrassment and sadness in her voice. Collecting quarters in a jar wasn’t going to do it this time.

She suggested I go into the military. “If you enlist, you can get the GI Bill, and you can pay for college that way.”

For young men looking to escape the dead-end world of Jennings, two acknowledged, acceptable methods existed. One was death itself—dying young by drink, from being killed in a car crash, or through violence. “Death by misadventure,” the coroner’s report would read. Joining the army was the other escape hatch. With the Vietnam War just then cranking up, the two methods often came to the same end.

Life in Jennings featured an almost complete news blackout. Around the time I entered high school our household finally got a black-and-white TV. Walter Cronkite reported on Vietnam, but I paid little attention, remaining blissfully unaware of the war as it ramped up.

Sequestered as I was beneath the dome, I never concerned myself much with goings-on in the wider world. The war I fought was a private, personal one, a partisan guerrilla battle against Jim Crow—and my stepfather. I made meaningless stabs at protest. I reserved my fiercest glare for when I stalked past the town library, which I found myself doing more and more, worrying the forbidden place like a bad tooth. How could we as Black people assert our human dignity when we couldn’t even qualify for a library card?

As far as the degree of danger involved, this kind of private war could prove as deadly as anything going on in Korea or Vietnam. Folks could get killed in Jennings—or in Montgomery or Selma—and be just as dead as the bodies that piled up around Khe Sanh.

Young and ignorant as I might have been, I knew enough to understand how military service usually played out. My father and several uncles had entered the U.S. Army. Soldiering certainly had its attractions, especially if you were dirt poor. Three squares, a bunk for the night, discipline, order, spit-shined shoes. The government even paid you some.

After two years, four years, six years of that, then what? Right back under the dome. Same old same old.

As far as I could tell, a stretch in the army didn’t set anyone on a new trajectory in life. I witnessed the story happen again and again to my relatives and to other men in town. Military recruiters promised to make boys into men. But when the Black troops returned to Jennings, they heard themselves again addressed as "boy." The dome worked its magic, changing men back into boys again.

The depressing situation didn't prevent everyone from sending me the same message. The military, the military, the military. Like a drumbeat. Didn't they see what I was seeing?

Wilbur Rochelle, the principal of Jefferson Davis High, stood only about five seven, but had a very strong, very deep voice that meant business. Rochelle's natural aura of sternness and discipline caused the community to respect him and the kids to fear him. Toward the end of my senior year, while walking the halls between classes, I heard Rochelle's voice boom over the school's PA system.

"Cleveland Francis, please report to the principal's office."

Normally, a message such as this would have been relayed by his secretary, but here was the man himself, reaching out. As president of the student body, I had visited Rochelle's office many times to discuss school events or other matters. We knew each other well, and I thought we respected each other.

Earlier that year, senior male students had been summoned to the library. School scuttlebutt had it that they would "take the test" under the watchful eyes of a captain from the U.S. Army recruiting center. The Armed Forces Qualification Test gauged an individual's suitability for enlistment in the U.S. Army. It was notoriously easy, not really much of a test at all. Basically, if you had a pulse, the army would take you.

I had not gone to the recruitment examination at the school library. John Fogerty's classic anthem "Fortunate Son" hadn't dropped yet, but the lyrics articulated my sentiments exactly. "It ain't me, it ain't me, I ain't no senator's son."

Because I had skipped out on the meeting, I had expected a call from Rochelle, or some sort of reaction, a discussion at least. The principal made no secret of his endorsement of the military as a viable next step for graduating students. For some of them, Rochelle considered going into uniform their last chance toward building a life.

I reported to his secretary. The principal came to the doorway of his inner office. "The captain told me that you didn't show up for the enlistment exam. What happened? Did you not know about it?"

I bowed my head, signaling respect. I acknowledged that I had not been at the library on the day in question.

"Why?" he asked.

"Because I chose to not be there," I said, trembling inwardly at my boldness.

"Why?" he asked again.

"I have no plans on going into the military."

"Why not? That would be a great opportunity for you!"

My nerve failed me. I couldn't bring myself to explain that my father and uncles had all gone into the army, and that I saw no great improvement in their lives because of it. Veterans they might be, but they still could not enter the front door of local businesses or use the public library.

"Mr. Rochelle, sir," I said instead, "I plan on attending college."

"But how?"

"Well, sir, I haven't figured that out just yet."

We stood there for a long beat, a stubborn student facing off with an Adult Who Knew Better.

"Son," Rochelle said, having the last word, "I think you are making a big mistake."

He turned on his heel back into his office, and I retreated the way I came. As soon as I was out of sight down the hall, I sank against a school locker and slid to the floor.

Could Wilbur Rochelle be right? Was I making a big mistake?

I thought about what the man had said, this authority figure hired by the community for the guidance of the young. But I also considered what he had not said. Rochelle had mentioned nothing about scholarships, nothing about sending an application to his alma mater, Southern University, a historically Black college located a hundred miles east of Jennings in Baton Rouge. He also failed to encourage me to check with the school's guidance counselor about other possibilities in higher education.

Even though I had been one of Jefferson Davis's top students that year and would serve as the class salutatorian at the graduation ceremony, the best Rochelle thought to offer me was a future as cannon fodder in Southeast Asia.

Refusing to join the military in no way represented a protest on my part. It was not an instance of being unpatriotic. As I said, most of the men in my family had gone to serve the country. In 1948, when I was all of three years old, Harry Truman issued an order to integrate the military. But the ranks were still ruled by Jim Crow. Everybody I personally knew who went into the army ended up as cooks, cleaners, or laborers. Some of them became servants or valets to officers.

Pete Francis told me inflated tales of his military service. "You know, Butch, the army sent me all over," he said proudly. "I was posted to the tropical island of Guam in the Pacific Ocean. Halfway around the world!"

Later I discovered that Pete had been assigned to a burial detail in Guam, retrieving corpses and body parts from the island's dense jungle, American soldiers who had perished in the Pacific theater. In Jennings, that gruesome work did not get Daddy so much as a "thanks for your service." Or a library card.

★ ★ ★

August came on, time was running out, and I still had not managed to take a definite step toward realizing my dream of a higher education. I had closed the door to the military but hadn't been able to pry open any alternative. As much as I prayed every night, as hard as I went at it asking the good Lord for direction, nothing ever seemed to result. I also wondered whether my path would lead me into the ministry, as Rev. Chaney had suggested.

The college application deadline passed. Yard work for the Holston family and menial tasks at home filled my days. Despair rose to challenge my faith. I feared I'd be marooned in Jennings forever.

That summer the heat became a physical thing, entering my skull and foxing my brain. During my walks on the way home from mowing lawns uptown, I had to plot my route carefully. Avoiding the sunny side of the street, I jumped from one spot of shade to another.

My path home always led me past a filling station, one of the few Black-owned businesses in town. The Gilbeaux brothers ran the place, both of them teachers at Jeff Davis High, moonlighting at the gas pumps. Harry Gilbeaux taught industrial arts and was the high school basketball coach. Wilbur taught math. I knew them casually, like I knew pretty much every member of the community.

Why did I decide that particular afternoon might be a good time for a sociable chat with the Gilbeaux brothers? What moved me to cross the street? To do it I had to step out of the shade.

"Hello, Cleveland!" Harry hailed me. "How's it going with you?" The chemical smell of gasoline hit my nostrils. We exchanged comments about the oppressive heat. None of us approved of it. Wilbur asked what my plans were now that I had graduated high school.

"I want to go to college," I said. "Mary Francis says they can't afford to send me."

"Hey, you ever look into this National Defense Loan thing?" Harry asked.

"National Defense Loan," I repeated back to them, clueless.

"It's a government program," he explained.

"Well, hey, Terry Blanchette over at Evangeline got into Grambling State University on that one," Wilbur rambled on. "I think it was Terry, anyway. You know him, Tom and Joan's son, Grandma Blanchette's people?"

"Was it him that went to Grambling?" Harry asked.

I didn't give a damn about the Blanchette family from Evangeline. I was more interested in those three words, "National Defense Loan"—or, actually, only the single magic word "loan."

The Gilbeaux brothers didn't know many details about the program, but they had said enough to send me back to Jefferson Davis High School. The place was closed for the summer, but a skeleton crew of cleaners and teachers were there, getting ready for the new year. I looted the files in the counselor's office looking for information about this golden ticket called the National Defense Loan.

Okay, all right, the door forward had opened a crack. When I tried to obtain an application to Southern University, the voice of a secretary on the other end of the phone line informed me that the deadline for the fall semester had already passed. The school mailed me the form anyway. I filled it out and sent it back.

There was no home delivery of mail in Jennings. Everybody got their mail from the main post office in town. The postal boxes there were "separate but equal," segregated by address. As a result, no white person ever had to stand next to a Black person to get their mail. I haunted the place like a ghost, checking two or three times a day for word from Southern. Waiting for my future to be decided.

"Butch, honey, you've got to allow time for the mail to work," Mary Francis said, taking pity on me. Days passed. I gave up hope.

Two weeks later, the mid-August heat wave finally lifted. At the same time a fat manila envelope landed in the Francis family's postal box.

I was in.

Being accepted at Southern did not necessarily mean escaping the dome. In Louisiana at that time, no Black person could legally attend any institution of higher learning except two historically Black schools, Southern University and Grambling State College.

During my days at James Ward Elementary and Jefferson Davis High, all of my teachers were graduates of either Southern or Grambling. Not one of them was free from the heavy hand of Jim Crow. To use an example fresh in my mind, not one of them could check out books in the public library.

As a graduate of Southern, a slightly more elevated social position might be available to me, but as a Black teacher in a Black primary or secondary school I would still remain under the same rigid rules and prohibitions that had long poisoned my life.

My biology teacher, Sidney Briscoe, might have been respected within the Black community, but outside of it he was strictly limited and constantly constrained. I admired him, but I didn't want to become him. At

Southern, I decided that I would seek a bachelor of arts in biology instead of the bachelor of science degree that could lead to an education career. I hadn't figured out my future plans just yet, but I would be off the teacher track for now.

You might consider it random, the encounter with the Gilbeaux brothers that wound up changing my life. I had crossed the street that afternoon on a whim.

I certainly didn't see it that way. From the day of my baptism forward I felt I had given myself over to God. I was never sure if I would become a minister when I grew to adulthood. The Little Preacher's diary was full of Bible verses. Just as I still believe to this day, I believed that I was in the hands of the Lord. My destiny was set even though I hadn't determined exactly what it was that destiny had in store for me.

I was not so prideful that I thought God focused his love on me to the exclusion of all others, or that he moved Butch the boy around like some random chess piece. I was content to believe that the divine power worked in mysterious ways. I did know that I had been praying hard and long for months, and the developments that August felt like an answer to my prayers. My faith was an important fuel that drove me into the unknown territory of higher education.

I'm with the gloomy Dane, Hamlet: "There's a divinity that shapes our ends." Shakespeare then adds a kicker, "roughhew them how we will."

A higher power shapes us, yes, but we also have the individual ability to shape our ends. Though we do it clumsily and only half effectively ("roughhew"), we exercise our free will all the same. Some force in the universe nudged me out of the shade to talk with the Gilbeaux brothers that afternoon. Afterwards, the obligation was all on me to track down and fill out the National Defense Loan forms and send in my application to Southern.

"Opportunity knocks." Mary Francis used to repeat the old saying to us all the time when I was growing up. "But if you're not there to answer, it'll go down the street to knock on somebody else's door."

The family of my girlfriend, Janice McZeal, was not wealthy. Her father, Huey, worked as a tradesman, and her mother, Ruby, did domestic service like my mother. But they were maybe a minor step up the economic ladder from the Francis family. The McZeals had managed to scrape together enough money to send their daughter to college, with no scholarship or government loans involved.

We were a pair, Janice and I, both good at school, both religiously minded. We pledged to each other that we would save intimacy for marriage. Everyone expected us to wed eventually, and most people expected me to enter the clergy. I would be a pastor and Janice would be a pastor's wife. Our lives were mapped out.

So come the fall of that year, it had the feeling of destiny when Janice's parents pulled up in front of the house on Pearl Street in their Volkswagen van. They would take me and their daughter east to Baton Rouge and Southern University, where we had both enrolled. Mary Francis would come with us to help get me settled. I recalled when she had brought me to my first day of school twelve years before, and I had followed her back home. There would be no following her back this time.

Huey and Ruby McZeal had known me for three years. Our families often visited with each other. I spent much of my free time with Janice, usually on weekends at the McZeal family's Lake Arthur home.

That day my five sisters lined up to give me a big send-off. Pete Francis was elsewhere, by happenstance or design, I didn't know. All I knew was that I had busted a hole in the Jennings dome just big enough to slip out into the wider world.

No one could have been happier than that full vanload of pilgrims. The dreams of the older generation had come true for the young. The Volkswagen featured three rows of bench seats. Janice's parents took the front, with Dad McZeal driving. My mother and Janice's brother sat in the second row. Janice and I rode in back. We held hands for most of the trip.

Nowadays the drive from Jennings to the state capital of Baton Rouge takes about ninety minutes on Interstate 10. In 1963 the trip took more than twice that long. We had to cross half the state of Louisiana. The two-lane blacktop of Highway 90 ran through a succession of small, blink-and-you'll-miss-'em towns. We finally passed the larger city of Lafayette, celebrated as the birthplace of zydeco music.

Everyone had been chattering happily for the first fifty miles or so. But after we left Lafayette behind Janice and I fell silent. I gazed out at the black bayous and silvery rivers of Têche country.

It began to rain, not a great downpour but a soft, gentle pattering. The rest of the passengers in the van went quiet, too. The soothing punctuation of small towns continued. Larabee, Breaux Bridge, Henderson. We crossed the Whiskey Bay Pilot Channel and the Atchafalaya River. Grosse Tete—Janice and I laughed at that one, the name of the town translating as "big head" or "fat head." Were we going to be guilty of getting big heads just because we had both been accepted at college?

The skies opened, with the storm drenching the roadway. The countryside outside the van's windows struck me as alien, primordial, biblical, like the mythical waters of Noah's flood.

All the fountains of the great deep broken up
And the windows of heaven were opened
And the rain was upon the earth forty days and forty nights

Genesis 7:11

I half expected to see a white dove of peace flying by.

And the dove came in to him in the evening
And, lo, in her mouth was an olive leaf plucked off

Genesis 8:11

Beyond thoughts of a corner turned, a turning point achieved, and beyond feeling the truth of the Lord's grace, I had a vague notion of another concept that would be very much in the air during the years that followed. The whole of American society would be transformed by it, and my own life as well.

Freedom.

All of us have a right to be free. All of us have the right to grasp the life within us, fully and with all the strength we can muster. I had taken along three treasured possessions when I climbed into that Volkswagen van alongside Janice. My guitar, my Bible, and a biology textbook. Music, the good Lord, and science. My holy trinity. I had the feeling I was rich.

★ ★ ★

Entering the community of Southern University felt wonderful. Everyone looked like me, and I mean *everyone*. The student body numbered ten thousand. I had never been around that many Black people in my life. The sensation was so pleasant that I walked around campus grinning loopily, overwhelmed with joy.

Right from day one, the atmosphere of Southern struck me as different from anything I had ever known. It was like breathing fresh air when I was used to choking on the stale suffocation of the dome. After eighteen years in Jennings under the heavy hand of Jim Crow, having to calibrate my behavior according to a rigid, unforgiving set of rules, always looking over my shoulder, always walking a strict line drawn by others, I could finally, *finally* relax.

Breathe in, breathe out, Brother Cleveland. Kick back. Take a load off. What a relief!

At Southern, I didn't have to think in terms of black and white. Blackness was assumed, blackness was the default position. The subject of race rarely came up. Racism, the elephant in the room, had vacated the premises. I could pass whole days at Southern without seeing a single white person.

There were a few professors of Asian descent, but other than that, it was all Black, all the time.

You will have to excuse my young self. Of course, I endorse the principle of diversity as a fundamental social ideal. I realize all too well that uniformity breeds suspicion of the "Other." Black and white isn't the only factor at play here. Racial differences represent only one aspect of diversity, and in a wider sense we are all different. Our differences have to be celebrated, not stigmatized.

But please understand what Southern University meant for me at that precise moment. Sleeping as I had been—and as the old blues tune has it—with "rocks in my bed," walking around for so long with shards of glass in my shoe, it just felt so good to relieve myself of the constant, nagging, irritating pain. I had been near enough rubbed raw ever since I asked my mother that childhood question, "Why are we colored?"

Archival nineteenth-century photographs show the punishing collars locked around the necks of enslaved humans. Some foul act of the imagination worked to invent such fiendish devices, which resembled the parking boots that nowadays are attached to the wheels of cars. How might those suffering souls have felt when the spikes and shackles and chains eventually came off?

That's what Southern University felt like for me. Does that sound like too extreme a comparison? So be it. The contrast between freedom and Jim Crow *is* extreme.

Not only were my fellow students Black men and women, but they also resembled me in another way—pretty much all of them were strivers. They came from throughout the United States, valedictorians, salutatorians, editors of high school yearbooks, varsity athletes, student body presidents. My people!

Professors with PhDs in music and chemistry and literature taught us in lectures and classes and seminars. We had teachers with law degrees, prestigious fellowships, doctorates, and every other variety of educational achievement. The whole spectrum of a new Black educational universe lay before me, a realm that I had never imagined existed. A Black man served as the president of Southern University.

Everyone around me seemed smarter than I was, but somehow that wasn't intimidating so much as energizing and inspiring. Most of us had similar backgrounds. Church was a common denominator more than anything else. A few students came from comparatively wealthy backgrounds. I met kids whose fathers were doctors, lawyers, or bankers. None of our differences mattered to me. Taking my place in an all-Black community felt new, exciting, and—dare I say it—revolutionary.

Here's how I think about it. I had spent eighteen years in a segregated town ruled by Jim Crow. My time at all-Black Southern University simply evened out the balance a bit.

"It used to go like that," Bob Dylan said. "Now it goes like this." "A change is gonna come," Sam Cooke sang. Was it surprising that while strolling around campus I felt as though a great weight had been lifted from my shoulders? There's a popular book about the psychology of race with an eye-catching title, "Why Are All the Black Kids Sitting Together in the Cafeteria?" I was sitting together with the Black kids. Given the polarized condition of American society at that time, do we really have to ask why?

CHAPTER 7

A Guitar, a Bible, and a Biology Textbook

MUSIC, RELIGION, AND SCIENCE. I would embrace all three during the next four years at Southern, but I would come to each in a different way.

Because of my devotion to science, I signed on at Southern to study biology. I loved the discipline, intricacy, and beauty of the science of life. Physics featured the tightest focus of all the scientific disciplines, studying atoms, protons, and neutrons. Chemistry zoomed out a bit, concerning itself with molecules, ions, valences, reactions, and interactions. Biology took it a step wider.

As a science major, I sensed an unspoken, begrudging respect from the students who were taking degrees in the humanities. Literature, history, sociology—those were the cream puff subjects of a liberal education. Science was tough, science was real, science meant you were serious.

Then a seemingly random happenstance proved to be a game changer for me. While at Southern I came down with a common cold. Was the hand of the Lord really involved here? Could an infinitesimal microbe really be working in the service of the divine? I make no claim, but I have my own reasons to believe.

"Are not five sparrows sold for two farthings, and not one of them is forgotten before God?" asks the book of Luke. "But even the very hairs of your head are all numbered. Fear not therefore: ye are of more value than many sparrows."

The very hairs on my head, the very sparrows in the sky, the very microbes in my nasal passages, causing me to sneeze and become congested. Seeking symptomatic relief, I went to the university infirmary.

The visit represented a novel experience. I had never been to a doctor's office before, never been treated by a single doctor over the entire course of my childhood. Within the Jennings dome, modern health care wasn't available to us. Whatever doctoring we received came from home remedies only. That day at Southern I signed in at the infirmary and a nurse directed me to take a seat in the waiting room.

"It will only be a few minutes," she said.

I certainly never expected to meet the kind of doctor who walked into the waiting room to greet me. For the first time in my life, I encountered a Black physician. There he was, summoning me to the examination room, a white-haired older gent wearing a white lab coat. My cold symptoms seemed to vanish, as if just the sight of him magically cured me.

Since I had never met a Black doctor before, their existence had remained vague, general, and theoretical. I knew that a few privileged students I'd met at Southern had doctors in their families. It never entered my mind that I could ever become a physician. I became so excited that the reason I had come to the infirmary went right out of my mind.

To this day I don't recall the doctor's name, but our meeting set me on a new course in life, one that would take me to unimaginable places. The diploma posted on the wall identified him as a graduate of Howard University's medical school. He patiently put a stethoscope to my chest and listened. I remember a minor detail of the examination. He briefly (and kindly) warmed the bell of the instrument with his hand before he placed the stethoscope on my skin, so the cold steel would not cause any discomfort.

We barely spoke at all. He did not remark on my elevated heartbeat, my heightened respiration, my whole chest practically heaving with inner turmoil. A Black physician! To me, this was a superhero, wearing a lab coat instead of a cape. But the medical marvel merely listened to my lungs and my heart, then prescribed treatment for cough and congestion.

Auscultation. I didn't know the meaning of the word. I didn't know what it would take to become a doctor. I didn't know anything, really, about the science of medicine. I only knew where I wanted to go and what I wanted to do.

When I returned to my dorm, my cold symptoms cured, the incredible vision of a Black physician was all I could talk about. A lightning bolt had hit me from on high. The next day, I changed my major to premedical biology. The study of medicine would take my science courses into a whole higher, more difficult level of intensity. I didn't care. All because of a cold virus, I had seen the light.

Rihanna recently displayed her world-class collection of works by Black artists at the Brooklyn Museum. Interviewed in the media, the singer said there was a reason for giving the public a chance to see the paintings she had collected over the years.

"When you are a little kid and you have all these dreams in your head, you don't even know what's possible," Rihanna said. "So if you see it happen, you know it can happen to anybody."

To imagine you can become an artist, you have to encounter art, especially works by artists who look like you. Before it ever occurred to me that a Black man like me could become a doctor, I had to see one in the flesh.

★ ★ ★

Minor miracles such as my encounter with the Black doctor kept cropping up at Southern, and they always were connected to seemingly random events. Because I had switched my major to premed, my coursework now had to include a humanities class. And because I took a humanities class, the hand of fate reached into my life once again. An astonishing development took place, not in medicine this time, but in music, an intervention as real and long-lasting as Mary Francis's purchase of that Silvertone, lo those many years past.

Yes, I had indeed arrived at college with my old willow tree guitar, but I kept the instrument carefully under wraps in a cloth covering. In my dorm room I stored it out of sight in a closet.

At Southern University, the idea of a guitar god had not attained wide popularity. If the instrument was thought about at all, it was not an acoustic guitar but an electric—Chank Willis or Robert White, for example, adding back-up fills to the Motown hits of the day. The nuclear bomb of Jimi Hendrix had yet to explode.

So I feared going public with my chosen instrument. I imagined being greeted with smirks and disdain. An acoustic guitar? That's nerd material, folkie territory, or corny hillbilly stuff. There were no beatnik coffeehouses in Baton Rouge. I did not gig around, and—God forbid—I didn't strum away wearing a beret in front of the student union, warbling "kumbaya my Lord, kumbaya." I was shy. When I played, I made sure I was alone in my room, with the door locked.

I don't know whether I was somehow ashamed of my musical ability, or if I just felt out of step with the popular taste on campus. My shyness arose because the guitar was a personal thing for me, a private means of expression. I was a creature of the willow tree, and in some sense I always remained there.

Males in general and Black males in particular were supposed to keep their emotions and creative impulses bottled up and in check, never to be displayed in public. When I sang, I tapped into my willow tree self, reaching back to the time when I was young and green and wore my heart on my sleeve.

Dr. Huel D. Perkins taught the humanities class I was now required to take. The dean of the College of Arts at Southern and the university's professor of music, Perkins was the kind of man who gave the concept of a liberal education a good name. What a genial, civilized gent he was, taking his classes on field trips to the Delgado Art Museum in New Orleans, referencing novels and poems, having us listen to operas. Watering parched earth, opening our minds, opening our worlds.

To Perkins it mattered that his students knew how to appreciate an eighteenth-century *capriccio* of Roman ruins painted by Sebastiano Ricci, or a two-thousand-year-old Shawabti bronze from Egypt. He modeled minor aspects of correct social behavior, such as how to avoid committing the faux pas of applauding between the movements of a concerto or symphony. But more than that, he was teaching us how to see, how to think, how to thrive in the wider world far beyond Southern.

The first words out of his mouth on the first day of the first class I ever took from him impressed me. "I know what the university brings to you, but what did you bring us? I seek to discover what you have brought to Southern University, whatever that may be."

The notion startled me, focused as I was on everything the university could provide for my benefit. What about the other way around? It was like John Kennedy's famous question during his inauguration three years before, asking not what our country could do for us, but what we could do for our country.

I had to think, what am I bringing to Southern? Not more than fifteen students shared Dr. Perkins's humanities seminar with me. I tried to picture how each one of them would respond to the proposition.

"I want to meet with you all for fifteen minutes or so," Perkins announced. "We'll sit down and I'll talk to each of you individually."

I thought of the Three Magi. *Tell me your gift*. What did I have to offer? I didn't know if plunking away at the guitar even qualified. As a kid I thought that the Little Drummer Boy, for example, had gotten it all wrong. If you're Mother Mary, and you've just ridden a donkey the hundred miles from Nazareth to Bethlehem, then spent hours giving birth, probably the last gift you want is a drum solo to wake a sleeping babe.

But I didn't have anything else. I wrapped up the Silvertone in its camouflaging cloth, snuck out of my dorm, and crossed campus to the building where the music department was located. For Dr. Perkins, I thought I'd be just another eighteen-year-old student, someone he had met for an hour in class a few days before. I imagined him wincing to himself, *Oh, no, he's got a guitar*.

Entering the office, I introduced myself and unwrapped the Silvertone. Nervous, awkward, and unable to speak coherently, instead I started to sing. I led off with a Hank Williams tune, "I Can't Help It (If I'm Still in Love with You)," a song I always thought sounded good with just an acoustic guitar and voice.

Perkins stared, not speaking. Did he like or hate what he was hearing? I could picture the good doctor's reaction going either way.

Not knowing what else to do, I plunged onward. Next up, Gordon Lightfoot's "Early Morning Rain." Then "If I Had a Hammer," a song Trini Lopez had a hit with that year, but which I had learned from the version done by Peter, Paul & Mary.

My humanities professor held up his hand. I hadn't had the nerve to look him in the face while I was singing, but when I stopped I realized Dr. Perkins wasn't grimacing. He was beaming.

"Wait, wait a moment, young man," he said. He called in his secretary and told her to cancel all his remaining appointments for the day. Then he requested that she find a tape recorder and bring it into him.

"Play some more," he said.

I did. Perkins began to summon other people in to listen, faculty members from the music department, other staffers, and professors. A whole parade came in over the course of the next few hours.

Usually, it's a bad sign if a performance is greeted by silence. When I sang "Amazing Grace," the room went still. The hymn holds a special significance for the African American community. Written by John Newton, a former slave ship captain, the lyrics were composed after the man had reformed his evil ways: "I once was lost but now I'm found." That afternoon I did the song slow and mournful, and I could hardly believe my ears when Perkins broke the silence by stifling a sob.

"Do you ever write songs yourself?" he asked, recovering.

I played an early version of a tribute I wrote celebrating the backyard refuge of my childhood.

So follow me and you will see
There's peace beneath the willow tree

"Why, you're doing folk music!" Dr. Perkins exclaimed, excited now. "How in the world did you get exposed to music like that?"

According to Dr. Perkins, the Black musical heritage in America rooted itself in prayers for a better life. Gospel music allowed direct communion with God. The blues spoke about hard times. Soul and R&B added in a sensual element, allowing expressions of love and heartache. Jazz originated in the African American community of New Orleans, often incorporating elements of gospel, blues, and ragtime. Coming out of the Black community, all these different kinds of music shared the sense of rising above trouble.

But Perkins pointed out that folk music was different because it tended to focus on people's relationships with each other. Here was a nuanced take on life, going beyond the theme of "woe is me" and "my baby done left me," and instead asking "what we can do about it?" Folk music lived at the intersection of self and society. Wallowing in pain and suffering can be pleasurable when it's put into song but attempting to inspire changes in the world can be thrilling, too.

Somehow, Perkins told me, I had stumbled into that lane. I didn't know folk music from rock & roll, Swiss yodeling, or French cabaret. I didn't know anything about the folk revival happening in the wider culture, nothing about Pete Seeger, the Weavers, and Lead Belly. I learned songs off the radio and wrote my own.

Local AM programs featured country and Cajun programming, but the big network radio stations played whatever was popular, no matter what pigeonhole the song might fit into. Playlists were different in those days. Most of the stations played Top Forty, pure and simple. Whatever topped the charts was what came over the airwaves. A DJ might cue up Peter, Paul & Mary's cover of Bob Dylan's "Blowin' in the Wind," follow it with Little Stevie Wonder's "Fingertips," and then segue into "Rhythm of the Rain" by the Cascades. For some reason, listeners didn't get motion sickness. They liked the mix. Genre didn't matter.

"There's only two kinds of music," Duke Ellington said. "Good music and the other kind."

I didn't know anything. I was like one of those self-taught folk artists, painters such as Grandma Moses (Anna Mary Robertson Moses), untrained in any school or academy. My willow tree sanctuary gave birth to a one-off, single-pressing, special edition singer-songwriter. Solitude nurtured and formed me, creating me from whole cloth, a hermit musician. After all, who first played the guitar? Lonely Spanish shepherds, alone with their flocks.

I had no flock. My public performance resume remained extremely spotty. I played tuba in the marching band at Jeff Davis High School, the instrument bigger than I was, able to blow me over in strong winds. As a prank my fellow band members used to toss apple cores into the brass bell of the horn, or wads of paper, bits of trash.

In the First Baptist choir, I had sung hymns and gospel songs. While in high school, I played guitar and sang with a gospel group called the Mid-South Spiritual Singers, touring tent revivals and churches on the weekends. My sisters and I formed a gospel group we called the Francis Family Singers. I was far from the best voice in that ensemble. My sisters outshone me, especially Faye. Also, when I pledged to a fraternity at Southern, a few frat brothers and I made up a little quartet and sang at parties, doing hits from the Temptations and other R&B groups.

That was about the extent of my credits. I had a different side of me, one that I kept hidden away. I sang alone and played guitar where no one could hear me. I had never appeared solo in public, not until that first audition in front of Dr. Perkins.

In between songs he grilled me about my background. I mentioned growing up in Jennings and he nodded as if he understood exactly what that meant. He asked if I was dating anyone.

"I have—I have—a girlfriend, Dr. Perkins, sir," I stammered, surprised by the question. "Her name is Jan-Jan-Janice, sir, sir, sir." I could sing okay. I just couldn't talk.

"You don't have to call me 'sir,'" he said. "Professor will do. Or why don't you just say 'Doc'? That's what my friends call me."

I nodded uncertainly.

"You know what you need to do one day, Cleveland?" he asked. "Take the guitar and go over to her dorm. Call this Miss Janice of yours down to the lobby and serenade her right there in the lobby."

"Well, I don't know about that, Doctor Perkins," I said. He cocked his head, and I corrected myself. "Doc."

A few days later, at his urging I wrapped my guitar in its protective cover again and trekked across campus to the women's dormitory where Janice lived. One of her dormmates went upstairs to let her know I was there.

"Cleve is down there with a guitar," the friend told her. "He wants to serenade you."

Janice refused to come down, hiding out from her oddball boyfriend.

Dr. Perkins went beyond doing questionable service as my romantic coach, also taking on the role of a booking agent for my first ever concert. I would sing before a hundred music majors, the largest audience I ever faced, at least as a solo artist.

The old Silvertone guitar had developed a large crack in the body. Perkins drove me to a downtown Baton Rouge music store, Werlein's for Music, and bought me a larger, better, brand-new guitar.

"I'll keep the old one," he joked. "I'll sell it back to you if you become famous."

"'If'?" I said, giving him some lip. "Don't you mean 'when'?" He laughed.

On the day of the concert, I hid myself in the wings of the school's auditorium, peeking out at the house. As the students began to fill the seats, a bout of stage fright hit me. My knees went jelly.

Doc Perkins took pity. "Take a deep breath," he said. "Exhale slowly, walk out on to the stage, sit on the stool, place the guitar in the proper position—and perform."

I did the ten songs that Doc had selected for me, a mix of gospel and folk. The audience remained politely quiet as I sang, but applauded generously after each number. The music and my enunciations came out crisp and clear over the hall's sound system. I ended the performance with "The Willow Tree," a song I had written and sung many times before, most often within my private childhood refuge.

When I finished, the students rose to their feet in a standing ovation. At that moment, if I had died and risen to heaven I would not have complained. I bowed my head in thanks and floated off stage. The power of music impressed me all over again, lodging itself deep in my soul. I grasped the intricate interplay of lyrics and melody, the ability of a song to find a home in the heart of strangers, with words and music connecting them to the story being told.

"It's a gift," Dr. Perkins said excitedly, embracing me. "It's yours for life."

About the time I got a real guitar I got a real song, too. Sam Cooke's "A Change Is Gonna Come" hit the radio in the summer of 1964, when I went home to Jennings on break.

The first time I heard it I knew it was mine. Cooke's voice is what struck me first, polished as mahogany and melancholy as rain. I went into my room and got my new guitar out, waited an hour for the song to come around again on the station's rotation, then put my mind to figuring out the chords. The lyrics weren't very complex. I memorized them on that first listen.

Learning to play the song took a few days. Figuring out what it all meant took longer. To me, "A Change Is Gonna Come" represented a pure example of folk music, in spite of its R&B and gospel arrangement. The power came through just fine without all that, with just me and my guitar. Writers at *Cash Box* music magazine labeled it a "message song." I felt the message deep in my bones.

Hope.

That's why I loved the song. Sam Cooke had cooked up a potent brew of weariness and determination. The playwright Samuel Beckett formulated the same sentiment: "You must go on. I can't go on. I'll go on."

I taught the song to my sister Faye and we started to do a gospel version at Union Baptist. The congregation took to it. The adults punctuated the chorus with plentiful "Amens" and "Uh-hums."

Mary Francis pronounced "A Change Is Gonna Come" her favorite of all the songs I did. After dinner she would finally be able to sit down after her twelve-hour day, tired and cored out from taking care of two families, one uptown and one of her own. Outside in the dark, the racket of crickets provided its own kind of concert. We would sit there silently and listen to that for a while.

Then she'd say, "Butch, play that 'born by the river' song." Sometimes as soon as I finished she'd ask for it again.

Daddy thought less of it. Pete Francis had lost his hope. Mesmerized by his own misery, he had formed a firm conviction that change wasn't ever gonna come, and there was no use offering hope that it would. Some people get so comfortable in their despair that they get ornery when you try to pull them out.

★ ★ ★

Like a lot of my fellow students, I brought my Bible with me when I came to college, a treasured talisman I had packed alongside my guitar and biology textbook.

Religion remained central to my life. When I returned to Baton Rouge for my second year at Southern, I served as president of the university's Sunday school and was generally known around campus as an upright, uptight churchman. Based on my work in religious organizations, I even warranted a listing in *Who's Who at American Colleges and Universities.*

At Southern University I first became aware of the "Divine Nine," a group of historically Black fraternities and sororities more formally called the National Pan-Hellenic Council. These Greek-letter organizations would earn a significant place not only in Black society and culture, but in American history as a whole.

Though other fraternities on the Southern campus invited us to join, my roommate William Horton and I agreed that the Phi Beta Sigma fraternity sounded best. Students on the campus of Howard University founded the first chapter of the "Sigmas" in 1914, followed in 1920 by its sister sorority, Zeta Phi Beta.

"To develop leadership and serve the community" stood as the pronounced goal of the fraternity, but just as importantly the organization provided lifelong social networking that extended far beyond college days. Behind only the Black church, Black Greek-letter societies helped provide organizing muscle for the era's civil rights push.

Just as Southern University represented a sanctuary of freedom after the oppressive atmosphere of the Jennings dome, the Sigmas offered a microcosmic safe space for me to spread my wings socially. I shared many of the same values with my soul brother William Horton, an army veteran who was majoring in English and philosophy.

Leadership qualities that I discovered and developed at Union Baptist and Jefferson Davis High carried over to the Sigmas, to the degree that my brothers elected me president of the fraternity. We weren't a wealthy Greek by any stretch and did not own a chapter house or anything like that, but we were recognized and active on campus.

When I pledged to the Phi Beta Sigma fraternity, I looked around and had thoughts of elevating its moral tone. While they attended to the mission of the organization, many of my frat brothers majored in partying. Meanwhile, Horton and I remained stuck in our "Little Preacher" modes. We sought to change the fraternity's outlook, style, and direction.

We summoned all the guys to a weekly Sunday school meditation hour. We convinced everyone to wear their emblematic spiffy blue blazers and neat white shirts. "Dress like the man you want to become" became an unofficial byword.

While I led the group in carrying out our mission, some of the brothers grumbled at the fraternity's new direction. Without my knowing, they organized a counterrevolution and fomented an uprising. One evening I found myself confronted in a general meeting of the whole fraternity.

"Man, Cleve, we are unhappy with the way things are going here," a self-appointed spokesman named Matty Piper said. "We're walking around campus decked out and looking like a sure-enough crew of fools, man."

Another of the mutineers chimed in. "In addition to all that scholarship and leadership, the purpose of a fraternity is also to impress women!"

The comment sparked a chorus of "yes!" and "right on!"

"Cleve has got us all in Sunday school," said another frat brother. "We're not impressing anybody with that Sunday school nonsense, man."

My dear frat brothers took up a chant. "Revote! Revote! Revote!" To my ears, it sounded like "Revolt! Revolt! Revolt!" The villagers were coming at me with torches and pitchforks. I got ousted as president by a near-unanimous majority. Matty Piper was selected to take my place. As a consolation prize, and maybe to show how they really felt about me, the brothers voted me in as chaplain.

But maybe my more worldly brothers had the last laugh on the Little Preacher. During my years at Southern, I came off my high horse, lost my virginity, and learned to enjoy the effects of a nice glass of wine.

Looking back, the situation reminds me of a Johnny Cash song:

You're shining your light, and shine it you should
But you're so heavenly minded, you're no earthly good

Protest was in the air, and not just at Phi Beta Sigma, either. A jolt of social justice electricity passed through the entire country, most dangerously in the Deep South. Just days before our drive to Southern in the Volkswagen van of Janice's parents, a quarter million people joined the March on Washington for Jobs and Freedom.

That Wednesday afternoon, August 28, 1963, Rev. Dr. Martin Luther King Jr.'s "I Have a Dream" speech transformed the American conversation on civil rights. I watched it all on the Francis family's black-and-white television.

Eighteen days later, as if in nightmarish response to King's words, a bomb blew up the 16th Street Baptist Church in Birmingham, Alabama. The town had so many attacks on Black homes and churches that it earned the nickname "Bombingham."

Killed in the church explosion were three fourteen-year-olds, Addie Mae Collins, Cynthia Wesley, and Carole Robertson, as well as eleven-year-old Denise McNair. Say their names.

It was time of decision. Ringing in my ears was Pete Seeger's pro-union song, written by activist and coal miner's daughter Florence Reece when she was only twelve years old.

> *Which side are you on, boys?*
> *Which side are you on?*

I had to choose. Stokely Carmichael, an early Freedom Rider in Mississippi and a prominent civil rights organizer, came by invitation to speak at Southern University. In remarks to the student body, he would directly confront my church, my rock, the institution that helped form me.

"What do we see in the Black church?" Carmichael asked the audience. "I see the pews full of Black parishioners. They're all looking up toward the front, toward the pulpit. And what's usually right there behind the pulpit? A giant portrait of Jesus, portrayed as a white man. A church full of Black people worshipping a white man."

Carmichael's challenge shook me to the core. Could that be true? I knew the Black church as the backbone of the civil rights movement. Slavery in America stole life and liberty from millions, but the enslaved laborers were allowed the consolation of religion and the Bible. That proved to be a crucial error by the slaveholders, since eventually the Christian church would make all the difference. No society that judged one group of human beings inferior to another could possibly withstand the withering moral judgment of Jesus.

Thinking about Carmichael, and thinking about the church, I remembered an incident from long before. I visited Southern University a couple of times in high school, once when I was fifteen. Sidney Briscoe, my biology teacher, organized a trip to a competitive, state-level science fair being held at the university. Briscoe smoked cigarettes, and on our way back to Jennings from Baton Rouge, he found that he had run out of matches.

Always eager to serve, I jumped up and offered to go out and get him some. We pulled over in front of a roadside bar in a small town. I saw the "Whites Only" sign on the door but decided to proceed inside anyway. The errand was minor enough, and brief enough, that I figured Lord James Crow would allow the transgression.

As soon as I entered, a lady rushed out from behind the bar. "What'd you want?" she demanded.

"Matches?" I responded, ducking my head as I had been conditioned to do. "I only need a penny box of matches."

One of the male patrons spoke curtly to the barkeeper lady. "Get him the matches." I felt the mood turn ominous, but it was too late.

A second male voice said, "Wait, I'll handle this."

The blow came down before I knew what was happening. I was blind-sided and knocked out, dropping in a heap, my unconscious form blocking the tavern door.

Briscoe and the other students rushed out to carry me back into the car. I came to, groggy and bleeding from the mouth. My fellow students and my chaperone teacher remained completely silent, as did I. As a measure of the incredible power of the taboo that gripped the South back then, we drove all the way back to Jennings with not one of us saying a single word about what had happened.

We arrived at Pearl Street. Briscoe brought me into the house and told my mother what had transpired. Later that night Mary Francis came into my room.

"Butch," she said gently, "I know what happened was terrible. That was a real bad man who hit you."

Hurt and angry, I couldn't speak.

"Tell me something, honey," she said, petting my head. "If that man fell into a well, would you pull him out? That man who hit you, would you help him?"

My soul rebelled. *Him, that cracker, fallen down a well? We're the ones in the bottom of a well, Mama! No one's extending a hand to help us out!*

But I didn't say any of that. I knew the answer Mary Francis wanted, knew it from years of Bible study and from hearing the Lord's word. "Take care of him," Jesus said in the parable of the Good Samaritan. "Whatsoever thou spendest more, when I come again, I will repay thee." Take care of him. Take care of the wounded, the poor, the helpless, all those fallen into the bottom of the well.

"Would you pull him out, Butch?" Mary Francis repeated gently.

I hesitated for another moment. "I would."

"Good," she said, and walked out of the room. Later, she explained that she did not want me to get caught up in hatred and vengeance.

"You'll probably never see this man again," she said.

"I didn't see him the first time, Mama!"

She told me not to let this single person dictate the rest of my life, this violent anonymous stranger who appeared out of nowhere only to do violence.

Mary Francis had a second level of motivation that night, beyond the Christian principle of "turn the other cheek." She knew it was not safe for a Black man in Louisiana to go about seething with anger. Such figures tended to meet with bad ends. Be angry, sure, but convert your anger into another form of energy, such as getting an education to gain independence.

I considered that long-ago roadside bar incident as I confronted the twists and turns of the civil rights movement from my perch at Southern University. The principle of nonviolence espoused by Dr. King vibrated on a deep sympathetic frequency within my mind. The idea simply felt right to me. The cool kids at Southern gravitated elsewhere, to the extremist fringes of the movement. That wasn't me.

The activist organization that Stokely Carmichael led enshrined "nonviolence" in its name: SNCC, the Student Nonviolent Coordinating Committee. The SNCC logo featured an interracial handclasp of brotherhood.

But I also understood the way things were trending in the movement. Black Power was on the horizon. Carmichael himself would become disillusioned with the snail's pace of the democratic process. The armed resistance of the Black Panther Party loomed only a few years in the future. They would display a different kind of logo.

Which side are you on? On one end of the political spectrum were the Black Power firebrands—Stokely Carmichael, H. Rap Brown, Malcolm X, the Black Panthers. On the other end stood a man of the church, mocked and maligned for being too cautious, too passive, too "soft."

I didn't have to rack my brains or belabor my decision. I already knew the one I would choose. Dr. King became my lodestar.

CHAPTER 8

Baton Rouge to Virginia

SOUTHERN UNIVERSITY EXISTED in a world of its own, not only culturally but geographically. To the west, the campus wedged itself up between a bend in the Mississippi River and a slough-like bayou called—I kid you not—Mulatto Bend.

The Big Muddy made for a spectacular sight to see. I often sat on the Scott Bluffs and dreamed as the current eddied and flowed below me, thick as soup. That river was history. I thought of the thousand-mile trip nineteen-year-old Abraham Lincoln took by flatboat from Indiana, down the Ohio and Mississippi Rivers, all the way to New Orleans.

Lincoln had to have passed the very spot where I was sitting. The journey was an eyeopener for young Abe, because for the first time he witnessed what was going on in the slave states—a situation that had to be seen to be believed. The experience marked him for life.

"Whenever I hear anyone arguing for slavery I feel a strong impulse to see it tried on him personally," the Great Emancipator said later.

On the opposite side of campus from the river, to the east, we were cut off by Highway 61, which according to bluesman Mississippi Fred McDowell "is the longest road I know." The road is known as "the Blues Highway" because of its long history in blues music. In the song "Highway 61 Revisited," Bob Dylan had a darker vision of the well-trafficked route, as an apocalyptic landscape where a promoter puts "bleachers out in the sun" for an audience to view "the next world war."

A set of railroad tracks ran alongside the highway, and none of us were going anywhere while the endless freight trains rolled through, two hundred tanker cars rumbling along one after another, all filled with gasoline or liquid natural gas.

Depending on how you want to see it, the location of the Southern campus represented either a protective sanctuary similar to my willow tree refuge, or an artificial, blocked-off cul-de-sac. The highway and river helped shield us from outside intruders, but also isolated us. The landscape proved toxic, situated downstream and downwind from a petrochemical refinery that was surrounded by other industrial installations. I studied for my classes with the scent of hydrocarbons in my nostrils.

Southern University had been founded during Reconstruction, when a group of African American leaders in Louisiana had urged the establishment of a college devoted to "the education of people of color." The state legislature chose a patch of land no one else wanted. Back then the concept of "environmental justice" hadn't been invented yet, but when I was at Southern the neighborhood could have done with a government Superfund cleanup. A nearby town sported the name "Brownfields," a term for land polluted by industry.

Southern was a "land-grant college," part of a federal system devoted to promoting agricultural and mechanical arts. A high-toned vocational school, in other words, instructing farmers which seed to plant and when. The school's formal name was "Southern University and A&M College," the "A&M" being the agricultural and mechanical part of the equation. Only later on did the school's curriculum expand to include the sciences and the liberal arts.

A clause in the federal land-grant program required military training for all males who attended such a school. We enrolled in two years of ROTC, the Reserve Officer Training Corps, a pipeline to active service military. Three afternoons a week after attending classes, I donned the khaki uniform, performed endless drills, and learned to disassemble and assemble an M-1 carbine upon command. We were an impotent army, issued no ammunition, possessing no live rounds.

The whole show summoned up memories of the toy army games I played as a kid in Jennings. Alongside my Pearl Street buddy, London White, I fought, crouched, ran, and crawled, ambushing pretend enemies, killing, exploding, stabbing, wreaking all sorts of havoc with childish glee. I still retain a vivid image of our mothers calling us in for dinner, often right in the middle of our mock battles, how their voices floated over the falling dark of the neighborhood.

Out of those memories came a song I would compose in 1970, written with my friend Victor Liguori: "War, A Children's Game."

I remember when our guns were made of wood
And bullets used to be rubber bands

The battlefield was our own back yard
And dead boys always lived to run again

In the real war, half a world away in Southeast Asia, the voices of mothers were calling their boys home, but a lot of the sons weren't answering. None of the dead lived to run again. Whenever I caught sight of the newspapers or watched the evening news, the casualty lists from Vietnam brought home the deadly reality of what was going down.

Upon graduating from ROTC, we were eligible for the Officers Training Corps (OTC), which would automatically lead to a commission as a second lieutenant in the U.S. Army. That sounded pretty good to a lot of people. Friends of mine went into the military. Success stories did happen. Donald Ray Pierre, a fellow graduate of Jefferson Davis High in Jennings, went to Vietnam as a medic, became a neurosurgeon, and retired with the rank of commander in the U.S. Navy.

I was trapped. As a land-grant college student, I had to take the OTC exam. I tried my best to fail but wound up just squeaking by with a single percentage point passing margin.

An army colonel called me into his office. "You passed the exam, son,"—they like to call you "son" in the military—"but you didn't pass it by much."

He gave me a hard stare. I could read his thoughts. *Is what we have here a malingering, self-sabotaging son of a bitch?*

"That score bothers me," he finally said. "So I will have to allow you to opt out."

Relevant in this case was the memorable last line in the antiwar novel *Catch 22*: "The knife came down, missing him by inches, and he took off." The knife had missed me by a single exam point. Those casualty lists from Vietnam? They were packed with the names of OTC second lieutenants.

Again, I had no beef against the military. But my future lay elsewhere. The current of change that passed through the whole country also electrified me. My personal life underwent a transformation. Janice McZeal and I broke up, got back together, and broke up once again. I could see where she wanted our life together to lead. We would marry, move back to Lake Arthur to be near her family, and raise kids of our own. It was a sweet vision, but I came to understand it was not for me. In my junior year we ended our relationship for good.

Janice was my first love. We dated all through high school and two years of college. She would always occupy a place in my heart. But the experience at Southern had changed me. It had set my soul free. I could not be held to promises I made while imprisoned in the unreal world inside the dome.

I went on to follow my own path. Janice returned to the dome, married, and raised a family. I was fortunate to meet her again in the mid-1980s, when

I returned to Jennings to speak at the Union Baptist Church for Black History Month. Seeing her, her husband, and her children brought me around full circle. I felt nothing but affection for the memories of our youth.

I was finding myself more and more under the wing of Dr. Perkins, who served first as my professor, then as a mentor, before finally becoming much more than that, a father figure whom I would come to love and treasure throughout our time together.

The Perkins residence became a second home. I had an open invitation to visit. While there I met and sang with other guests, many of them professional musicians. Dr. Felton G. Clark, the president of the university, often came by. Frequently I went over after classes on Friday and spent the whole weekend. Not only musicians showed up, but doctoral scholars, other students, friends, and prominent notables from across the country. I became familiar enough with Perkins to address him as "Doc." Thelma, his wife, made for a gracious presence.

Civilization lived at Doc's. I wasn't familiar with the term "salon," but those evenings were the closest Southern University would come to having one. Talk was general, sophisticated, and high-minded. I found myself in the mix, surrounded by love and brotherhood. At times I had to catch myself and ask if it was really happening. I always brought my guitar, and usually gave impromptu concerts.

What I recall most from those evenings was the connection I made with the audience, an exhilarating sense of harmony and communion that I would seek forever afterwards. When I sang spirituals such as "Wade in the Water," "Were You There?," or "Down by the Riverside," a deep and emotional mood would settle on the group in the Perkins's living room. Music brings people together, and so does the recognition of a common history. Most of those present had come up through the church. They had all heard the songs before. To see someone like Dr. Felton Clark sit back, misty-eyed, and allow himself to be carried away by the music—well, there was nothing better.

Children wade in the water
God's gonna trouble the water
If you don't believe I did begin to wade in the water
Just see the holy ghost looking for me
God's gonna trouble the water

Everyone listening during those evenings was descended from enslaved Africans. These old songs had been the balm of our ancestors. The Mississippi, the river of memory and forgetfulness, flowed by right outside the door.

I'm gonna lay down my sword and shield
Down by the riverside down by the riverside
Down by the riverside I ain't gonna study war no more

Beyond that sanctuary of peace and culture, the Vietnam War raged, killing off young men by the thousands—more than a few of them young graduates from Southern University. Antiwar protests roiled streets and campuses all over the country, all over the world. The emotional toll ran deep and heavy.

There I was, singing my songs, adding my voice to the conversation.

This is it, I thought. *I will always need to have this in my life.*

★ ★ ★

The passage of the Civil Rights Act of 1964 meant that the gates of higher education had swung open for everyone. My sisters Barbara and Lois were able to attend Louisiana State University as undergraduates.

During my senior year at Southern, riding on a wave of elation for all that I had accomplished, I got busy. One after another, I filled out and mailed twelve applications to medical schools located in every region of the country, north to south, east to west. I cast my net wide.

My grades were solid and my extracurriculars were stellar. Roll the dice twelve times, and you are bound to come up seven at least once. In my imaginings, I saw myself having a choice of schools, everybody clamoring to add Cleveland Francis Jr. to their honor rolls. I'd have to beat them off with a stick.

Johns Hopkins University in Baltimore, Case Western Reserve University in Cleveland, Duke University in North Carolina—I didn't hold back, I applied everywhere. In those days the two most viable medical schools at historically Black colleges were Howard University in DC and Meharry Medical College in Nashville. I considered those two my "safety school" options, certain that if I bombed out at the others, Howard or Meharry would take me.

But I wasn't planning on bombing out. I didn't even consider alternative futures. I would earn my MD and become a physician. The example of the Black doctor at the campus infirmary remained fresh in my mind, a personal touchstone for success.

Man makes plans, and God laughs. When the first rejection landed in my campus mailbox, I remained unruffled. Okay, all right, it's their loss. Then another envelope hit, and another, then two at once. Disappointment gave way to a rising sense of dread and panic. Twelve applications, twelve rejections. In my mind I thought of them as the dirty dozen. Even Howard and Meharry had turned me down.

As it turned out, my two "safety" schools had actually proved more difficult to get into, not less. They increasingly served as legacy schools, with slots reserved for children of doctors who were alumni. They were also virtually the only medical schools in the country enrolling Black students. The one-two punch—the legacy situation, plus competing with every other Black applicant in America—worked to shut me out.

The golden future I had so optimistically laid out for myself was not to be. What was I going to do now?

At one of Doc's social gatherings I laid my troubles out to the host himself. He first commiserated with me, but then quickly shifted into a practical mode, attacking the problem briskly and without sentiment.

"Well, you know, Cleveland, I'd say you're going have to reenroll here at Southern. You'll need to convert your degree into an education degree, so you're not totally at a loss, just hanging out there with a bachelor's degree and nowhere to go."

For some reason Doc's sober-minded approach only increased my frustration. I was confronting a crash-and-burn vision of the future, and I thought he should have recognized my predicament as a Shakespearean-level tragedy. *Oh my God*, I thought. *I'm headed right back into the dome.*

"An education degree will require a year of student teaching," Doc continued. "You will have to secure some funding, and perhaps find scholarships for at least the next six months."

I couldn't stand it. My skin felt like it was being stung by a swarm of London White's yellow jackets. I got to my feet and hurried to put on my coat.

"Cleveland?" Thelma Perkins asked. "You're leaving us?"

"The problem is I'm *not* leaving you," I muttered. "I'm not going anywhere."

I busted out of Doc's house and headed for Scott Bluffs, sitting there with the dark Mississippi River at my feet.

An education degree. A picture of Sidney Briscoe formed in mind, my beloved science teacher at Jeff Davis. He had risen as far as a person of color could within the confines of the dome. Half of my fellow graduates at Southern were headed for similar jobs teaching high school. The cast-iron ceiling of Jim Crow did not allow for any higher expectations.

They were the Black elite of Jennings, secondary school teachers such as Briscoe and the Gilbeaux brothers, folks without day laborer calluses on their hands or dirt beneath their fingernails, professionals with offices and salaries and high standing in the community. Their redbrick homes signified their success, while the rest of us lived in wooden-framed houses set on concrete blocks. Like the Francis home on Pearl Street.

The truth was, in the strict hierarchy of Jennings, there were gradations even within the Black community. The elites looked down on folks like Mary and Pete Francis and everyone else who worked with their hands. She never let on in public, but I know my mother felt their scorn. The caste system was heartless. Someone gets a leg up, first thing they do is put a boot on the neck of the fellow below.

So that was it. That was as far as I was allowed to go, aspiring to brick instead of wood. The last four years at Southern had been a fool's paradise, an aberration, a dead-end detour. I felt the hands of Jennings reaching out, seeking to drag me back home.

Bruce Springsteen tells a story of growing up in New Jersey, and his father recommending that he get a safe, nine-to-five job. "You work hard, you play it straight, you get a little something for yourself." Springsteen commented: "But I didn't want 'a little something.' I wanted it all!" That was me. I wanted all my dreams, medicine, music, everything.

Walking around campus in a daze during those days, I couldn't bring myself to confess to my family what had happened. Pete Francis, I thought bitterly, would give me an "I told you so" sneer. Mary Francis might pronounce herself happy to see me settled in a teaching position. Perhaps one day I could rise to become a high school principal like Wilbur Rochelle, advising graduates to go into the military.

One evening, feeling miserable and lost, I wandered the hallways of the biology building, a familiar home during my time at Southern, heavy with the formaldehyde odor of the labs, so comforting and inspiring to me. *That's the smell of success*, I used to tell myself. Idly glancing at the bulletin board outside the biology department offices, I noticed a pack of postcards stapled to the brown cork.

"SEEKING APPLICANTS," ran the all-caps heading. "Apply for graduate school at The College of William & Mary in Virginia." The cards listed an address in somewhere called Williamsburg, Virginia. I could not have pointed to the place on a map. The main feature of the cards that attracted me was the fact that they were postpaid. What did I have to lose? Not even the price of a stamp. I filled out the form and mailed it.

A few weeks later a package arrived at the campus post office, an application for graduate school in biology at William & Mary. I filled it out and mailed that, too.

I got in.

★ ★ ★

Mary Francis came to my graduation ceremony at Southern. Well, of course she did. Proud of me, yeah, but I also think she had a sense of satisfaction that she had managed to triumph over the Black elites in Jennings. Let them keep their brick houses. Her son Butch was going places, with a college diploma in his pocket and a bright future in graduate school. She wouldn't go as far as gloating in Wilbur Rochelle's face, or to any of the rest of them, but she knew what she knew. At least as far as her first child went, she had won.

Meanwhile I was trying to figure out where Williamsburg, Virginia was and who in the world William and Mary were. I found out that William & Mary was chartered by an English king and queen in 1693, making it the second oldest college in America, behind Harvard.

The College of William & Mary was always styled around campus simply as William & Mary, or W&M. The more I dug into research about the school, the more I had the feeling of ghosts walking across my grave. The fun pair of royals after whom the school was named, King William III and Queen Mary II of England, were actually first cousins. Among the school's graduates were two American presidents, Thomas Jefferson and James Monroe.

None of those names or dates meant that much to me. But I discovered that next door to campus, on the same Virginia peninsula as Williamsburg, lay a finger of land that used to be called Point Comfort. The name strikes a darkly tragic note. In August 1619, twenty or thirty enslaved Africans (the exact number is lost to history) landed at Point Comfort aboard an English privateer ship called *White Lion*. A couple of days later, a second ship, *Treasurer*, arrived with additional enslaved Africans.

These people were stolen from an area near today's Angola, probably from the Ndongo or Kongo kingdoms. Portuguese slavers kidnapped them, then hastened the captives off to labor and die in the gold mines of Mexico. Halfway across the Atlantic, in a development that sounds like a good news–bad news joke, pirates attacked the Portuguese ship, *São João Bautista*.

Great, right? Freedom! Not so fast. The privateers diverted the human cargo to Point Comfort.

So human trafficking in America began. A contemporary account gives this note: "The governor and cape merchant bought the Africans for victuals." I'm sure this doesn't mean they were purchased to eat. More likely they were traded for food and put to work in the tobacco fields.

The whole neighborhood of my new school would be haunted. Here was me, marked with a caul from birth, gifted with the sixth sense of seeing ghosts, headed to a place that was no doubt crawling with them.

Point Comfort was the Plymouth Rock for African Americans.

I wasn't about to let history stop me from pursuing my destiny in higher education. A plan came into focus. I would study at William & Mary for a master's degree in biology, which would lead to a doctoral thesis and a PhD. With that I could land a professorship at any junior college that would have me. It wasn't my dream of an MD, but a PhD would be the next best thing. I would be able to put a "Dr." before my name after all.

Goodbye Southern, goodbye Big Muddy, goodbye Louisiana. Farewell to Dr. Huel Perkins, who had taken his place as the most important adult male in my life. Doc and I had an emotional leave-taking. He had recorded a traditional spiritual that I performed with another Southern student, George West, called "Beams of Heaven."

Beams of heaven, as I go
Through this wilderness below
Guide my feet in peaceful ways
Turn my midnights into days
When in the darkness I would grope
Faith always sees a star of hope
And soon from all life's grief and danger
I shall be free some day

Perkins was aware that I was leaving for William & Mary. "Cleveland, I want you to make me a promise," he said.

"Yeah, hey, Doc, we'll be getting together again, plenty of times, I know."

"No, I want you to promise me you will continue developing your gift of music."

"Well, sure," I said. "You showed me the way."

"A second promise, too. When the time comes, I want you to sing 'Beams of Heaven' at my funeral."

"Aw, man, Doc," I said, embarrassed as one tends to be when someone suggests they'll die one day. "You're going to be around for a long time yet."

"Promise me," he repeated.

I said that I would. Years later, in 2013, I kept that second promise, playing at his memorial service. I like to think I tried to keep the first one, too, keeping my hand in music. And eventually I realized that my friend and mentor had left me with one last lesson. I hadn't realized that "Beams of Heaven" was written by the "father of African American hymnody," Charles Albert Tindley, a pastor, orator, poet, writer, theologian, and social activist.

Tindley claims a place in the secret history of American song along with eminent contributors forgotten or erased because of their skin color. So "Beams of Heaven," one of my mother's all-time favorites, wasn't some random choice for memorial music. At my own passing, I'm going to have mourners serenaded with a recording of me singing the hymn that Tindley wrote and that both my teacher and my mother treasured.

Dr. Huel Perkins was a good man, a towering figure in higher education, one of the unsung American heroes. There are dozens, hundreds, maybe thousands of Doc's students out there, his spiritual children, spreading his influence and passing on his heritage, down through the years and all over the country.

★ ★ ★

Traveling by train, you tend to experience scenery in a different way than you do traveling by automobile. Interstates have a sameness to them. All highway interchanges seem pretty much interchangeable.

With train travel, the routes take you through landscapes that somehow feel like they're out of an earlier time. You have a chance to see a countryside not malled up, truck-stopped, and billboarded out. From the windows of a train, you encounter not superhighways but dirt road byways, sandlot ballfields, backyard clotheslines strung with laundry, abandoned Pentecostal churches, turpentine camps, and freshly ploughed back-forties. Some of it is ugly, but most of it is quite beautiful. It's like seeing the country without makeup.

At the end of summer in 1967, Mary Francis met me at Union Passenger Terminal in downtown New Orleans. She wanted to see me off for my cross-country journey to William & Mary.

At this point neither one of us had ever left Louisiana. The fifty dollars she slipped me for the trip, a tight wad of tens, fives, and ones, probably represented months of scrimping. I was headed for the Great Unknown, but I did my best to put on a brave face. This lady was my rock, and I knew we wouldn't be seeing each other face to face any time soon.

My mother pointed out that one of her sayings had come true once again: "He may not arrive when you want him, but He's always right on time."

"So's the Southerner streamliner," I said, trying to keep the tone light. "That's right on time, too." I looked away, sizing up the magnificent silver locomotive that to me resembled an earthbound rocket ship.

When I turned back to Mary Francis, both of us had tears in our eyes.

"We did it, Mama," I whispered, hugging her tight.

"Well, you got to keep on doing it, up there in Virginia," she said. She released the embrace before I did. "Be good and remember the Lord, Butch."

I started to walk away, but my mother had one last word of advice. "Remember to find the church when you get there."

The Black church was a vibrant American support network like no other, surpassing the Masons, the Shriners, or the Toastmasters. The church served as a modern-day underground railroad. Wherever I went, I knew a safe haven would be somewhere nearby.

"You'll be fine if you just find the church," Mary Francis called after me.

With that I boarded the silver rocket for a new life. My single brown metal suitcase and the guitar Doc had given me seemed to be the only things connecting me with the past, the only moorings that kept me from floating off into space.

I found my seat, a single economy fare with no one else around me. I gazed out the window at the passing landscape. The Southerner streamliner had station stops in Picayune, Hattiesburg, Laurel, and Meridian in Mississippi, and Tuscaloosa and Birmingham in Alabama. We were heading for Georgia and the swing north along the East Coast—all places I had never been.

The rhythmic, clickety-clack song of the rails mesmerized me.

Good morning, America, how are you?
Don't you know me?
I'm your native son

Was I? Steve Goodman hadn't yet written "The City of New Orleans" at that point, but I had a similar question as we traveled east toward Atlanta. Was I a native son of America? Richard Wright asked the same question in his 1940 novel, *Native Son*. At times it seemed the nation had disowned and disinherited me and others like me. I was taking a leap without knowing what I would find when I landed.

Hope told me I was headed for a better place. I had little knowledge about Virginia or Williamsburg. But after all, wasn't pretty much any place preferable to Jennings, Louisiana? I recalled something that Frederick Douglass wrote: "I prayed for twenty years but received no answer until I prayed with my legs." I had prayed for twenty years, and now I was praying with my legs.

On and on the Southerner rolled. Day turned to dusk. The country seemed too immense to make any sort of sense out of it. America the endless would swallow me whole. I would disappear into it and never be found again.

Along past houses, farms, and fields
Passing towns that have no name
And freight yards full of old Black men
And the graveyards of the rusted automobiles

I fell asleep while we were passing through Atlanta and didn't wake until a conductor shook me by the shoulder hours later.

"Charlottesville," he said. "You change trains here."

Foggy-headed and still clueless, I grabbed my guitar and suitcase and stumbled off onto the platform. I was that green—I hadn't realized I needed to switch trains. Where was I? What time was it? Near midnight by the big station clock. With a hiss of airbrakes the big streamliner pulled out, headed for DC and eventually New York City. Both the platform and the station were deserted. Despair, loneliness, and fear settled in, feeling like an illness coming on.

Nothing for it, I thought. Rolling up my suit jacket for a pillow, I laid down on the varnished mahogany benches of Charlottesville Union Station. I was exhausted, but sleep eluded me.

Charlottesville, I thought. Site of Monticello. I had a nickel in my pocket and there it was on the reverse side of the coin, the elegant home of Thomas Jefferson. He had graduated from William & Mary, the same school I would attend, the man who wrote the words, "All men are created equal."

My restless brain wouldn't quit, parading random images through my mind, stray facts, scraps of song lyrics, whole train cars of memories. Charlottesville. Site of Monticello, yes, but also the major hub for slave trading in the antebellum South. From 1790 to 1865, thousands upon thousands of people were trafficked at the slave market in the town's Court Square. "The entrepôt of evil," the scholar Henry Louis Gates Jr. labeled it.

In the empty train station, I heard an echo of the folksinger Odetta, in full voice at her famous 1960 concert at Carnegie Hall.

No more auction block for me
No more, no more
No more auction block for me
Many thousands gone

Oh, stop it, I commanded myself. Not all places are haunted. *Yes, they are.* Not everything relates. *Yes, it all relates.* No, it doesn't. Get some sleep.

★ ★ ★

The next morning, as we boarded a train bound for the Virginia Peninsula cities of Richmond, Williamsburg, and Newport News, I happened to help a lady heft her heavy bag up to an overhead rack. I felt self-conscious doing it, since despite a quick sponge bath in the Charlottesville station restroom, I figured I still had an air of travel funk on me.

"Oh, thank you," said the nice blonde lady.

"Happy to help," I mumbled.

After we disembarked at the Williamsburg Transportation Center, I lugged my stuff to the street outside the station. Feeling like a little lost sheep, I stood attempting to figure out my next move. The woman who I had helped stow luggage pulled up in a car beside me.

"Hello?" she called out. "You were so nice to me on the train that I wonder if I might give you a ride."

The situation was a new one to me. I tried to imagine anything similar happening in Jennings or even Baton Rouge. I approached the driver's side window.

"Where are you headed?" she asked.

"I'm not real familiar with the town," I said. "Where do Black folks live?"

"Hop in," she said.

Maybe this is just how things happen in strange-ass Virginia, I thought. I slid my suitcase and guitar into the back seat of her shiny new Buick. Should I get in back with my baggage? Or do the unimaginable, and sit up front next to a white woman? She reached over and opened the front passenger door for me.

"Is there a Black church in town?" I asked, getting in. "Maybe you could take me there."

"There are two, First Baptist and New Zion Baptist Church."

In my clueless state of mind, I couldn't decide.

"You want to go to the First Baptist Church on Scotland Street," she said authoritatively, deciding for me. "That's the oldest one, one of the oldest Black churches in the country, I think."

She dropped me off at a solid redbrick edifice in the colonial style that didn't look all that old to me. I thanked her and waved as we said goodbye. She drove off down Scotland Street. I never saw the woman again. I think the heart spiritually grows with every act of kindness.

I had arrived in Williamsburg as a stranger in a strange land. "Just find the church and you'll be fine," Mary Francis had said, her last words to me.

This particular Black church proved to be closed up tight, with no one there to answer my knocks. I was so close to being home that I could near enough taste it, but I wasn't there yet. I dropped my bags and sat down on the front steps. Then I got up and read the nearby historical plaque. First Baptist was indeed one of the oldest continuous congregations formed by African Americans, founded by enslaved worshippers gathering in brush arbor meetings in 1776. The same year the country itself was founded. *"We hold these truths to be self-evident . . . "*

Somehow, in some way, I had faith that First Baptist would magically open its doors to me. *God will hear*, I thought. I knocked again. No answer. It was Saturday, the pastor's traditional day off. Of course no one was around. What now?

Well, if I can't get into the church, I'll pray with my legs again. I knocked on the front door of the gracious white clapboard house next door to the church. A middle-aged Black woman in a sundress answered.

"I was just over at First Baptist," I said. "I wanted to speak to the pastor."

"Oh, you know, I heard someone say Reverend Collins has the weekend off," she said. "He's not preaching this weekend."

"Well, I just came in from Louisiana, and I'm enrolled at William & Mary."

"From Louisiana? Well, that's a long way. You know, Reverend Collins—Reverend David Collins—he's from Louisiana, too! Where are you staying in Williamsburg?"

I shifted my feet, unsure how to answer. Seeing my blank look, she jumped in with an offer of hospitality. "Well, hey, you know what? You can stay here with us tonight."

I made a weak attempt to beg off, but I wasn't about to argue with her.

"In the morning," she said, "I'll contact the minister. We will get you two together."

Well, yes, the Lord works in mysterious ways, and oftentimes extremely generous ways. This stranger I had just met took me in and introduced me to her family. I was served an excellent home-cooked meal and given the opportunity to take a hot shower. The next morning I got up and there was a big family breakfast waiting. My host telephoned Reverend Collins.

"Bring him over to the parsonage on Monday," the pastor told her.

CHAPTER 9

Back to the Past

IF IT WASN'T GOD who was looking out for me when I landed in Williamsburg, I sure wish I knew who it was, because I want to shake that man's hand. An anonymous lady gave me a ride. A second stranger invited me into her home, fed me, and provided a feather bed to rest my travel-weary bones. Then I met a new friend, the pastor, who invited me to stay in his palace.

Well, okay, it wasn't really a palace, only the parsonage for the First Baptist Church. But it was kind of majestic—big, well appointed, and comfortable, a white wooden colonial home with a giant front porch and high ceilings inside. Southern living at its finest. Rev. David Collins, a single divorced preacher, rattled around in the place all alone.

I told him I had just arrived in town, from New Orleans by way of Charlottesville. "I'm just looking for a place to study," I said.

"You need look no further," he said. "You can stay with me. From here, you're only two blocks from the college. We have plenty of room."

Plenty of room, yes. We sat in the parsonage's immense back parlor, a space designed to host church socials, choir meetings, or impromptu touch football games. It was a cocoon of bourgeoise splendor. Lace doilies lay on every surface—in fact, some of the doilies had doilies on them, no doubt crocheted by the women of the First Baptist ladies auxiliary.

"Hey, you have to pay rent," Rev. Collins said, as if the idea had just occurred to him. "I'm not going to charge you an arm and a leg, but I'm cheap, and it'll be on the principle of the thing. Not going to gouge a poor young scholar. I can help you."

Neither one of us actually quoted the verse in the book of Matthew, but it's what we were both thinking. "Truly I tell you, whatever you did for one of the least of these brothers and sisters of mine, you did for me."

Everything was just right in line with the two of us. Collins was from Louisiana. I was from Louisiana. Collins led a life in the Baptist Church, I led a life in the Baptist Church. That morning we became fast friends. The pastor came across as a mild-mannered churchman, balding, with horned-rimmed glasses. But I soon learned the man had a steel will underneath all that, as well as being a powerful preacher.

Collins told me that the entrance steps at First Baptist, the ones I had rested upon the afternoon I came into town, were hallowed ground. Those same stone steps had been trod by his hero and mine, Rev. Dr. Martin Luther King Jr., during a celebrated visit to Williamsburg in June 1962. Collins himself had serious civil right bona fides, assuming an executive position in the Southern Christian Leadership Conference, leading lunch counter demonstrations, mentoring local high school students in the doctrine of nonviolence. He was my type of guy.

"I notice you've got a guitar with you," he said.

"Well, I sing," I told him.

He looked pleased and excited. "What do you sing?"

"Oh, you know, spirituals, gospel, and folk music. I was raised in the church, my sisters and I all sang in the choir. We had a small gospel group known as the Francis Singers."

He eyed me and eyed the guitar, which rested alongside my brown metal suitcase. I took the hint, got out the instrument Doc Perkins had gifted me with, and did my folkie version of "Amazing Grace." When I finished it felt as though Rev. Collins and I were going to be ascending to heaven, if not right away, then sometime soon.

That song tends to transport people. The good reverend certainly reacted strongly. He looked like he was about to give me a break on the rent, thought the better of it, and shook my hand instead.

The following Sunday at First Baptist, Collins set me up to sing in front of the congregation. He urged the members of the congregation to go out of their way to introduce me to the Black community of Williamsburg, to let folks know who I was and what I was doing.

"We've got a newcomer that came in from my home state," he said. "Finally, one of our own students is going to be able to attend college right here at William & Mary. He needs our support. He's also a singer and he is going to lead us all in 'Amazing Grace.'"

My passport. Even though I was "a certain man," as the Bible labels an unknown newcomer, music allowed me entry into Williamsburg society. First the Black community, then later into the town and campus as a whole.

The folks in the congregation enjoyed having me sing up in front of the congregation, accompanied by the church's musical director on piano. I enjoyed it, too. We got along well, the church members and me. They were not solemn and silent, but liked to make a joyful noise unto the Lord every once in a while, injecting a participatory "Amen!" or "Yes, Lord!" into the proceedings.

Right away, from that first Sunday on, my songs turned into a regular feature in the First Baptist order of service. Each Sunday before Rev. Collins delivered his sermon, he'd have me up to sing a spiritual, a gospel number, or an old-style hymn.

An aspect I liked about Collins was that although he was no doubt a man of the cloth, he lived in the real world. He liked to impart secular life lessons to me just as much as scriptural ones. The preacher owned a big Lincoln Continental, and he'd let me drive the monster as we went around town. Occasionally, we had dinner out, and once we were approached by a very striking woman who had friends in the First Baptist congregation. She sat with us for a while, we shared a coffee, and then Collins got up and announced it was time for us to go.

"Sorry to leave you, ma'am, but we have another meeting," Collins said.

Outside the restaurant, I confronted him. "What are we doing? Why'd you tell her that? We don't have another meeting."

"I'll give you a good piece of advice, Cleve," he said, climbing into the Lincoln. "Whenever you're in a conversation with a very beautiful woman, you be the first to leave, and that way she'll remember you with favor."

Two blocks away from the parsonage lay the green expanse of the W&M campus. I bought a bike and started exploring the environs. My residency at the parsonage lasted only for one year. Collins soon took another church posting and moved on, but for my first year at William & Mary he provided a soft landing.

★ ★ ★

Williamsburg threw me into a history book. Let's round it off and make it an even thousand miles from Jennings to my new home in Virginia. I didn't realize that while I had moved a measurable distance across the country, I also effectively traveled back in time.

In the center of town sat a three-hundred-acre living-history museum called Colonial Williamsburg. Everything was ye olde this and ye olde that, bonnets and bodices and cocked tricornes. An aura of unreality enveloped what was essentially a theme park of the past.

Rev. Collins told me that when the Rockefeller family endowed the Colonial Williamsburg Foundation in the 1920s, the founders razed a historic Black neighborhood to make way for the development. The process included flattening the earliest First Baptist Church site from the 1700s. The land was then used as a parking lot.

Recently, an archeological dig at the site turned up the brick foundation of the original meeting house, as well as a cemetery with sixty graves. Researchers selected three individuals for exhumation and DNA testing, revealing all three to be male and of African descent.

According to a report on the dig, the analysis yielded the following:

> One subject died between the ages of 16 and 18, and had experienced early childhood stressors, such as malnutrition or disease. A garment button made from animal bone was recovered from his grave. . . . Skeletal analysis of the remains of the two other less well-preserved individuals revealed that both were male and aged between 35 and 45 years old. One appears to have been buried dressed in trousers and a vest, and a button from his clothing still had cotton fibers attached.

Ghosts! Ghosts and hauntings all around me! Who will protect from harm the boy born with a caul? Animal bone buttons? Are you kidding me? Trousers and a vest? Cotton fibers? Superstitious Pete Francis would have a witchcraft field day.

I had traveled a thousand miles on the ground, and two centuries through time. In Colonial Williamsburg I encountered place names such as Duke of Gloucester Street and the Palace Green. Reconstructed buildings and restored originals summoned up a facsimile of an earlier era: Raleigh Tavern, the Governor's Palace, the Wythe House, the Bruton Parish Church.

The grand families of the American power establishment underwrote the whole affair—the Rockefellers, of course, but also Lila and DeWitt Wallace, the couple behind *Reader's Digest*, and Walter Annenberg, a philanthropist, ambassador to the UK, and publisher (*Racing Form*, *TV Guide*, *Seventeen*).

Wandering amid groups of historical reenactors wearing colonial period costumes, I felt torn between finding the presentations cool and interesting, and judging them to be a skewed view of the past. Forgive a Black man for not being sentimental and nostalgic about colonial America.

I stood looking on as a blacksmith banged away with a huge hammer, shaping a horseshoe next to a coal-fired forge. He performed a memorized spiel to the family of tourists that surrounded him, telling them what a colonial farrier's life was like, but occasionally going off script to slip in choice tidbits of political commentary.

"I actually don't think the Civil War was about slavery at all," he said, punctuating the observation with a terrific hammer blow on his anvil. *Uh-huh*, I thought, recognizing the blacksmith's comment as an example of what gets thrown around in common everyday speech without considering who it might affect. It's one of those lines we hear consistently when someone doesn't want to discuss the issue of slavery. I shook my head and moved on to the butter-churning exhibit.

Colonial Williamsburg bordered on the College Yard of William & Mary. In fact, William & Mary was essentially next door and to the immediate west of Williamsburg. The campus itself represented something of a culture shock. I had gone from Southern University, an environment where pretty much everyone looked like me, to W&M, where no one did.

Well, almost no one. While I was indeed the only African American in the biology graduate program, there were other Black students at the school. A total of five of us, in fact, on the whole campus. We counted. Three female undergraduates, a female law student, and me. I referred to us as the William & Mary Five.

Though the atmosphere of Williamsburg seemed designed to put white culture on display, I never once experienced any racial ugliness the whole time I was there. I was never denied access to the college's library, never had the N-word flung at me from a passing car. Virginia remained segregated, to be sure. But somehow the state pulled off the uncanny trick of just happening to have become that way. Jim Crow had been rendered into a ghostly background presence.

I felt none of the constant undertone of fear I grew up with. If I was a stranger in this community, it was because I made myself feel like one. But the change in environment took some getting used to. The customs were different. I noticed little things, like the fact that folks didn't make up plates of food and pass them around the way we tended to do in Louisiana. We called it "fixing a plate," as in, "Say, honey-child, can you fix me a plate?" In Virginia, the dishes were passed for each diner to help themselves.

Being a graduate student proved to be a whole separate ballgame from my undergraduate work at Southern. For the first time, I got involved in doing original science research. Dr. Garnett Brooks, my professor, was a brilliant herpetologist. Meanwhile I was frightened by snakes—and I mean I had a real, Indiana Jones–level of fear left over from my Louisiana childhood. What was I doing assisting a herpetologist? It felt as though fate was playing a cruel joke.

My very first day on campus, a secretary in the biology department offices told me to meet Dr. Brooks at his lab. Following directions, I came upon a door bearing his name and knocked.

"It's open! Come in."

I found him sitting at his desk in a room filled with snakes, jars of dead snakes in formaldehyde and cage upon cage of live snakes.

"Hey, Black man!" he called out, and tossed a three-foot long rat snake at my feet. Later on, I learned that Prof. Brooks performed the same snake-tossing trial by fire with all of his grad students, no matter the color of their skin.

For reasons that could be attributed only to my intestinal fortitude, spinal integrity, and instinctual paralysis, I didn't flinch, didn't leap up onto a chair and holler. I stood there, a little shocked but otherwise okay. The snake slithered off. It was not small.

Dr. Garnett Brooks busted out laughing. "It's a good thing you aren't scared of snakes because we've got nothing but snakes around here. One of your jobs will be feeding them." He gave me a serious look and added ominously, "Not all of them are as harmless as the *P. obsoletus* I just pitched at you."

You have to understand, this incident represented virtually my debut encounter with a white man, or least with a white stranger. I mean, I knew white folks could be different, but this reptile-tossing business outdid everything. I used to tell people that the first time I ever met my professor, he called out, "Hey, Black man!" and threw a snake at my feet.

We got on well. His fellow faculty members always called him by his nickname, Jack. By reason of my standing as his research assistant, I didn't think I qualified for the informality, and always addressed him formally as "Dr. Brooks." His primary research focused not on snakes but on the species *Sceloporus occidentalis*, the western fence lizard. (For many years, his e-mail address included the tag "lizardwidowmaker.") The professor's interest centered on evolutionary biology. He sought a better understanding of an anatomical oddity shared by several varieties of lizard.

A third eye.

Gurus and yogis in Eastern religion talk about the mystical power of a symbolic third eye, but at William & Mary we were studying the real thing, an actual physical attribute. Our research showed that the lizard's third eye represented an evolutionary forerunner of the pineal gland, which in mammals plays a crucial role in internally regulating sleep-wake cycles and circadian rhythms. These reptiles would evolve into mammals that are able to control their own internal temperature. The fence lizards we studied burrowed under the sand, with only the third eye exposed to help the animals gauge ambient heat.

Caged lizards and snakes outnumbered human beings in the lab by a ratio of maybe a few hundred to one. I worked under the direction of Dr. Brooks, feeding and taking care of the creatures.

We had three groups of lizards, one with the eye surgically removed, another with the eye covered with tin foil to serve as a sham operation, and a third control group without any intervention. I collected lizards shipped from an exotic animal emporium in California, keeping them fat and happy with a steady diet of crickets. The schedule demanded I stop by the lab in the middle of every night to ensure the heat lamps were working properly and to check which of my lizard charges were up and about.

Life is funny. I wanted more than anything to become a medical doctor who treated human beings. And there I was, a grad student working with lizards.

The novelty of the gig did have certain side benefits. One night I took a date up to the lab, hoping to show off the impressive nature of our research. At that point in my life, I might not have had a firm grasp on what constituted a romantic evening.

"Do they bite?" my date asked, examining the motionless research subjects.

Impulsively, I stuck a finger into one of the cages to demonstrate to her that the creatures were harmless. A large resident lizard lunged forward, snapped its jaws down on my finger, and refused to let go.

My date started screaming. I yanked open the cage. The lizard stood its ground.

"This is—this is—unusual," I stammered. I reached my other hand into the cage and attempted to pry the lizard off my finger. In the struggle, the poor creature's tail dropped off.

The woman beside me fainted.

At least unconsciousness put an end to her screaming. I was torn between checking on the poor girl—she had fallen to the floor—and making sure I didn't lose my index finger to a lizard bite. Or worse, lose my research subject.

"Loss of a tail—the, the loss of the tail—no, no big deal," I babbled nervously to no one. "They regrow, regrow—regenerate the tail."

With an audible champagne cork thwock! my finger popped from the lizard's maw. I was unscathed, and I knew the tail would grow back whole within a month. The fainting maiden also recovered, shaken but unharmed. I suspected the night at the lab would be my last date with her.

★ ★ ★

Only a special kind of crazy will propel a person onstage with only a guitar to hide behind. Nobody is ever more alone. Singer-songwriters resemble standup comedians in that way. Not for nothing does the language of performance invoke extreme terms. "I died up there tonight." "I really killed it just now." Having an audience stare silently or seeing folks flee toward the exits really does feel like a sort of death.

As I settled in at Williamsburg, I had the best motivation in the world to head out and try to find music gigs. I was broke. A graduate student's stipend leads to weight loss and eventual starvation. To make some spending money, I searched around for bars, nightclubs, and restaurants that were looking to hire an itinerant troubadour.

As far as that went, I was in the right place at the right time. The folk revival that began in the 1950s didn't die when Bob Dylan went electric at the Newport Folk Festival in July 1965. I had that surprised exclamation of Doc Perkins ringing in my ears: "You're doing folk music!" I came to the realization that I could rightfully claim a place amid the hordes of bearded, finger-snapping, acoustic guitar–strumming coffeehouse poets, the children of Woody Guthrie, Lead Belly, and Pete Seeger.

Word of mouth among my fellow students served as my booking agent. I sang a couple of times at Hoi Polloi, a small coffeehouse lounge located within the student union. Then I heard of a bar called Castaways located on Route 17, the busy main stem of the city of Newport News. Not to mince words, the joint was a redneck place, packing in Virginia good ole boys as well as sailors from the nearby naval hubs at Norfolk. The couple who ran the place, Brenda and Danny Grubaugh, took to me right away.

Though I had a difficult time believing it myself, I actually became a popular act at Castaways. The more I played there, the more I built an audience, and the more the Grubaughs asked me back. I'd gaze out from the small stage at the alcohol-fueled, borderline raucous crowd and ask, *Are these really my people?* Then they'd applaud like crazy after a song and I'd think, *Yeah, these are my people.*

The bouncer at the place looked like he came out of a tractor commercial, but he had my back. "Ever anyone says anything, just tell me," he said. We both knew what he was talking about. "In fact, anyone even looks at you cross-eyed, they's out." He jerked a thumb toward the door and made a quick whistling noise with his teeth.

Nothing ever happened. No bar-brawl incidents, no cross-eyed looks. In fact, just the opposite. I made a lot of personal friends simply by virtue of being the lead singer. One of my fans, a white construction worker who came in every time I performed, brought his wife and invited me to sit next to her in one of the booths.

"You know," he said, marveling. "This is the first time my wife ever sat next to an N-word." Only he didn't use the polite euphemism. He came right out with the full monty.

He laughed, half-embarrassed, and extended an invitation for dinner at their mobile home. The situation was too pathetic for me to get angry. Here was a fan who had shown up almost every night that I performed at the club, but he was limited by his background. All he had heard during his upbringing was that two-syllable descriptor. The gent knew of no other word to describe me. I respected his impulse, his effort to forge a human connection—bringing his wife in to meet me, insisting that I, a Black man, sit next to her, a white woman.

But I have been called "nigger" my whole life. I certainly wished my Castaways fan had used another word. I understood what the term could mean and what it had meant in history. But I also knew who I was, and I wasn't that. In this context, the usage wasn't disrespect. It was ignorance.

Ah, America, I thought. Nothing like it in the world.

CHAPTER 10

Follow Me

PERFORMING ALL OVER the Tidewater area, I experienced something of an identity crisis. Students stopped me on campus to ask for an autograph. Audience members at Castaways became familiar enough with what I was doing that some of them would request specific songs. The identity crisis came when a middle-aged Black gent approached me after a set.

"You're doing real good, man, but I'm wondering something," he said.

"What's that?" I sort of knew what was coming.

"Why in the hell are you playing all this white music? Hanks Williams, that's cracker country, and then that Peter Paul and Mary folkie stuff? Joni Mitchell? Judy Collins? C'mon, man, that ain't you. That ain't us. You sound like Mr. Man has taken y'all over."

He came off not so much angry as puzzled. I just smiled politely and responded with some neutral comment that I didn't recall afterwards. But I did remember his words, and took them with me back to campus. The problem was that I had similar questions buzzing around in my own mind.

What I was doing felt nothing but right. The music I played rose straight out of the willow tree refuge in the Francis backyard. No "Mr. Man" was involved in its creation at all. But was I somehow unconsciously channeling the wrong kind of material? Was I a Black man with white tastes?

The question sent me off on a research jag at the campus library. I dove into the stacks, tracking down the history of folk music in books, magazines, encyclopedia entries, anything, everything. A university library is one of my favorite places in the world. If the library doesn't have something, the librarians will hunt a book or article down like the Feds after an outlaw, canvassing other collections all over the country. Interlibrary loan became my gold mine.

What I found opened my eyes. Folk music had a deep African American background—I mean, of course it did. Specific kinds of music have the reputation of being the exclusive property of the Caucasian race, but that idea could not be more wrong. It took some digging, but I uncovered a secret history that revealed a stunning level of diversity everywhere I looked.

We're taught that music is made up of several rivers. Folk flows over there, country runs here, classical is somewhere separate, as are the wild currents of jazz. But music is an ocean. The waters mix and flood and merge. And all the various peoples on earth have had a free hand in it.

The term "folk music" itself began as a description of the music of Black America. Early mentions stretch back to 1913, describing the work of Will Marion Cook, a composer and violinist who directed a group called the Afro-American Folk Singers. Cook used spirituals as the basis of his concert compositions. I also discovered Black singers who had preceded me more recently, including Terry Callier, who in 1964 recorded an album called *The New Folk Sound of Terry Callier*.

The roots of folk snaked out from the blues, a music that was Black as it could be, its beginnings reaching back to Africa. From colonial times onward, Anglo-Celtic balladry cross-fertilized with hymns of the Black church to create an entire repertoire of commonly known songs.

Figures among the Black intelligentsia had long weighed in on the subject. James Weldon Johnson, composer of "Lift Every Voice and Sing," often called the Black national anthem, spoke about "unknown bards" in reference to the anonymous creators of tunes that had been passed down over generations. W. E. B. Du Bois described folk music as "weird old songs in which the soul of the Black slave spoke."

During my childhood, I witnessed the cross-fertilization process happen firsthand. A neighbor played harmonica, someone a few streets over played blues guitar. One of the teachers at Jefferson Davis High did jazz. We had magnificent gospel singing in church, some of it contributed by my own sisters.

I knew Cajun music intimately from family roots in Têche country, and saw with my own eyes all different sorts of people participating—Black, white, Creole, and Native American. My grandfather Jimmy Bobb played a mean *fais-dodo* accordion, the zydeco music for Saturday night country dance parties. I also grew up on the western music of Roy Rogers and Gene Autry.

How can we separate the strands? It's impossible. Shape-note singing came from Africa. The banjo has African roots. Work chanteys, field hollers, murder ballads—you sure can't pull apart the strands and assign origins there. It's all too tangled. Wonderfully tangled, I thought, marveling at the sheer humanity on display in the history of folk, the incredible variety.

Artists are like sponges. My own music blended influences of every singer I had ever heard and liked, superimposed with my own style. I loved the soul of Sam Cooke, the clarity of Nat King Cole, the heart of Harry Chapin, the songwriting of Brook Benton, the spirit of Mahalia Jackson, the smoothness of Johnny Mathis, and the country honesty of Hank Williams and Merle Haggard.

The last person who had tried to parse out what I was doing, Dr. Huel Perkins at Southern University, had settled on the term "folk music." All right, I thought, okay. But I knew my sound developed independently under a giant backyard willow tree in Jennings, Louisiana. It might as well be classified as its own separate category, as "300 Pearl Street Music."

People had been trying to jam me into a pigeonhole my whole life. But pigeonholes are for pigeons, and I resurfaced from my deep dive at the campus library with a new sense of confidence. Genre is a lie. Segregation is a lie. A border is a lie. In an interview in *DownBeat* magazine, Joni Mitchell said, "I want the full hyphen: folk-rock-country-jazz-classical. So finally when you get all the hyphens in, maybe they'll drop them all, and get down to just some American music." My sentiments exactly.

I decided that I could play the classification game as well as anyone. I began describing my music as its own distinct category. I labeled it "soul-folk" and dared anyone to call me out for it.

★ ★ ★

At Hoi Polloi, the little coffeehouse lounge at W&M, I began noticing a professorial gent a few years older than me who always came alone, the same face in the audience every night I performed. He'd sometimes shout out requests. The student crowd tended to be pretty casual and vocal, so this guy fit right in. He smiled a lot and gave off a friendly, enthusiastic vibe, so I couldn't begrudge him the random catcall. In my mind I fondly nicknamed him the Heckler.

In the middle of a rendition of Jose Feliciano's "Rain," the Heckler stood up and called out a challenge.

"Can you hit the high note?" he shouted, pointing his finger to the sky.

Damn-slamma-bamma, man, what are you doing, interrupting the set? But he had thrown down the gauntlet, and I picked it up, hitting him with a full octave high vocal that pretty near blew him right through the back wall of the lounge.

The Heckler looked professorial because he actually *was* a professor, and a nationally prominent, full-tenured one at that. Dr. Victor Liguori taught sociology and anthropology courses at William & Mary. His wide-ranging interests included race relations and environmentalism, and he offered popular courses in both. He was single and had a lot of time on his hands in the evenings. At Hoi Polloi, Castaways, and area music festivals, Victor developed into my most devoted fan.

In the months that followed our first meeting, Victor proved to be much more than a fan, becoming a friend and mentor, serving as my unofficial manager. We began hanging out almost every day. I'd drop by his office in the sociology department after work, or we would meet up somewhere and talk. Growing up I never had a brother, which was close to what Victor Liguori came to be for me.

The first time I dropped by his office, I was mistaken for the janitorial help. The professor himself wasn't in yet.

"So, hey, yeah, you're here," called out one of the other sociology professors. "I need this cabinet moved and they only sent one person?"

"Moved where?" I asked, not letting on. Seeing how small-statured I was, he offered to assist me.

Together we dragged the big file cabinet from one side of the office to the other. When we finished, he thanked me.

"Actually, I'm here to see Victor," I told him. He became speechless. When Victor showed up ten minutes later, we had a good laugh about it. Sometimes the only thing you can do is laugh. The incident proved even funnier when he informed me that the professor specialized in the study of social stereotypes.

Never before did I have white friends, surely not in Jennings, and not at Southern University, either. Neither was I used to acting as an authority figure to white people, which I did every day teaching undergraduate classes in biology. The novelty of the more relaxed interracial relationships at W&M made me a little nervous. I kept wanting to look over my shoulder. But I liked it, and eventually I came to a conclusion that shaped the rest of my life.

In a glass-half-full moment of clarity, I realized that as much as I hated racism and prejudice, I loved brotherhood and sisterhood more. The positives of integration far outweighed the negatives of segregation. It wasn't even close. I realized I considered Victor Liguori my brother. I looked into my soul and understood I couldn't in all conscience describe our connection in any other way.

The two years I spent at William & Mary proved to be a watershed in my life. For the first time I made dear friends who were not Black. Victor Liguori, yes, but two others as well, both fellow students.

When I needed new digs after my cushy parsonage residence ended, I asked a fellow grad student in the biology department named David Gapp if he wanted to pitch in together as roommates. What we had in common was that Dr. Brooks supervised our progress on our graduate work. We weren't much more than casual study partners, but we agreed to look for a place in the Williamsburg community near campus.

The search did not proceed straightforwardly. A Black guy and a white guy, two grad students looking for housing? Tidewater Virginia might have been a bit more culturally advanced than Jennings, but there were still local limits to the boundaries of brotherhood. After getting doors shut in our faces in several different neighborhoods, we finally rented a house in the Black part of town.

Dave's biology research centered on turtles in the nearby James River. I accompanied him on one of his trips, rowing a flatboat along the same landscape where the first enslaved Africans in the country had arrived over three hundred years earlier. Dave had set up turtle traps on the river shoreline. He would lift the poor turtles by their tails and—you might want to avert your eyes for this—perform enemas and place the poop in petri dishes. Back at the lab, Dave would analyze the gut bacteria of his research subjects, examining the flora for changes as an index of industrial pollution affecting wildlife.

We made quite a team, he and I, me fooling with the third eye of the western fence lizard, him dealing with the butt ends of the striped mud turtle. Hurray for the unstoppable march of science.

Dave noodled some on the guitar, nothing fancy, just basic stuff. We often played together during the rare times we weren't hitting the books. When I found out that duos were sometimes paid twice the money as a solo act, I suggested he might join me onstage.

Dave might have qualified as the shyest person I had ever met. His immediate reaction: "What? No way!" I waited another few days and asked him again.

"You really don't have to do anything but strike a few notes now and then," I said. "No stage patter, no nothing. Just do some of those guitar runs you do."

He looked dubious. We tried out the act in a dining room at the Williamsburg Inn, and he was indeed as stiff as a board. But the inn and other clubs paid us double. The duo of Cleve & Dave was born. The bump to fifty dollars from twenty-five still sounds minor, until you realize that the higher amount is equivalent to $450 in today's dollars. Enough to keep both of us afloat for the week.

After a few weeks at coffeehouses, bars, and other venues, Dave actually got into performing. He never exactly loosened up, but he did provide tasty back-up fills. Gradually, we widened our selection of entertainment venues. We did gigs at a few Tidewater music festivals. Even more raucous than Castaways, the Wharf, a popular club on the Yorktown waterfront, asked us back repeatedly. We ignored the constant barfights and kept on playing, needing to get paid.

A second friend at W&M, Lorna Totman, might have been closer to me than Dave Gapp. Dave and I roomed together, worked together, and played music together, but our connection remained near the surface. While Lorna and I never had a romantic relationship, I developed a deeper friendship with her than with any other person I knew at Williamsburg. She was a senior biology major. I only knew her for a single year before she graduated, but during that time we became friends for life.

She would come to every one of my shows that she could. We had serious conversations about any topic at all—politics, race, the war, whatever. I don't know how many Black people Lorna knew, but she more or less "adopted" me like a big sister. She was engaged to a guy in the military and they planned on marrying after graduation. Lorna stood tall and skinny with straight, long black hair. Her most noticeable feature had to be her clear, piercing eyes. She spoke the truth at all costs.

"I'm always afraid the campus police will mess with you, Cleve," she told me.

"I'll be all right," I reassured her. I never experienced any problems, including during those late-night walks across campus to babysit the fence lizards.

I asked Rev. Collins if it would be okay to invite Lorna to First Baptist.

"Yes, of course, son," he responded. "All are welcome in our church." The empathetic treatment of strangers always moved me as a prominent aspect of the Christian faith. As far as I know, the same principle holds true in Islam, Hinduism, and Buddhism.

As was the custom, that day a deacon rose to ask a question at the beginning of the service. "Do we have visitors to the church this morning?"

Lorna stood and said her name. "I'm a member of Oakton Methodist Church of Oakton, Virginia." She looked like a light bulb in the sea of Black faces.

Lorna never did marry her soldier. I happened to be present on the biology field trip to the Shenandoah Mountains where she met her eventual husband, who was also from northern Virginia. Both Dave Gapp and Lorna Totman hailed from the same area of the state, Dave from Falls Church and Lorna from Oakton.

One weekend in spring 1968, we coordinated our schedules, and I spent a couple days at each of their homes, being squired around the neighborhoods where they grew up. If you want to get to know someone better, meet their family. Lorna and her parents took me to Sunday worship, where I stood out just as much as she had at First Baptist in Williamsburg.

Overstaying the weekend visit for a few days, Dave and I headed back to W&M on Thursday, April 4, 1968. We discussed the status of our biology research and traded lightly comic comments about our Cleve & Dave performances. He drove while I flipped through the AM radio stations, dialing between WWDC 1260 and WEAM 1390, searching for possible songs we could include in our act. We had just passed Fredericksburg along I-95 when a news bulletin broke into the music.

"The president of the United States is expected to give a statement shortly, in a matter of seconds, about the death this evening of Martin Luther King in Memphis, Tennessee. . . . King was shot on the balcony of the Lorraine Motel in Memphis."

Dave and I fell silent, stunned. Not President Lyndon Johnson but Vice President Hubert Humphrey's voice came on air with a statement. "I'm sure some of you in the audience know that a great tragedy has taken place in America tonight. One of the renowned and active leaders in the cause of civil rights has been struck down by an assassin's bullet. Martin Luther King has been shot, and he is dead."

I turned to Dave—not my friend and brother David Gapp at that moment, but the white dude sitting in the driver's seat next to me—and blurted out an anguished cry from the heart.

"How much more of this do you people think we can stand?"

Dave stayed silent, not quite knowing what to say to me. We passed the last hour of the trip in complete silence, both lost in sorrowful thoughts, neither one of us speaking a single word.

When we arrived back at our apartment, I took my guitar around the corner and sat on the steps of the First Baptist Church. In 1962 Dr. King had walked up these very steps when he visited Williamsburg. Still shell-shocked and grief-stricken, I began to lightly strum the guitar. Out of my emotional trauma came a song, "The Ballad of Martin Luther King."

With faith in God and humanity
He said, "I have a dream"
It was a dream that had come from above
And lodged deep within
A dream that a man could be free
Regardless of the color of his skin

★ ★ ★

In the wake of the King assassination, other songs took on new levels of meaning, including spirituals like "Motherless Child" and "Wade in the Water," as well as folk music originals such as Dick Holler's "Abraham, Martin and John," made popular that year by Dion.

Didn't you love the things that they stood for?
Didn't they try to find some good for you and me?
And we'll be free
Someday soon, it's gonna be one day

That song got covered by pretty much everyone, from Bob Dylan, Emmylou Harris, Kenny Rogers, Marvin Gaye, and Ray Charles to the venerable standup comic Moms Mabley. I heard Dick Holler's lyrics as a plaintive echo of Sam Cooke's "A Change Is Gonna Come," which I began to include in every set Dave and I played.

The local audience for our act had grown to the point where folks were asking where they could buy our music. In performance we received requests over and over for certain songs. People were following us and actually had developed favorites, which knocked me out.

"Man, you sang the hell out of that song," Victor Liguori said to me one evening after we performed "Early Morning Rain" at Hoi Polloi. "Did you see their faces? You could have heard a pin drop. You're killing them!"

The crowd had been jam-packed and enthusiastic, but with the war, the election, and the assassinations—two months after King was murdered, Robert F. Kennedy was shot and killed in Los Angeles—the folk music scene turned both more somber and more determined.

"You've got to do a record," Victor said, insistent. "Look at this, you have people coming up and asking you for autographs. You need to have something to sign—that's what a record is good for."

I gave Dave a sideways look. "We don't have any money to record, Victor," I said.

A little matter like a shortage of funds was not going to slow Victor down. Diving into his role as the informal manager of the act, he went out and raised enough coin to record a Cleve & Dave 45-rpm single. My song "The Willow Tree" took the A-side, with another self-penned tune, "It's Got to Get Better," on the B-side.

So we finally had something to autograph for fans. Then the question became, "Where's the album?" "Oh, y'all have to do an album!"

"People have been wearing out the grooves in that 45 single," Victor said. "We'll have to get you into a recording studio and put something proper together." In addition to Victor putting in some of his own money, the owners of Castaways, Brenda and Danny Grubaugh, also contributed financially to the project. It takes a village.

No thrill in the world exists like holding that first album in your hands. I suppose I might feel the same when this memoir comes off the printing press, but the release of the album *Follow Me* brought tears to my eyes. The psychedelic font of the title graphic perfectly reflected the peace-and-love period. We put it out under the label of "Soulfolk Records," an entity that did not really exist. Even the slightly chemical smell of the vinyl added to the transcendent experience.

My artist's statement in the liner notes was rendered in all-lowercase letters, also fashionable back then (Bob Dylan did his album-cover poetry that way). The sentiments bring something of a cringe when I read them today, but they also represent a time-travel moment bringing me straight back to where I was and who I was in 1970.

> i sing because i have some things i want to say to you. i feel some things i want you to feel. i call it soulfolk, a blend of rock gospel and traditional folk music. i want to share with you the messages of folk music in the sounds of a soul style—my style. i have written eighteen songs so far. some of them tell you the things a black american knows. some of them, like "the willow tree" and "just think about it for a while," speak of emotions felt by all people. "the hot sun," the first song i wrote, is for my father, and all fathers who work in the hope that their sons will know a better life.

Oh, yes. In the words of Bob Dylan, I was so much older then, I'm younger than that now. Twelve songs, eight covers and four of my originals. The credits listed David Gapp on lead guitar, Victor Liguori as producer, and on bass Kenny Zeigler, a friend of my sister Nancy. Listening to it now represents a trip back in time. I hear the depth and quality of my young voice from over a half century ago.

Here is the album's track listing with the songwriter credits and comments:

"The Willow Tree" (Cleveland Francis—*the song I played for Dr. Perkins back in 1963*)

"Little Green Apples" (Bobby Russell—after *O. C. Smith's 1968 hit version*)

"Early Morning Rain" (Gordon Lightfoot)

"When I'm Sixty-Four" (Lennon-McCartney)

"Hot Sun" (Cleveland Francis—*a song I dedicated to the hardworking fathers of the South*)

"Hey Jude" (Lennon-McCartney)

"Just Think About It for a While" (Cleveland Francis—*about the cruelty of love*)

"Both Sides Now" (Joni Mitchell)
"Rain" (J. & H. Feliciano)
"Time" (Michael Merchant—*the Pozo-Seco Singers had a folk hit with this in 1966, and Don Williams recorded a country version later*)
"Getting Ready for Tomorrow" (Willie Hutchison)
"With God on Our Side" (Bob Dylan)

Over fifty years after the album's limited local release, the good folks at Forager Records in Los Angeles rediscovered it on the internet. Forager reissued a newly remastered double vinyl and digital recording of the original songs, adding in material from demo tapes that Victor Liguori had preserved. Released under a new title, *Beyond the Willow Tree*, the little-album-that-could thus found a worldwide audience. My sadness is that Victor did not live to witness the reissue.

★ ★ ★

I often took advantage of the many opportunities that Colonial Williamsburg offered to anyone who roamed the grounds deep in thought, looking to soak up the historical vibes of the place. I did some thinking while sitting on a bench in the garden of the Governor's Palace or in the garden of the famous Wren Building. My thoughts centered on my past travels and travails. Faith, music, and science had brought me a long way from the willow tree in Jennings.

While I was getting deeper and deeper into music, I was also plunging deeper into the study of science. The facts of biology were one thing, but even more moving to me was getting a sense of what life represented on its most fundamental level. What were the elemental building blocks of living organisms? What manifold intricacies and mysteries were involved?

Slowly, gradually, with me only half knowing it, my personal holy trinity of music, science, and religion began to change. The transformation felt subtle but irrevocable.

"Science brings men nearer to God," stated Louis Pasteur, one of the giants of the scientific method. I felt the truth of that sentiment.

Biology provided a new lens with which to see. I could experience the world at a cellular level, the tiny furnaces of existence firing away, invisible to the naked eye. *If that isn't God*, I thought to myself, *I don't know what is*. Something as ordinary as a dragonfly's flight became a miracle. I could see the phenomenon in terms of the insect's transfer of stored energy into motion.

I did not lose my religion. Not at all, and far from it. I simply felt my spiritual life transform, like a butterfly coming out of a chrysalis. Science, religion, and music merged together into some sort of personal unified field theory. Each seemed a beautiful facet of the same harmonious whole.

People have long used religion to explain the unknown. When crops were failing, or the great hurricanes came, they would say, well, God was angry. But the more knowledge we assemble through science, the less we have to trouble God with ignorant questions. We can allow the Great Mystery to stand. To me, acceptance of the scientific method is vital to appreciating the miracle of God.

Biology is the science of life, and the deeper we peer into the complexity of existence, the more miraculous it appears. I take my place among the small percentage of the populace who have witnessed a person die, who have seen firsthand an individual passing from life to death. I know the limits of science. Once a life is terminated, we cannot reverse the mechanism, cannot reanimate what is gone. I've seen the coldness that comes across the corpus, the slack muscles, the draining color.

We remain unable to harness human knowledge to solve the puzzle of mortality. Life is sacred. As I grew to adulthood, I found it more and more difficult to kill any living thing, even a fly. I came to recognize that with that act I would be taking away something that only God can give or take away.

Lest it sound like I am going all New Age on you, I had my feet firmly planted on the ground. I still knew where I was going and how I would get there. That spring I defended my thesis and received my master's degree. The world was my oyster or, more accurately, the world was my cloister. I would become a monk within the sacred precincts of academia. A PhD would come next, then more teaching, and then a tenured professorship, preferably at a prestigious institution of higher learning.

My future rolled out before me, sunlit and golden. I might have heard a small nagging voice within, a regret that I had not realized my dream of becoming a medical doctor, but that voice got quieter and quieter as time went on. I had achieved not that specific dream but another. Who could say whether it might not be a better one? Mary Francis's hopes for her son would attain realization all the same.

What is that true saying that I quoted when I was describing my medical school rejection? *Man makes plans, and God laughs*. Or, to cite a different sphere of religious belief, when his followers asked the Buddha to sum up his philosophy in two words, he said, "Everything changes."

Truth, bro, truth. As soon as I graduated from W&M, a trio of fastballs came at me, none of which I saw coming. Changes came from all directions, from Mary Francis, from the U.S. military, and from the discipline of science. I didn't have enough time to duck.

CHAPTER 11

What Are We Fighting For?

AROUND JENNINGS WHEN I was growing up, I would encounter them every once in a while, women who wore sunglasses inside, on cloudy days, or at night. I always thought they were just styling, until my oldest sister Fayester clued me in.

"Black eyes," she said significantly. "Those shades mean she's got a man who's beating on her." Sometimes these domestic abuse victims wore long sleeves, scarves, or turtlenecks even in the heat of summer, the better to hide bruises inflicted upon them by their mates.

I flew back for a visit to Jennings a single time while I was living in Williamsburg, my first trip ever on a plane. I arrived and arranged to pick up Mary Francis at her maid's job at the Holston family home. She emerged from the house wearing sunglasses, although a heavy overcast clouded the sky. I didn't want to think what my mother's choice of eyewear implied, but I couldn't avoid concluding that the situation had gone from bad to worse between her and Pete Francis.

When his whipping boy (that would be me) left home, my dad had to find another target. Conveniently, he didn't have to look much beyond 300 Pearl Street. My parents had always fought, loud and often. Mary Francis always gave as good as she got. But the arguments involved pushing and shoving at most, never escalating to physical blows. Now it looked as though they had.

We drove back home to Pearl Street from the Holstons' house. I simmered with anger at the idea of my mother going into work with shades on, and Marge Holston never asking her what was going on. Silence was stitched deep into the social code of the South. Don't ask, don't tell. Plus Mary Francis was a proud woman and would be upset at being confronted about her private affairs.

I would have to tread carefully myself. "You know, Mama," I said, "if it ever gets too bad around here, you should consider moving out by me in Virginia."

She shook her head, saying that she had to think of my little sisters. Faye, Barbara, and Lois were all safely launched in college, but Nancy was fifteen and Liz was only ten, and they were both still at home.

"I can't just abandon them," Mary Francis said. We were in the kitchen at the Pearl Street house, she sitting at the table still in her shades, me leaning against the counter near the stove.

"I have to tell you, Williamsburg is a real wonderful place"—I didn't have to spell out "especially compared to Jennings," since that premise was assumed by both of us. "Virginia's still the South," I added, "but it isn't the Deep South."

Again, we both knew what I was talking about. Talk always had to be coded in the Jim Crow era. I told her that jobs were plentiful in Williamsburg, and she would be able to find a better opportunity than doing housework for the Holstons. She was only in her mid-forties, with half of her life before her, too much time to spend suffering my stepfather's nonsense.

"Life could be different for you, and Liz and Nancy could have a better chance." I felt like a real estate agent, extolling the charms of a move to a new neighborhood.

We had a long talk that day before Daddy and my younger sisters came home. Mary Francis remained quiet and unmoved for most of it. I never thought for a minute she'd take me up on the idea of relocating. Crashing out of the Jennings dome was for her children, not for her. Old habits die hard.

I returned to Williamsburg. Flying over the American countryside put me in the same meditative mood as train travel did. My mother had been my rock, and I had just seen the rock crumbling before my eyes. *He'll kill her*, the voice of doom spoke into my ear. The prospect seemed too awful to contemplate, but I knew the toll domestic violence could take. *She will never leave*, whispered an answering voice.

The situation simmered for the remaining year I had in grad school. Then a series of developments occurred, each one more unexpected than the other, sending my life and my mother's spinning off in an entirely new direction. Soon after the graduation ceremonies completed, and with my diploma in hand, I experienced a sensational send-off from William & Mary that had me leaving the school in a cloud of glory.

Putting on his artist manager's hat, Victor Liguori acted as mover and shaker for this turning point in my life. "We'll have to do a farewell concert, Cleve," he said to me that spring. I imagined a low-key, casual affair, maybe a warm group of friends and fans gathering at Hoi Polloi, with some wine and cheese. Victor had bigger plans.

The Phi Beta Kappa Society had been founded at William & Mary in the momentous year of 1776. It was the country's first academic honor program, later evolving into a nationwide phenomenon with hundreds of chapters. The theater arts building on campus was named after the group. With a proscenium stage and seating for five hundred, the main theater in Phi Beta Kappa Hall normally hosted symphonic orchestras, operas, and nationally recognized touring companies.

"No, Victor, no," I responded when he proposed that I appear there.

"Yes, Cleveland, yes," he said. "It'll be great!"

"We'll never be able to fill that place."

"There's only one way to find out," he said. Victor Liguori was not one to be stopped when he formed a plan of action. With the help of Sam Sadler, vice president of student affairs at William & Mary, the concert became a reality.

At any college, the mood during graduation time turns celebratory, almost giddy. I underestimated the name that the duo of Cleve & Dave had established around campus. When the date for the concert arrived, we walked out on stage and stopped short, stunned to see a standing-room-only audience, every seat filled, the crowd spilling into the aisles and onto every available patch of floor.

We killed. Standing ovations, multiple encores. You have to appreciate the atmosphere in the country in 1969, especially on college campuses. Antiwar protests roiled not only the United States but the entire globe. Folk music provided the soundtrack of the era, focusing student sentiment, lending a sense of a shared common cause. The vibe in Phi Beta Kappa Hall that night felt electric. We were one big, determined family, collectively gathered together not just for music but to help change the world.

Some of the numbers turned into audience sing-alongs. Hearing hundreds of voices raised with mine transported me to a realm of brotherhood and sisterhood that I didn't want to let go of.

How many roads must a man walk down
Before you call him a man?
How many seas must a white dove sail
Before she sleeps in the sand?
How many times must the cannonballs fly
Before they're forever banned?
The answer, my friend, is blowin' in the wind
The answer is blowin' in the wind

★ ★ ★

In the aftermath of that high, I rattled around campus in a bittersweet mood, somewhat at loose ends. One phase of my life was over, but my new life hadn't begun. I'll never know what sent me wandering into the biology building at W&M that morning in May. I had no reason to be there. The warmth of the season should have lured me outside, since springtime in Williamsburg is paradise on earth. Students walked hand in hand, lending truth to the state's new tourism slogan, just coined that year: "Virginia is for lovers."

Curiosity might have killed the cat, but as an element of my personality it has always served me well. When I passed the biology building's main lecture hall, I heard voices and peeked inside.

The big room was empty but for a dozen or so undergrads occupying the first couple rows of seats. In front of them stood a tall, bland-looking gent in a suit jacket whom I didn't recognize as a professor, but who was nonetheless giving some sort of lecture or presentation. I stepped down the hall's steeply raked set of stairs to listen.

"There's a wide array of opportunities at MCV," the gent said. "We're a nationally ranked medical school and one of the world's premier academic health centers."

What was he talking about? I didn't understand. What was MCV? I slipped into a chair off to the side.

A pitch. The guy was giving a recruitment pitch, trying to attract students to MCV, the Medical College of Virginia, located in Richmond, the state capital (and the old capital of the Confederacy). Fifty miles north on Interstate 64. So close I could almost taste it.

Piled on a table in front of the hall were applications to MCV, and the recruiter was urging the assembled undergrads each to take one. Urging? Actually, he begged the students to fill out an application. He came off like a car salesman, earnest but casual, tieless, friendly.

At that juncture in my life, I'd forgotten all about medical school, forcing it from my mind. The sting of those dozen rejection letters had made a deep impression on me. *Oh,* I had concluded, *maybe this wasn't the path the good Lord wanted me to travel.*

Here was something new. Perhaps my future path toward a PhD would prove not to be set in stone after all. In fact, at the moment that prospect, so certain just a few minutes before, seemed to vanish in the wind. I was transported straight back into the excited mood of six years earlier, when I first met that anonymous Black physician in the campus infirmary at Southern University.

Medical school. Medical school! A dream deferred, a dream abandoned—now a dream reborn.

I approached the recruiter as the meeting broke up. He eyed me. I wondered if he was going to mistake me for the help, perhaps ask me to move the table with all the paperwork on it back against the wall.

"May I have one of those applications?" I asked.

"Sure thing!" he said. In my experience recruiters and salespeople always speak in exclamation points. "Good to see you! What's your background?"

I told him I had just taken my master's degree in biology. His eyes went wide. Suddenly I had his entire attention. I didn't realize it at the time, but the powers that be in the Virginia statehouse had recently mandated a push to integrate all the state's institutions of higher learning. The recruiter's focus widened to include minorities. Without me knowing it, I had become a hot prospect.

The man's sales pitch kicked up a few notches. He had been fishing for sunfish and had suddenly found a trophy bass on his line. The undergrads had all taken their paperwork and left. It was just me and Mr. Salesman. Demonstrating the school's interest in enrolling minorities—"really super-qualified minorities like you!"—he walked me through the application. I couldn't believe it. Here he was, coaching me on how to game the process, how to more or less short-circuit the levels of bureaucracy at the school and submit my application directly to the "deciders," as he called them.

"You'll hear back from us, truly, within a week!"

The recruiter made good on his promise. Ten days later I found myself riding a bus north on I-64, making the trip from Williamsburg to the state capital. Richmond is one of those places that suffers from having a little too much history. To find my way through Jackson Ward, the traditional Black district, and then to the MCV facilities, I had to pass the so-called White House of the Confederacy. But this was a new day, I told myself, a new era and a new me.

The initial morning meeting I had with an instructor in the department of medicine made me think I might have been mistaken. "I'll tell you right up, son—you won't get in here. They are certainly not going to give you a white student's slot."

At the Medical College of Virginia, it seemed, life was the same old same old, the zero-sum game that had been shutting me out of opportunity for what felt like forever. I wanted to say to him, "I'm not your 'son,' *Daddy-o*!" But I didn't. If I let myself get angry about every hope-deflating, balloon-puncturing experience I encountered along the way, then I wouldn't have time to be anything *but* angry.

A trip to Richmond wasted. Back to Williamsburg and back onto the PhD in biology track. I had a second interview scheduled later in the afternoon, and I would just skip it. I had already gotten MCV's message, loud and clear. *I don't need this,* I thought.

But my bus didn't leave until later in the afternoon, and the school offered lunch to all the applicants that day. When I stayed for that, I decided I might as well go to the second interview meeting.

The two sessions were as different as night and day. The second was with the dean of students himself. "We're looking for qualified people who are ready to take this on. We were impressed with your credentials, and if you enroll, we will have a position for you."

The magic words. The dean wanted to sign me up right then and there, producing a letter of commitment form and passing it across his desk. I couldn't sign that puppy fast enough. I felt as though I were in a dream. Medical school!

"I can promise for certain you will get in," the dean said, after I scrawled my John Hancock on the dotted line. "But I have to be honest with you. This is a rigorous four-year course of study, and you will get no favored status here. We will accept you with pleasure, but whether you succeed and make it all the way through the program to graduate is entirely up to you. You will also have the opportunity to flunk out."

"I wouldn't have it any other way." I said, looking him in the eye and rising from my seat to shake his hand. "You don't know this about me, but I am the son of Mary Francis of Jennings, Louisiana, and I will graduate from this school."

It wasn't a Greyhound bus that took me to Williamsburg that day—I floated back there. I was too psyched to thumb my nose at the Confederate White House as I passed by on my way out of Richmond.

By that time, I knew some of the school's history. The Medical College of Virginia had been burned flat at the end of the Civil War. McGuire Hall on campus honored the man who resurrected and rebuilt the school, a physician named Hunter Holmes McGuire. A personal friend of Stonewall Jackson, he was the surgeon who had performed the amputation of the Confederate general's left arm in 1863, at the Battle of Chancellorsville.

As a Black man I didn't have many predecessors at MCV, but I would find out about one of the trailblazers, Dr. Charles Christian. In the late fifties, he had graduated first in his class. The school did not allow him to attend the graduation ceremonies and instead sent him his diploma in the mail. The thing about old Jim Crow, he's petty.

None of that mattered, or at least, it didn't matter much. I was in. Medical school!

When I stopped in at the biology department the next day, a note waited for me.

Call your mother.

★ ★ ★

I didn't have a chance to tell Mary Francis my news before she told me hers. "Butch, if the offer is still good, I'll take you up on coming there to be with you."

My stepfather's violence had finally reached a trigger point. That phrase might become a literal truth, since although we didn't have guns in our house, Pete Francis could easily get his hands on one.

On the phone that day I told my mother that yes, of course, she should move to Williamsburg immediately. Meanwhile, my mind raced. How in the world was I going to make that happen? Mary Francis had never once stepped foot outside the state of Louisiana. She was an ultimately capable woman, but even so, how would it work? How would we get this fortysomething woman and her two adolescent daughters a thousand miles across the country?

We knew we would have to conduct the move in total secrecy. The three older girls were away at college, and we did not even involve them in the planning. In my darkest imaginings I didn't think Pete Francis would actually murder my mother if she tried to leave him, but even the faint possibility frightened me. My mother had to coordinate her departure carefully to avoid any suspicion on Pete's part, sparking rage or anger that could result in bodily harm. It would have to be a stealth maneuver all the way.

I began to plan the move as a D-Day–style operation. I was not a military guy, but it would be a dangerous undertaking. The Steve McQueen movie *The Great Escape* had been a huge hit in the early 1960s. In my mind I termed it the Great Escape, getting Mary Francis and my two youngest sisters from Jennings to Williamsburg. I earned money from my gigs and sent enough home for three bus tickets, but used a General Delivery drop box to avoid the chance of my stepfather catching on.

My mother packed only the essentials, abandoning many possessions she treasured, including photographs, clothes, and mementoes. She would be leaving her longtime job with the Holstons for a leap into the unknown. I worried about my sisters, too. Kids are creatures of habit. They hate being uprooted and separated from their friends. But when my mother announced to Liz and Nancy that she was quitting Pete Francis and taking them with her to Williamsburg, they did not put up any resistance. They too had their fill of life with Daddy.

In the soupy heat of a Jennings summer, the three pilgrims boarded the Big Grey Dog for the thirty-hour bus trip across America. In those days before cellphones, we had no "comms," as the military always termed communications. Keeping in touch would prove impossible. I didn't know whether they had successfully left Jennings. I didn't know if Pete Francis had discovered the plan. I spent the time fretting.

The Williamsburg bus station was near the train station where I had arrived in town myself, only two and a half years before. After the daylong communications blackout, I felt a flood of relief when the doors of the Greyhound opened and the three of them stepped off the bus.

My oldest sister Faye, then at Southern University, fielded a call from Pete Francis. "I can't find your mama!" he wailed. I recalled a line from Paul Gauguin, the painter. "Life being what it is, one dreams of revenge." I was just glad to get Mary Francis out from under my stepfather's heavy hand.

The timing of the Great Escape proved perfect. Although I was caught up in planning my own move, transferring to Richmond and medical school, I took on the added job of settling Mary Francis and my sisters in Williamsburg. I already had an apartment and would not have to look for another one for them.

For a short while, we were all crowded in together. The place was small, with two bedrooms, a living room, a small kitchen, and a single bathroom. My roommate Dave Gapp graciously accommodated the Francis family, landing on him out of nowhere. My mother slept in one room with the girls. I took the other bedroom. Dave slept on the couch for a few weeks until he found new digs for himself.

Mary Francis had her kids young, so she was only forty-five years old when she pulled up stakes and totally changed her life. I admired my mother for her bravery, determination, and enterprise. Within a week of arriving she found a job, initially as custodian at Colonial Williamsburg. But her employers recognized potential when they saw it, and they trained her as a waitress and gave her a bump in pay. The tips rolled in, too, not only because of her careful attention to detail but simply because she could charm the pants off anyone when she wanted to. The girls signed up at a local school and adapted well, eventually rising to the top of their classes.

So all was well, right? My mother felt secure, even more so since her son had been accepted to medical school in Richmond, only an hour away. It was almost spooky how everything seemed to have fallen into place. Life was good.

Man makes plans . . .

I graduated from William & Mary in spring of 1969 and would not matriculate at the Medical College of Virginia until later that fall. Beyond enjoying the summer, gigging around with Dave, and spending time with my mother, I didn't think anything of the gap between schools.

Someone was paying attention, though—a draft board a thousand miles away in Jennings. The demand-to-appear letter landed in my mailbox with a thud. I had been receiving a college deferment for my entire time at Southern and W&M, over such an extended stretch of time that I no longer even thought about it. Now for a brief four-month period I had left myself exposed.

"You will report to the U.S. Army induction center in New Orleans, Louisiana at 0800 hours on the date listed below. . . . "

Once again, I want to state forcefully my feelings of allegiance to my country. I would have never fled to Canada to avoid the draft as others did, and would have accepted entering the military as my patriotic duty. I honored the example of the men in my family who had served. When I saw that induction notice, though, I could not help but feel despair.

The bloody conflict in Vietnam raged on. The Tet Offensive of the previous year gave the lie to the Pentagon's claims that America and its South Vietnamese allies were winning the war. The military needed more warm bodies. I immediately contacted the Jennings draft board.

"You have received multiple deferments, son," said the voice on the other end of the telephone line, shading the word "son" so that it sounded like "boy" to my ears.

"I've been accepted to the Medical College of Virginia," I said. "I'll be starting classes in September." It seemed obvious to me that my worth to society as a doctor exceeded my worth as cannon fodder.

"I would be happy to sign an agreement to serve my time in the military as a doctor, if you'll just defer so I can get my medical degree."

"We can't possibly allow another deferment. Your time is up."

I pleaded. I begged. I wrote letters. Employing an argument well known to be a losing strategy, I appealed to the U.S. Army's sense of reason and fair play. My advisor Dr. Brooks and Dr. Byrd, the head of the biology department at W&M, pled my case. The dean of MCV wrote to confirm my matriculation. The draft board responded harshly, imperiously ordering me to report. No excuses allowed.

Managing to get the induction center changed from New Orleans to Richmond, I hopped on a bus to appear at the designated address—McGuire Veterans Hospital. It felt like the ghost of Hunter McGuire, the Confederacy's amputating surgeon, had somehow reached out to grab me.

Hundreds of draftees showed up to be processed that morning. I joined the group as uniformed enlisted men and women herded us from room to room, test to test, physical and mental exams, one after another. I passed them all. Everything operated as smoothly as a sausage maker.

Right around that time, Country Joe debuted his acidly sarcastic "Fixin' to Die Rag" at Woodstock, the peace-and-love festival happening four hundred miles to the north in upstate New York.

And it's one, two, three, what're we fighting for?
Don't ask me, I don't give a damn
Next stop is Vietnam
And it's five, six, seven, open up the pearly gates
Well there ain't no time to wonder why
Whoopee! We're all gonna die

The sausage links reassembled in a large waiting room, a nervous pause before taking the oath and being formally inducted into the U.S. Army. Nobody looked exactly happy. A military orderly entered carrying a clipboard. He called out three names, and mine was one of them. A nurse handed us each a folder and led the way down a dizzying series of hallways into yet another examination room.

A doctor in full officer's uniform sitting at a small, rickety-looking table called out my name. I walked over and stood in front of the table, handing him the folder as I tried to assume a posture somewhat resembling ramrod straight attention. He never looked at me but bent his head to examine the documents.

"How long have you had the inguinal hernia?" he asked.

Shocked, not really knowing what a hernia was or whether or not I suffered from one, I couldn't summon a response.

He continued without looking up. "The military will give you a year to have this fixed. If not done by then, you'll be inducted in our service, and we will fix it for you."

A uniformed aide directed me to the exit door. What was *Catch-22*'s last sentence again? *The knife came down, missing him by inches, and he took off.* I seemed to be quoting that line all too often in my life. At least the present problem was resolved. I would be safely enrolled in medical school by the army's one-year deadline. After that, and if it came to pass, I would willingly enter the military as a physician. A great load lifted off my back.

It turned out that I did not suffer from a hernia, inguinal or any other kind. A congenital condition called a scrotal varicocele—a tangled collection of blood vessels in the testicular sac—can sometimes mimic an inguinal hernia during a physical exam. The condition is usually benign, and I've lived all my life with it without a problem.

Running through my mind on the bus ride back to Williamsburg was the soothing promise of the Catholic saint Mother Julian of Norwich: "All shall be well, and all shall be well, and all manner of things shall be well." I checked my mail when I got home, and MCV had sent me the name and contact information of my future roommate. We would communicate by mail over the summer.

CHAPTER 12

Dr. Cleveland Francis Jr.

DRIVING NORTH TO RICHMOND to settle in at medical school, I presented the perfect picture of 1969 America. I was a twentysomething folksinger driving a used VW bug that I had bought from Victor Liguori and given a cute nickname ("Zeke"). I could not have been more emblematic if I tried.

At W&M I had accomplished my debut in the world of white folks, entering a realm of society that had been closed off to me before. Musically and academically, the inaugural voyage had been a success. Through Victor Liguori, Dave Gapp, Lorna Totman, and Dr. Brooks, I moved fully into an integrated world. I had no fear of losing my identity as a Black man, and I resisted basing my interpersonal relations solely on race.

Not only friendships, but also folk music declared me as something of an outlier. The kind of music deeply embedded inside me happened to bring out audiences that were 99 percent white. The conundrum held true throughout my years in music. I didn't have a choice. I couldn't do anything else but maintain allegiance to my music and my racial identity at the same time. As it worked out, I gradually gained a substantial Black following with my own brand of soulfolk.

As I pulled Zeke into the MCV campus, giving an ironic acknowledgment of the Confederate White House as I passed by, I found my dorm and searched out my assigned room. I looked forward to meeting the roommate with whom I had been communicating by mail for weeks. But I knew I was in trouble the moment I walked in the door.

If it's not too obvious, let's call my erstwhile roommate "Bob White" to keep him anonymous and save him from embarrassment. His family—his mother, father, and two little sisters—were there in the room with him. All five of them stood frozen in place, the looks on their faces identical and priceless. I almost laughed out loud. The White family appeared as though they were acting out a *tableau vivant* scene called "Surprised He's Black."

All minorities develop a special kind of radar to gauge reactions to their presence in an unfamiliar environment. It's part of our survival mechanism. My antennae go up, my Spider sense tingles. Is this situation going to go south, or isn't it?

Bob had moved whole hog into the dorm room. He chose the desk closest to the window, the bed farthest from the door. The open door of the closet revealed what looked like his entire wardrobe. I held out my hand, shook his, and introduced myself. No one else spoke. I knew exactly what was going on without anyone saying a word.

"I'll be right back in a few," I said. "I've got some more of my stuff down in the car."

Giving the White family plenty of time to get themselves sorted, I took more than a few minutes, just sitting in Zeke the green bug and enjoying the warm fall weather. When I did finally return, I climbed the stairway and entered without knocking.

The room was entirely empty. All of Bob's belongings had vanished. His trousers, shirts, and suits, hung in the closet with such care, disappeared. The whole five-person assembly who had been there just minutes before had skulked out via the back stairs.

Having read the family's faces the instant I walked in the door, I can't say I was surprised by the abrupt leave-taking. From growing up in Louisiana, I certainly knew such reactions were possible. I had been somewhat lulled by my time at William & Mary and the fairly complacent reception I had received there. I had allowed myself to forget that as a culture we were still mired in ignorance.

But the incident didn't faze me much. I had been beaten and battered by Jim Crow for what seemed like forever. This? A kid choosing to vamoose rather than room with me? That was nothing. I had developed the skin of a rhino against such nonsense. I was not bothered at all.

Whatever cloud rolled across my sky that day had a delightful silver lining. Not by design, I'm sure, but whatever else he did, Bob White had gifted me with a private dorm room. No worry about my roommate's study habits conflicting with my own. No unexpected guests. No hats hung on an outside doorknob to indicate a romantic tryst going on inside. I pulled the two beds together and took advantage of two whole closets, two desks, and my own space to pace the floor or sing my songs to myself. Without saying a word to the college administration, I happily settled in.

Later on during classes at MCV, I did run into Bob White occasionally. He apologized for the dorm room incident but blamed his family. His father threatened to remove Bob from school before he'd see him with a Black roommate. Charitably, I wrote the whole thing off as the hidebound attitudes of the older generation. Bob was okay. He was the son of bigots, not a bigot himself. Or so I assured myself.

My snubbing by Bob's family was truly the least of my problems. I had been through Jefferson Davis High School, Southern University, the grad school at the College of William & Mary, and nothing, *nothing* in my experience prepared me for the rigors of medical school. MCV wasn't just studying, it was studying on steroids. The syllabus weighed in at twice the size of a large Yellow Pages phone book, if by chance you remember what a Yellow Pages phone book was, and if you don't, just know that the damned things were huge. Folks used to stand on them to reach the upper shelves in the kitchen.

At the beginning of each course, I received a half-foot-thick binder with outlines, illustrations, and readings. I had to digest all the material in four weeks, followed by an exam given once a month on a pass or fail basis. I felt like the cartoon character from the sixties, Tooter Turtle, who needed a Mr. Wizard the Lizard to rescue me from my predicament. "Help, Mr. Wizard! I don't know if I can make it as a medical student anymore!"

The sheer volume of work stunned me. I decided I had to do something, anything, formulate some sort of strategy to help me handle it all. I was drowning in facts, figures, and concepts. I had to learn how to study all over again.

All right, okay, I said to myself. What did we have here? Each course of study concerned itself with a single system of the human body: musculoskeletal, cardiovascular, digestive, respiratory, endocrine, and all the other systems as well. The only way I could manage was to break out the material system by system. Sitting down with markers and sheets of paper, I physically charted out the body's systems on paper, listing every aspect of each one. Then I pounded the information into my skull like John Henry, the steel-drivin' man.

Gross anatomy lab almost killed me. That's "gross" in the sense of "large," not in the sense of disgusting—though it was a little of that, too. Professors split the class into groups of four students, assigning each group a single cadaver to work on for the year. Other groups named their study cadavers. I was not planning on becoming so friendly with mine.

Old Louisiana superstitions came back to haunt me. Not to put too fine a point on it, but the dead bodies gave me the creeps. MCV had a basement anatomy lab—I mean, of course it was in a basement, smack dab in steampipe Freddy Krueger territory. I took an ancient, creaky elevator to get down to the lab.

Rows and rows of stainless steel tanks the size of dumpsters contained the cadavers for dissection and study. Inside the tanks, bodies floated in formaldehyde, resembling, to my eyes, the enormous pale dead catfish that sometimes bobbed up in the bayous.

To be able to deal with the dissection process I had to steel my nerves. *Now Cleve, you are a man of reason and science. Your fears are not rooted in fact—you must banish them entirely from your mind.*

Easier said than done. Prepping for an anatomy examination, I ventured down to the lab alone one Sunday night. The exam would cover the brachial plexus, a group of nerves passing from the spine through the axilla on the way to controlling the motor and sensory function of the arms and hands. To commence my study, I carefully fixed the arm of my anatomical subject in a brace. While working with a scalpel on the axilla area (more familiarly known as the armpit), I accidentally bumped the brace. The arm of the cadaver dropped to wrap itself casually around my shoulders.

Yow! I must've jumped a mile. Telling myself how foolish I was being didn't stop me from fleeing the lab and heading home. The following Monday morning the professor complained to the class that someone had left a body uncovered.

★ ★ ★

My experiences in the gross anatomy lab might have been to blame for the nightmares that began to plague me horribly, the same one every time. But in fact, it could not have been dissecting corpses that brought on the bad dreams. I had experienced the same terrifying dreams once or twice before, before med school, back when I was at Southern University. Now the demons had returned.

Rather, it was demon, singular. Every night I imagined physically battling with Pete Francis, trying my best to kill him. I never succeeded. I'd wake up in a cold sweat. The violence and fury of the dreams always frightened me awake, panting and helpless. I somehow knew that I had been bellowing in my sleep.

Exhausted by day and shell-shocked at night, I tried everything to pull myself out of the spiral. Sleeping aids, exercise, leaving the light on. Nothing helped, nothing ended the vivid nightmares. I dreaded falling asleep. When I did, there I was, stalking my daddy, weapon in hand, murder on my mind.

My studying began to suffer, along with my performance in class. Where before I had been a top student, I began a gradual descent into the lower rankings. The homicidal nighttime visions forced everything else out of my brain. After laboriously learning how to study, I felt as though I had suddenly forgotten how.

"What's wrong, Mr. Francis?" The dean of students had called me into his office. "You don't seem yourself, certainly not in respect to your studies."

"I'm sorry," I said. This was the same dean who had said I had a secure spot at MCV, but whether I graduated would be up to me. Now I felt like I was in danger of washing out.

"Are you having family issues? Perhaps a bad breakup with a girl?"

I told him no. Did the nightly urge to kill my stepfather qualify as a "family issue"?

"I can't sleep," I said. "I'm having difficulties sleeping well, going to sleep, staying asleep."

The dean nodded, assessing my bloodshot eyes and ashen skin. He offered to get me a tutor.

"I don't think that would do any good," I said miserably. "I know how to study, Dean, but I just can't seem to do it."

"I'll tell you what," he said. "Why don't you go see Dr. Christian? He's the head of the outpatient psychiatry department here. Get yourself checked out. You're not one of those who resist the whole idea of mental health therapy, are you?"

Dr. Christian turned out to be one of the few Black men on the faculty. He was the gent who back in the 1950s had graduated first in his class at MCV, the one they would not let appear at graduation. I laid out my difficulties to him. He queried me extensively about my background. He seemed to judge it important that the nightmares became frequent only when I had entered medical school.

"Not 'frequent,' Doctor," I said. "Every. Single. Night."

He gazed at me, silent for a long beat. Sitting there, for the first time fully confessing what had been happening, I experienced my suffering more deeply than ever before.

"Why are you here, Cleveland?" he finally asked.

I didn't understand. "Why am I 'here'? You mean why am I meeting with you, Doctor?" I thought we had covered that. He and I were meeting because my life had gone into a tailspin.

"Let me try something out to you, see if it makes sense," he said. "Let's assume that you've been going along in your life, and your main motivation has always been to prove this man wrong, this authority figure who raised you, who belittled you and said you'd never make anything of yourself."

That was indeed Pete Francis all the way. "Yes?" I didn't know exactly where the good doctor was going with this.

"That's why you excelled, in high school at home, at Southern, and then at William & Mary. Subconsciously, you wanted desperately to establish that the man was wrong, back when he was abusing you. And now you've done that, haven't you? You've already proved Pete Francis wrong."

"Yes." I was afraid of busting out crying.

"I mean, that business is over with. How could you possibly be more successful at rejecting this false image of yourself that he painted for you? So you no longer have that as a motivation to succeed."

According to Dr. Christian, much of my drive had come from early trauma and hatred for my stepfather. I nodded, feeling a dawning realization, an aha! moment. Excitement began to mix with my mood of misery.

"So I have to ask you once again, why are you here, Cleveland? Why are you with us at the Medical College of Virginia? What is your motivation now? Because you have to find a new one or the nightmares won't quit, and we might lose you. We don't want to lose you because you are too valuable to us. Can you find a new reason why you want to be a doctor?"

Why was I at medical school? I didn't have to search very long for the answer. My soul practically shouted it out to me.

"I want to help people," I whispered.

"What?" Dr. Christian asked. "What did you just say?"

"I want to help heal people who are ill." Louder this time, prouder and more certain.

I had found my true purpose. It had been within me all along. Talk therapy can be magic—in a single session, Dr. Christian had effectively, definitively, and once and for all set me straight. The homicidal nightmares never again visited, my performance in class improved, and studying, though still difficult, was now doable. In modern terms, I had suffered PTSD, not from a war in Southeast Asia or Afghanistan but from the war that Pete Francis had declared on me for the first eighteen years of my life. Through therapy Dr. Christian alleviated my symptoms.

A concept came back to me that my classmates and I had spoken about during our late night deep-think conversations at W&M. *We ourselves play every character in our dreams.* The truth was, Pete Francis, the real flesh-and-blood Pete Francis, never entered my nighttime sleep. He remained safely a thousand miles away in Louisiana. It was my own image of my abusive stepfather that tormented me.

I had internalized the demon of my childhood. Since I created him, I realized I could just as well kick him the hell out. Alternatively, I could throw open the doors of my heart and kindly usher Pete Francis into the vaults of memory.

★ ★ ★

Three Black men entered the first-year class at MCV in 1969. One flunked out, and then there were only two, me and a Virginia-born guy with the splendid Sherlock Holmes–style name of Archer Baskerville. He had graduated from MCV's school of pharmacy and then remained on campus to attain his MD. Birds of a feather, we became acquainted. I found Arch to be a shy but brilliant guy who stood a half-foot taller than I did.

"Hey, brother—we should room together," he said, upon finding out that I lived solo in a dorm just like he did.

"I'm good as I am," I told him. He persisted, repeating the suggestion several times over the beginning months of our first year together in med school.

One day I returned from class and found he had somehow got his hands on a key to my room and moved himself in. I walked in and then almost walked out, thinking I was in the wrong room. There he stood, though, grinning like a fool. I decided to accept the *fait accompli*. We laughed about it later and remained roommates until we graduated, spending two years in the dorm and the last two years in a shared apartment off campus.

When the class met to get organized, I ran for vice president and won. This continued for the four years of study. Many of the students were legacies who had relatives that had attended MCV before them. These beneficiaries of educational nepotism possessed copies of pretty much every exam that had ever been given at the school, going back years.

To us, the file of test papers represented a treasure trove, like a family heirloom passed down from generation to generation. As Archer and I got to know the legacy students, they shared the precious old exams with us. It wasn't exactly cheating, just a way to get a leg up.

For the first time during my education, music took a back seat to learning. I didn't have much time to search out gigs. In a limited way, I kept my hand in. Several of my fellow students played guitar. We'd gather in the lobby of the women's dorm on Friday nights for informal jam sessions. During the summer breaks I would return to Williamsburg and join musician friends to play the Tidewater restaurants, bars, and Colonial Williamsburg establishments. The tips and gig money I earned allowed me to help support my mother and my sisters.

With the extra money I was making and my mother's increase in her pay, we were able to move the family from the tiny apartment to a larger place in the Carver's Garden neighborhood of Williamsburg. Nancy and Liz were growing up and needed more room. My sisters Barbara and Lois would visit during their summer breaks from college in Louisiana. They too found summer work in Colonial Williamsburg, dressing up in period dress and acting as tour guides.

I was lucky to be only fifty miles from the family. I could pop down from Richmond on a Friday night, then return on Saturday night for all-day study on Sunday. Mary Francis liked her job at Colonial Williamsburg. Nancy and Liz were doing well in school. So I could concentrate on my studies with the knowledge that the family was safe, sound, and all set.

A few incidents happened at MCV that stand out in my mind. A real dragon of a professor named Dr. Charley Thompson inspired fear in the hearts of all medical students and trainees. As an attending physician, he seemed to relish selecting specific students to rake over the coals. I witnessed Dr. Thompson's modus operandi and did my best to avoid him but anticipated that my day as a target would come eventually.

During a rotation at McGuire Veterans Hospital, I joined a group of medical students presenting a patient with cirrhosis of the liver, a common enough diagnosis at the time. I had gone deep to study everything there was to know about cirrhosis. I even looked at the global data and tried to ferret out unusual facts about the international scope of the disease. Though alcohol was by far the number one cause of cirrhosis at the VA hospital, it turned out not to be the leading contributing factor worldwide.

That morning my number finally came up. Dr. Thompson arrived in his white lab coat, sporting a bowtie and the well-shined black footwear students used to call "FBI shoes." As a group, the other students and I presented the cirrhosis case. He looked us over and lifted his hand to choose a victim. For some reason I stood out. Could it have been that I was the only Black face in the bunch? I had the uncanny sense of a roulette wheel rotating. The wheel turned, the little pill rattled and dropped, and the slot came up black.

The doctor glanced at my name tag. "Okay, Dr. Francis, what is the number one—"

I interrupted him before he could complete the question. "Malaria," I said.

Thompson appeared dumbfounded. "How in the world did you know what I was going to ask you?"

"The number one cause of cirrhosis in the world is malaria." This was one of the odd facts that I had picked up in my deep dive studies.

"You are right," Thompson said, a little begrudgingly.

The other students in the group could hardly contain themselves. I had no further encounter with Dr. Thompson for the remainder of my time at MCV.

Another incident at medical school did not have such a gotcha!-style outcome—in fact, quite the opposite. The MCV facility had five separate emergency rooms. One was for general intake and the others were for treating specialties. In the final week of my rotation, I worked in the obstetrics-gynecology section of the ER.

A woman presented to the general emergency area with a complaint of having a "discharge." Without obtaining any more information from the patient, the clerk gave her directions to the OBGYN emergency room. There a nurse readied the patient for an evaluation by a physician.

"This is your last day on the rotation," the resident who was training me said. "I'm going to let you take this case."

For a medical student, being allowed to serve as lead physician for the first time represented a defining moment. I gave instructions for the nurses and orderlies to set up the patient for an exam. I watched as my orders sent everyone scrambling. The nurses helped the patient onto a special exam table equipped with stirrups, preparing for me to perform a pelvic examination.

I came in with my sterile gown, gloves, and mask, taking a seat on a stool to begin the exam. I appraised the vaginal area and saw no evidence of anything wrong.

"How long have you had this discharge?" I asked the woman.

"Doctor, I don't know what you are doing," she responded. "I've been trying to tell everybody all night that I have a discharge in my ear!"

The situation had proved comical enough to have the nurses convulse with laughter. But a deeper lesson lay behind the comedy. Listen to the patient. Whatever else is going on, listen to the patient. I took that principle forward throughout my medical career.

Despite such incidents and setbacks—there were others that I hesitate to confess—I soldiered on through the four years of medical school. Once the plague of nightmares ended, I maintained my academic standing with no backsliding.

The medical school process amazed me—how over the course of four years ordinary humans can be transformed into healers. I became transformed myself. Now that I had become a healer, the idea of skin color and segregated domes and fear of the other seemed unimportant and foolish. I somehow felt protective of the entire human species. I would never again be able to look at another human being without going beyond the superficial to understand so much more about them.

The knowledge of how we all resembled each other beneath our skins enthralled me. I knew how brain matter appeared in different shades, how the heart looked and how it functioned. Physicians can diagnose a stroke by patient's movement or handshake. They can tell by a certain swelling in the legs that a person was in heart failure. They could look in a patient's eyes and detect anemia or diabetes.

A common meme on the internet displays a collection of nine human hearts, exposed in all their venous glory. Each heart carries a label: Muslim heart, Christian heart, Black heart, atheist heart, Jewish heart, white heart, and so on. All the pictures are identical.

When I strode across the stage at my medical school graduation, I finally joined the same fraternity as that aging Black doctor I encountered in the school infirmary at Southern University ten years before. In the audience sat my mother, looking proud enough to burst.

The same memory floated up in my mind as when Mary Francis came to my graduation from Southern. I once again recalled the first day of school, when at age six I followed her after she left to go home.

"Oh, Butch, you have to stay in school," she told me back then, returning me like a prodigal son to James Ward Sr. Elementary School. I took my mother at her word. Since that day, I had stayed in school with a vengeance, spending a total of twenty-two years educating myself.

I was not done yet.

"Matching" was the process of placing a medical school graduate with a training program at a specific hospital, taking into account the needs and wants of both the graduate and the program. I requested an internship and residency in internal medicine at George Washington University Hospital in Washington, DC.

Those casual folk music gatherings in the lobby of the women's dorm had become more and more popular. I met my wife-to-be at one of those musical evenings. Elizabeth Delahoussaye originally hailed from New Orleans, so I found her an easy person to talk to. We had a few dates, but the school year ended and after graduation I assumed I would never see Liz again.

Left: My mother and me, 1945.

Below: The Francis home at 300 Pearl Street in Jennings, Louisiana, where I lived with my mother, stepfather, and five sisters until I graduated high school.

Cleveland Francis Jr., age nine, 1954.

My Southern University graduation portrait, 1967.

With Dr. Huel Perkins, who was my mentor at Southern University, 2010.

Left: Fledgling soulfolk singer at William & Mary, 1967.

Below: A shot of me as a street musician, drawing a crowd in Williamsburg, Virginia.

Right: With my roommate and musical partner Dave Gapp at William & Mary, 1969. Note the biology lab apparatus in the background.

Below: Performing at William & Mary for the Martin Luther King Jr. Scholarship Fund, 1970.

Above: With my friend Victor Liguori, a one-time heckler who became a mentor, informal manager, and devoted fan, 1982.

Left: Performing at William & Mary, 1970.

Right: A young Dr. Cleveland Francis Jr.

Below: Denzel Washington and Chris Rock have shared this street wisdom: “You’ve got to buy your mama a house!” So I did.

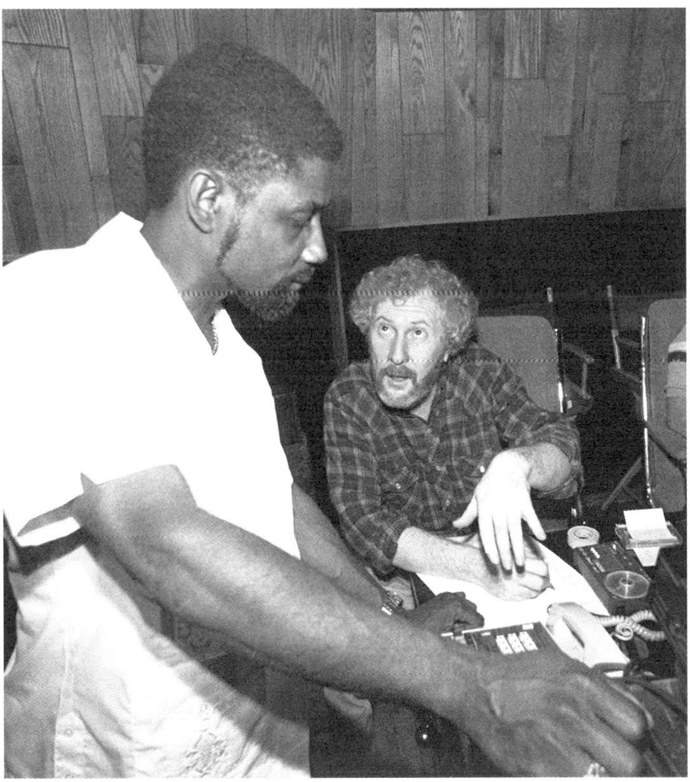

Above: At an American Heart Association show in 1985.

Left: In the studio with my producer and friend Arthur Lisi as we recorded "Reflections on the Wall," 1987.

Standing at the Vietnam Veterans Memorial in Washington, DC, which inspired my song “Reflections on the Wall.”

Heaven and earth to me: onstage at the Birchmere, my home club in Alexandria, Virginia, 1993.

Working on the video for “Love Light” with my director, David Schweitzer, 1990.

Publicity photo for Playback Records, 1990.

Publicity photo for Capitol Records Nashville, 1991.

Jimmy Bowen, the head of my record label in Nashville, Liberty Records, as he looked when I first met him.

Just some of the news media that greeted my arrival as a country music artist in 1992.

Appearing on The Nashville Network's show *Video Morning* with Katie Haas and Al Winter.

Yee haw! Jumping for joy at the start of my first country music tour.

With my trusty road manager Tony Hamrick.

Above: Appearing on *Larry King Live* in 1993.

Right: Publicity photo from 1993, by which time Capitol Nashville had been renamed Liberty Records.

Meeting the great Charley Pride (left), one of my heroes, in 1993.

Hanging out during the recording of my third country album, *You've Got Me Now*. From left: songwriter Robert Byrne (who produced the album), me, Vince Gill (who contributed wonderful background vocals), and recording engineer Bob Bullock, 1994.

Signing an autograph for a young fan.

Right: Good morning, America, how are you? Onstage in 1995.

Below: With some of my country music heroes and forerunners. We were at a celebration of the release of the box set *From Where I Stand: The Black Experience in Country Music* by the Country Music Hall of Fame and Museum and Warner Bros. Records. From left: Dobie Gray, Big Al Downing, Aaron Neville, Charley Pride, and me, 1998. Photo by Raeanne Rubenstein.

Left: Performing at the Grand Ole Opry in 1995.

Below: With my colleagues at Mount Vernon Cardiology Associates, 2015.

With my wonderful wife, Hardeep, at the Birchmere in 2010.

CHAPTER 13

Murmurs of the Heart

HERE'S HOW IT GOES when you're training to be a physician: four years in med school, a year as an intern, then two years working in a hospital as a resident. I did both my internship and residency in internal medicine at George Washington University Hospital. After that, I officially became an internist and could have practiced anywhere I wished.

But I was a glutton for punishment. A fellowship in cardiology would represent the capper on my education, the cherry on top of the sundae. Upon completion of the fellowship, I would be more than just a doctor. I'd be a specialist in internal medicine, a cardiologist.

Richard Pryor has a famous comedy routine in which his own heart actually speaks to him in the midst of a heart attack. "You're thinking about dying now, aren't you?" the heart asks, with Pryor nodding "yes, yes" and whimpering in pain. "You didn't think about that when you were eating all that pork!"

Pork is cheap, pork is plentiful. Seared into my memory were the pig slaughtering days on my grandparents' farm. Pork has been a staple of the African American diet since forever. For this and other reasons, heart disease stalks the Black community like the grim reaper. While I understood that basic fact well enough, it wasn't the primary reason I went in for cardiology.

My goal was simple and clear. I didn't want to be a Black doctor working only with Black patients in the Black community. I wanted to be a doctor treating patients, period, with no qualifiers or modifiers necessary.

During my lengthy postgraduate education, I hadn't worked alongside many people who looked like me. Was I bent on integrating the segregated profession of cardiology? Serving as a dome-buster once again? But even if that might have been true, it didn't represent my main motivation, either.

Cardiology hooked me way back in med school, years before I ever took a fellowship in the specialty. During a random, idle moment walking down a corridor at North Hospital in Richmond, I suddenly found myself swept into a "code blue" emergency. Such an event is more often called an "MSET" nowadays, but whatever the term, the situation triggers an all-hands-on-deck response.

As I stood immobilized, everything around me seemed to happen at once. Nurses and physicians rushed—really, they *sprinted*—into the patient's room. Many of them pushed along emergency apparatuses designed to intervene in a heart attack: respirators, monitors, a portable defibrillator.

As a medical student and a silent spectator to all this, there was no help I could offer, no part for me to play. I marveled at the chaos and intensity of the scrubs crowded around at bedside. Beyond the emergency team pumping on the lady's chest, I could not even see the patient. I imagined the sound of a flatline on the heart monitor, an ugly, despairing monotone. The words "patient mortality" went through my mind. No matter the rush, I thought, no matter the lightning level of response, they were going to lose her.

Then from behind me I saw three figures heading down the hall, not rushing, merely walking at a pretty good pace. They were the cardiologists who had been called in on the case, an attending physician and two residents. The head cardiologist entered the room and behaved like Jesus calming the waters.

He observed the patient and the scene for a moment. "Stop whatever you are doing," he said to the half dozen staffers present, speaking in a loud, firm voice. He halted all the activity and moved to check the woman's pulse.

"Who was the first one here?" he asked. "Who triggered the alarm?"

A young nurse's aide raised her hand. "I came in and she wasn't breathing."

"This woman is awake," the cardiologist said, stating the obvious. The lady was elderly, and at times when patients of advanced age drop off to sleep, respiration can slow almost to a standstill. The aide happened to enter the room during one of those long pauses between breaths, concluded the patient was dying, and triggered the code blue.

The bedside crowd broke up. Everyone but the cardiology team left the room. The patient reached out and held the attending cardiologist's hand. "Thank you," she breathed, more a whisper than anything fully articulated. I knew the patient definitely had reason to give thanks. If the cardiologist had failed to intervene, the vigorous CPR compressions performed on her could have broken ribs or caused other damage.

So, a false alarm. Even so, what impressed me most was the way the attending cardiologist had cut through the chaos, instantly organizing the whole situation. *Wow*, I thought, my mind working at a very basic level. *A cardiologist would be a great thing to be.*

I kept that thought in mind throughout the remainder of my medical education, through internship and residency. Experience reaffirmed that initial impulse. I saw a lot of cardiac patients during my years of training in internal medicine. I witnessed the intricacy of their care and met many cardiologists. The intensity of the field still attracted me, the life and death decisions involved. I had climbed my way up the medical school mountain. Now I experienced the mountaineer's desire to summit.

I applied for a cardiology fellowship with George Washington University Hospital.

"That isn't available for you here at GW," said the head of the department of internal medicine. "What's a second choice?"

I didn't have one. The admin told me there were three applicants ahead of me in line for the single cardiology fellowship available at the hospital.

I reached out to Dr. George A. Kelser, director of the cardiology division at George Washington. He should be able to help me, I figured. But I was disappointed.

"The doctors ahead of you in line have excellent Ivy League credentials," Kelser said. "They graduated from Harvard, Yale, and Duke, I believe."

"Surely not all three at once," I said, making a weak attempt at humor.

For better or worse, and outmoded as it was, the words "Ivy League" remained a powerful password in higher education. But I doubted the Harvard and Yale boys would be interested in taking a step down to accept a fellowship at George Washington U. And the Duke graduate—well, I knew Blue Devils tended to be fanatical about their school. Like salmon swimming upstream to the place of their birth, Duke grads would always figure out a way to get back to Duke.

I informed Kelser that I would take my chances with my fourth-in-line fellowship application.

He frowned. "I'm not sure that would be your best decision, Dr. Francis," he said. Kelser then suggested that I check out opportunities at Howard University, the famous historically Black institution located nearby in the heart of DC.

"Well, do you have a name of someone I can connect with at Howard?" I asked.

"No, I don't really know anyone specifically, not over at Howard, no," Dr. Kelser said. "Not well enough to give you a name, no." The man could pack more noes into a sentence than anyone I had ever met.

"Why would you tell me to go somewhere when you don't know anyone?" I was fed up. People had been suggesting Howard to me ever since I came to the East Coast. I knew it to be a great school. I've always harbored deep respect for Howard University and other HBCUs. Many of my professors at Southern graduated from Howard, and it was the school of the doctor who made me want to go to medical school in the first place.

My determination to desegregate places such as W&M and MCV came to me as a conscious choice. I would pave the way for others and demolish the notion that Black applicants were somehow not academically equal. At the same time, I resented the kneejerk impulse to match me with a Black institution, as if it were the only game in town. Total strangers would sometimes make assumptions. "What year did you go to Howard?" I delighted in setting them straight.

My predicament felt familiar. I had been in this position before. A high school principal informing me that the military was the only choice I had. A secretary at Southern University saying the application deadline had already passed. The dirty dozen medical school rejections. My first interview at MCV: "They are certainly not going to give you a white student's slot."

Cleve Francis, the odds maker's nightmare. No sane-minded gambler would ever have bet good money on a kid from Jennings being able to rack up advanced degrees, much less land a cardiology fellowship. But once again, as had happened before in my life, the unlikely happened and the impossible transpired. One by one, the three doctors-in-training that had requested the George Washington fellowship dropped out. For the umpteenth time, I could pronounce those three charmed words, *I am in*.

During my fellowship I spent two years listening to the murmurs of the human heart. Cardiology seemed to align magically with my goals, my personality, my philosophy of life. At its core—I want to say at its heart—I discovered a deeply human element that spoke eloquently to me.

Surgeons work with patients so unresponsive they might as well be dead. Anesthesiologists put people to sleep. Dermatologists go skin deep. On and on through the long list of medical specialties, each one displays an essential quality. But what could be more human than the heart?

Even the brain, widely considered the most complex piece of real estate in the universe, even the mighty brain appears too fussy when compared to the heart, somehow not as basic, not as fundamental. The brain's model is complex: a computer. The heart's model is simpler: an engine. Humans can be brain dead, clinically and legally dead, yet the heart still pumps, warming the skin, making the chest rise and fall with the rhythm of being alive. When the heart goes, it's over.

Being matched with a cardiology fellowship at a DC hospital had personal as well as professional implications. Instead of going back home to Louisiana after MCV graduation, Elizabeth Delahoussaye had taken a job in northern Virginia. Fate or kismet threw us together once more. We resumed dating, began living together, and married in 1977.

Some events in my life seemed to develop spontaneously. They weren't planned—they just occurred. When Liz and I first met and dated, we never discussed a long-term relationship. We found common ground in our shared passion for music. Like me, she had grown up in the segregated Deep South. Unlike me, she experienced Jim Crow from the perspective of a white woman. She had few other Black people in her life, none as friends or significant others.

During the initial period of us dating, Liz and Mary Francis got along famously. They enjoyed each other's company. But when I told my mother we were going to marry, Mary Francis surprised me with the vehemence of her response.

"Don't expect me to approve," she said abruptly. "I will not come to that wedding."

Though I was somewhat blindsided, when I considered Mary Francis's reaction to our marriage, I thought I understood. My mother still had leftover attitudes that had been drummed into her brain over the course of years spent in the Jennings dome. Marriage between a white woman and a Black man represented the taboo to end all taboos. Mary Francis feared for me. Dancing in her head were visions of Emmet Till and the murder of my Uncle Theophile.

Liz and I made sure we knew what we were getting into. We even broke up and started dating others for a while before we got back together. There was nothing for it, we decided. We were in love.

Mary Francis came to our wedding after all. "How could I miss the marriage of my only son?"

As soon as Liz and I settled in together, we were forced to weather a storm that felt all too familiar, one that I had faced several times before in my life.

★ ★ ★

When I completed my cardiology fellowship in 1978, my brain so full of learning it felt top-heavy, I stood poised on a threshold. Dozens of cardiology practices operated in northern Virginia, Maryland, and the District of Columbia. Surely every one of them would stand ready to welcome me with open arms.

It didn't happen. Doors slammed in my face one after another. The old blues phrase: "If you're white, all right. If you're brown, stick around. If you're Black, get back, get back, get back." I remember standing on the steps of GW Hospital, tears of frustration in my eyes. After all these years, after all the education I had acquired, prejudice and fear blocked my path forward once again.

The few positions offered to me were at cardiology practices nicknamed "Beltway Bandits," due to their ambulance-chasing methods on the highway that encircled DC. Unable to stomach that kind of buzzard work, I took a temporary position at a local ER.

Located right on the Maryland line, Greater Southeast Community Hospital allowed me a harsh glimpse of one of the area's deepest, bleakest ghettos. I treated patients who viewed the ER as their own private doctor's office. Folks waited hours to be seen for heart attack symptoms. The uninsured residents of the neighborhood had few other health-care options. As I had told Dr. Christian, helping people who needed help was the kind of work that gave my life purpose.

Southeast Community Hospital surely wasn't upscale. Several staffers had cars stolen out of the hospital's parking lot. I bought a steering-wheel lock and placed my hub caps in my trunk. A few of the surgeons came out of military service in Vietnam, where as army medics they had become skilled at triaging gunshot victims. Their experience in combat proved helpful in the drug-fueled street wars of the neighborhood.

Between my earnings as an ER doctor and Liz's salary as a physical therapist, we made a decent living. But I felt lost and blocked. This was where three decades of schooling had put me? I yearned for a human connection with my patients, something I could never have working at an ER. I wanted to be able to interact with those I treated, to know them as people, to develop long-term relationships. All that proved impossible in the rushed, chaotic atmosphere of the emergency room.

Elizabeth saved me. She had taken a job helping a physiatrist—a specialist in physical medicine and rehabilitation—who was setting up a physical therapy department at Mount Vernon Hospital (now Inova Mount Vernon Hospital). The new, 180-bed facility, founded only a few years before, served the Mount Vernon neighborhood of Fairfax County, a booming suburban region southwest of DC. Elizabeth had worked at the place for a year and was thriving. She witnessed my struggles in sticking a landing after completing my fellowship, and she encouraged me to think outside the box.

"You know, Cleve, if you'd ever want to start a practice of your own, Mount Vernon might be a good place," she said.

Checking with every cardiology practice in the region, I had failed to land a position. The barrage of rejections reminded me of getting turned down by a dozen medical schools when I graduated from Southern. Why was I going out hat in hand, asking people to hire me? I possessed everything I needed to start my own practice. *I'll do it my own damned self.*

One of my mother's folk-wisdom sayings resurfaced. "If you want to catch a fish, you have to put your hook in the water." There was also another piece of wisdom kicking around the civil rights movement at the time, from Mahatma Gandhi: "Be the change you want to see in the world." I wanted to establish a multicultural cardiology practice that would hire qualified physicians regardless of race or ethnic background. We would serve the multicultural community where we practiced.

Elizabeth ran interference at Mount Vernon Hospital. She spoke to the staff doctors. "My husband is a cardiologist," she told them. "Would you support him if he came down here?"

On her recommendation I talked to the Mount Vernon physicians myself. It was one of those symmetrical situations where I was interviewing them as they were interviewing me. At the time I didn't realize that I was choosing the facility that would serve as a home base for the rest of my professional life.

"This is a new hospital," said Dr. John Titus, the head of family medicine. "We need a cardiologist here. If you would come over to us, we would certainly send you patients."

Thus began a brutal two-year stretch as the 1970s closed out, a harrowing period of long hours and unrelenting work that pretty near killed me. The doctors, especially internists who styled themselves cardiologists, did not readily accept my presence. Privately, I termed them "the Medical Mafia." It was as if I sought entry into the Genovese family.

But at least it was not simple prejudice. I didn't think the other physicians closed me out because of the color of my skin. Instead, the dynamic involved economics and power. There existed only a finite pool of patients. With racial bias removed as a factor, I figured the battle for success represented a fair fight. I just had to put up a good one, and I'd do that by resolving to be the best doctor my patients had ever seen.

On call twenty-four hours a day, seven days a week, I had no time for relaxation, no time for music, no time for Liz. Day and night did not matter anymore. Ask me about defibrillating a patient and I could answer. Only don't ask me what day of the week it was.

Borrowing $30,000 from a local bank, I opened a practice and gave it a name, Mount Vernon Cardiology Associates, a grand title for an outfit with only a lone doctor. I rented a small office, seventy-five hundred square feet of space across the street from the hospital. The first thing I needed to do was hire a staff. Among the many applicants I interviewed was a middle-aged white woman, Karen Daniel, a military wife who was seeking to get back into the workforce. I asked her the same question I posed to everyone I interviewed.

"Who is the most important person in the office?"

She answered without hesitation. "The patient, of course." I hired her on the spot as my office manager. I convinced a couple of experienced nurses from the hospital to cross the street and come work for me. I hired an accountant and lawyer.

Dating back to my medical school days and continuing throughout my postgraduate training, I always held nursing in very high regard. Nurses are the lifeblood of medicine. They spend much more time with patients than doctors do, and know much more about the patients as people than anyone else in health care. Patients tend to share much more information with nurses than with their doctor.

Whenever I had a new patient in the hospital, I always made a practice of tracking down the nurse to get her opinion on my treatment plan. Nurses respect doctors (mostly) but their first allegiance is to the patient. A nurse is usually the best judge of a doctor's character. Nurses interact with many physicians, both general practitioners and specialists, and can detect the slightest hints of arrogance or disrespect. Word can get around in the hothouse environment of a hospital. The community respects a nurse's opinions about a doctor, good or bad, depending on physician's behavior.

The cadre of nurses at Mount Vernon practically adopted me as a fresh-out-of-fellowship newcomer. They made it easy for me to survive and prosper as a solo practitioner. I see them as unheralded, undercelebrated angels of the human community, incredibly hardworking, unfailingly caring, and blessed with deep wells of practical and scientific knowledge.

From the start, I needed nurses to be there for me. They served as my eyes and ears for the many patients I was following. I'd arrive at the hospital at 6:00 a.m. for rounds in the critical care unit, then see new consults until 9:30 a.m. Then I would head over to the office to see patients until noon, shuttling back and forth from hospital to office until evening. I normally did not get home for dinner until 9:00 p.m. On weekends I would get to the hospital at seven o'clock in the morning for a twelve- to fourteen-hour day. This was in addition to being on call to the emergency room 24/7 for cardiology problems.

Getting my bearings after a few months, I came to realize that Mount Vernon was in reality a small town. Sure, it was part of the massive East Coast urban area that ran all the way from Boston through New York City, Philadelphia, Baltimore, and DC. But in terms of population, Mount Vernon outranked Jennings by only a few thousand people. The town wedged itself into the same kind of geographical cul-de-sac that I recognized from the location of Southern University. Interstate highways cut it off on the west and north. A wide loop of the Potomac River formed a boundary to the east.

Good lord, I thought, was I back inside a dome? Like Richmond and Williamsburg, Mount Vernon suffered from being burdened with too much history. The town took its name from George Washington's estate, located barely five miles south of the hospital where I was practicing medicine.

When he died in 1799, the Father of Our Country deeded part of his land holdings to his enslaved workers, the Mount Vernon neighborhood of Gum Springs, where their descendants live to this day. I used to joke that I had tried to leave the plantations of Louisiana, only to move to the old plantation of George Washington.

For a first case on my first day at the hospital, a nephrologist, Dr. Steve Goldberger, requested help with a very sick woman who had gone into heart failure. The call came at 2:00 a.m. I threw on a shirt and pants, grabbed my stethoscope, and raced to the hospital. When I arrived, I first stopped in at radiology to check the patient's X-rays. A security guard saw me entering the radiology department and called the Fairfax County police.

When I approached the elevator to the sixth-floor intensive care unit, three officers stood speaking to the guard. I realized at once what had happened. Still carrying the X-rays, I walked up to the gathering and introduced myself as "Dr. Francis, the new cardiologist." I pushed the elevator button for the sixth floor and got on. No other words were spoken. From that point forward, I always made sure I was dressed properly whenever I was on call.

I worked, and worked, and barely slept. In fact, I barely existed at all outside the fluorescent settings of the hospital and office. I had no life. But I was stubborn. I wasn't going to seek another, more established practice to join. I would also refuse to be doomed to work in an ER. Nobody gives you anything in this world, I told myself. I would have to earn everything on my own.

I took the lessons of the civil rights movement and applied them to my own situation. Members of the Black community needed to be in control of their own destinies. Dr. King and others had forced open doors, and society needed someone to walk through them. I would be that person. I had never marched, never protested. I was too busy getting educated. Now I would serve the movement in my own personal, limited way.

Word began to get around that there was a new cardiologist in town. Referrals slowly started to trickle in. A surprising one came from Dr. Kelser, the cardiology director at George Washington Hospital who had advised me to seek employment via Howard University. He didn't just refer a woman suffering from heart problems and living in the Mount Vernon area to me, he actually drove her medical records over to my office. He told her that I was one of the best cardiologists he had trained. She became one of my favorite patients, and I wound up taking care of her for fifteen years.

Prospective patients would call the office to confirm that I was "the Black doctor with the beard." My popularity grew to where appointments had to be booked weeks in advance. For the first time, I started making good money. Comedian Chris Rock asked the question, what do rap stars do when they hit their first jackpot payday? "They buy their mama a house!"

So that's what Liz and I did, purchasing a four-bedroom place in a pleasant Williamsburg neighborhood, with a screened-in back porch and a rocking-chair front porch, too. Not a palace by any means, but compared to 300 Pearl in Jennings and every other place in which Mary Francis grew up, the new house was a mansion. I happily inhabited the role of the good son. My steadily rising income represented a solid means of support for my mother and sisters.

The pace of work did not let up. Not until the beginning of the 1980s could I come up for air. I finally decided that it was time to bring a new partner into the practice. I had known Dr. Bruce Tinker at George Washington Hospital. He was married to a physical therapist who had been hired by my wife. When we first talked, Tinker was still in cardiology training at the University of West Virginia. I promised that I would hold a position open for him at Mount Vernon Cardiology Associates.

Dr. Tinker joined the practice as a partner in 1981. After two years of going it alone, I was completely exhausted. But I had somehow held my ground to become an established, go-to cardiologist for the entire region.

★ ★ ★

Put anything on the back burner long enough, and sooner or later it's going to boil over. Caught up in schooling, I stepped back from music for almost a half-decade after leaving Williamsburg. The town had done me well, serving as a perfect proving ground with its comfortable Cleve & Dave gigs, the coffeehouse home base of Hoi Polloi, Victor Liguori functioning as an enthusiastic informal manager, and a built-in audience of students, followers, and fans that could fill a whole concert hall.

With Bruce Tinker on board at Mount Vernon Cardiology Associates (justifying the plural in the name of the practice for the first time), I was no longer burdened with a 24/7 schedule. It was more like 24/3½. Instead of every night, I was now on call every other night, and I had at least a couple of days every week to call my own. More importantly, with a few gaps opening in my evening schedule, I could arrange to fit in the occasional weekend music gig.

Back when I worked in the ER at Greater Southeast Community Hospital, I met an ER technician there who was also a musician. Billy Pierce played a mean lead guitar. He and I began performing frequently at the Singer's Studio, a small club in Georgetown. But while getting my practice up and running, I had little time to devote to music.

Now we picked up the thread again, with the duo Dave & Cleve reincarnated as Billy & Cleve. I bought a twelve-string guitar, and with Billy backing me up, we sounded like a full orchestra. An enthusiastic musician-songwriter-chaplain named James William "Will" Flanders operated the Singer's Studio. He invited us to appear so often we developed a returning audience.

Throughout the 1980s, my public profile steadily rose within the community, both as a cardiologist and a musician. Area schools requested that I sing and speak at commencement ceremonies. Local churches tugged on my sleeve to appear at services. Newspapers, magazines, radio, and TV stations all piled on. Hungry for stories, reporters recognized a good hook when they saw one.

For the media, I fit perfectly into the "lifestyle" feature slot as something of a curiosity. A flavor of the frivolous came through in the articles and TV news programs, an "isn't this cute?" element that would prove to have negative repercussions later on. At the moment, I saw the press attention for the minor blip that it was, and didn't allow it to inflate my ego too much.

Why did I do music? For the attention, popularity, celebrity? My growing reputation as a musician certainly bolstered my medical practice. People all over the Washington, DC area began to recognize my name. I didn't have to make up business cards for Mount Vernon Cardiology Associates, because music served as my calling card. Some folks who called the office still asked for "the Black doctor with the beard," but now others requested "that doctor guy who sings."

★ ★ ★

I never did music only for the publicity, or the strokes, or the good feeling it engendered in my soul. I always saw singing as a lever for change. "A folksong is what's wrong and how to fix it," said Woody Guthrie. The sense of reaching out and connecting with the moral conscience of an audience member always did the trick for me. I didn't see it as Little Preacher–style proselytizing. To me it felt more like bonding.

Ever since my days at Southern I took direction from Martin Luther King Jr. He powered the civil rights movement by appealing to the moral conscience of everyone in America, everyone in the world. He stood on the shoulders of Gandhi. Both men knew that anger will never make for an effective human connection, that hate won't do it, and that guilt-tripping won't accomplish much, either.

Inside every human being, King knew, was a kernel of good conscience, a moral center. Every religion and spiritual practice recognized this truth, and it applied despite the political opinions a person held, or how their lives had shaped them for prejudice or bias. However corrupt or estranged you are from your true self, that little shard of the sacred remains within you.

KKK hood wearers, slavers, traffickers, gunrunning mercenaries, it didn't matter who you were. Anyone could change. Let me cite Bob Dylan again, something he said at the Grammys in 1991, quoting his dad, Abram Zimmerman. "It's possible to become so defiled in this world that your own father and mother will abandon you and if that happens, God will always believe in your ability to mend your ways."

Onstage I wasn't trying to get anyone to change their ways. I would never presume. What I looked for was a link to that moral core I believed existed within everyone. I stayed away from overt references to political candidates and concentrated mainly on causes—civil rights, of course, Vietnam veteran issues, mentorship of children, support for AIDS research, or helping indigent patients in cardiac rehab.

Woody Guthrie once suggested a rule of thumb for musicians: "Do one concert for yourself, and one for the other guy." Meaning do benefit concerts to the extent that you donate to charity 50 percent of your efforts as an artist.

The person I most revered in this respect was Harry Chapin, whose songs I performed in almost every set I ever played. He was the most effective folksinger I ever encountered when it came to the day-to-day work of connecting with his audience's moral center. That's what Chapin's saying here, in his song "Circle."

It seems like I've been here before
I can't remember when
But I have this funny feeling
That we'll all be together again
No straight lines make up my life
And all my roads have bends
There's no clearcut beginning
And so far no dead-end.

Finding ways to connect within the immediate community always interested me. Through Elizabeth I got to know a secretary in the physical therapy department who also volunteered for the Mount Vernon Hospital Auxiliary.

"We have something called the Lights of Love ceremony every year at the Christmas holidays," she told me. Stringing lights of every color, auxiliary volunteers decorated the large cedar tree on the hospital grounds. Members of the community donated five or ten dollars to sponsor a light in memory of loved ones who had died or were in the hospital. It was a homey, warm-cider-and-cookies occasion. Kids from the neighborhood high school would read poems.

I wrote a song called "Light Up the Night." Billy and I debuted it at the ceremony in 1982. This brought a flurry of publicity in local media. We would perform at the event for the next five years. The song proved so popular that the auxiliary paid the expenses for us to record it. Tape cassettes of "Light Up the Night" went on sale in the gift shop as part of fundraising efforts for the hospital.

Somehow in darkness, men cannot see
Love can't survive, men cannot be free
But there is a way to a brighter day
Love is the answer, hear what I say,
Let's light up the night
Light up the light
Light up the night with love

For my outreach work I always tried to emulate the motto "think global, act local." The local "Light Up the Night" effort wasn't big, wasn't grand, but it reached into the hearts of a few people who were hurting and in need of healing, and it reached into my own, too. Sometimes that's enough.

I have always believed that in this great big world of ours, the efforts of one person can make a difference. History has proven this to be true over and over, from Jesus of Nazareth, to Florence Nightingale, Mahatma Gandhi, and Rev. Dr. Martin Luther King Jr. As Charles Dickens wrote, "A very little key will open a very heavy door."

And besides, bigger things were coming my way, larger, far-reaching efforts that occurred on the national stage.

CHAPTER 14

Timeless

WHILE I WAS WORKING long hours every day of the week trying to get Mount Vernon Cardiology Associates off the ground, my personal life suffered. Elizabeth stood as my first supporter and ardent advocate, but those two years of me being on call 24/7 took its toll on our marriage. Even though she was always a loyal fan, the time I spent involved with music often took me away from home.

Elizabeth and I stayed married for eight years before separating in 1985 and divorcing in 1986. I was sorry we didn't make it, but I considered our time together to be a respectable run. I owe her so much for placing me on the path toward starting a private practice. We did not have any children and parted as friends, coming to a mutual agreement simply to go our separate ways.

The divorce was not an easy thing for me. I was never a big guy, weighing in at around 145 pounds, but I lost a lot of weight during that period, a change noticed by several friends. I enrolled in personal counseling, which helped me move on with my life, my work, and my music. I'd remain single until I remarried in 2009.

In a future reckoning beyond the pearly gates somewhere, I'll be asked what I gave up in return for a life devoted to music and medicine. I will not have to think too long, because the answer is on the tip of my tongue every single day. I sacrificed having a family, having children. There's no such thing as a free lunch, I guess, but some of those lunches extract a heavier toll than others.

My cardiology practice grew to include a total of five cardiologists, including myself. Now divorced and with the on-call burden being shared, I poured myself into work and music.

How can I explain what happened with my music in the mid-1980s? I had time, a little money, and the drive to employ both in the service of song. For an artist, time plus money equals freedom.

In quick order, I found myself invited to perform atop the wall of the Vietnam Veterans Memorial, at the headquarters of the International Red Cross, at the headquarters of the Pan American Health Organization, at the U.S. Capitol Rotunda, at the National Theatre, and—at the request of incarcerated Vietnam veterans—within the walls of a high-security prison. The extent of the connection I experienced during those days floored me, humbled me, exhilarated me.

All the appearances arose from songs I had written. The opportunities came via pure inspiration, motivated by topical issues or social causes.

For my community musical projects, I fortuitously met someone who would take my songwriting and performances to an entirely different level. One of the critical care nurses at Mount Vernon Hospital, Ann Marie Gorman, put me on to him. "Oh, you do music?" she asked. "You've got to meet Arthur Lisi."

Arthur and I struck up a strong friendship. Wisconsin born, from an Italian background, Lisi acted as musical director for Van McCoy during the disco years of the 1970s. McCoy toured worldwide on his massive hit "The Hustle," and Arthur was right there with him. Then Arthur signed on as the co-musical director on *The Cosby Show*, the #1 TV program in the country at the time. While Arthur might have had more professional credentials than Victor Liguori, the two men shared a quality that endeared me to them. They both liked my music.

"If you're ever interested in doing some projects, let me know," Lisi said at our first meeting. "We'll work together."

Back when I was at Southern University, I asked Dr. Huel Perkins if I should learn to read music. Self-taught as I was, I had only a vague idea of what reading music might entail.

"Normally, I would tell you yes, you should," Perkins had responded. "But at this point, you're not aiming to become a professional. You know, if things develop differently, there are always people out there who know music."

He reminded me that Sammy Davis Jr. couldn't read a note of music either. "He had an arranger, Marty Paich, helping him out. There's always a guy around that works with these kinds of musicians. With your talent, you can sing with a damned orchestra."

Tall and thin, with crazy red hair, Arthur Lisi became my Marty Paich, Nelson Riddle, and Quincy Jones, all rolled into one. He determined what songs fit my repertoire, choosing the range that suited my voice. We would go over the tunes together, then he'd work as the intermediary between the band and me. Understanding the language that musicians employ at that level proved vital for me to step up as a professional singer, as a musician, as an "act."

My performance at the Vietnam Memorial Wall had its roots in my feelings about war and country. I saw how Martin Luther King Jr.'s stance against the Vietnam War earned him even more enemies than he already had. I always harbored deeply conflicted feelings about the carnage happening in Southeast Asia. I knew many people who fought and served, and many people who protested, and a few who did both. But from the day I rejected my high school principal's advice to join the army, I stood apart from the military. I harbored some guilt about it, an unresolved sense that I had ducked out of my duty.

The acid-tongued writer William S. Burroughs passed a darkly humorous judgment on folks like me. "There are no innocent bystanders," he said. "What are they doing there in the first place?"

Long after the war's end, wounds from Vietnam still festered, both literally and figuratively. I developed a "hate the war, love the soldier" attitude, and at the same time felt fury over the waste of young life. "A rich man's war," I thought to myself, "but a poor man's fight."

Looking to wrestle with my own ambivalence, I naturally gravitated to the famous Vietnam Memorial Wall, designed by architect Maya Lin and located in the Constitution Gardens, just northeast of the Lincoln Memorial and adjacent to the National Mall in the heart of Washington, DC. I wasn't the only one drawn to the site. Since its completion in 1982, the Wall had become a focal point for grieving and healing, and sometimes for political demonstrations. Not knowing exactly why I was doing it, I began to make weekly pilgrimages to the memorial, a trip north from my home of some twenty-five miles.

The Wall functioned as a kind of spiritual magnet. There were always veterans and family members of veterans present, even at night, since the Mall is always open. I encountered some purposeful faces, determined to honor the dead, and some dazed faces, glazed with grief.

Many times I'd stick around until ten or eleven at night. I remember evenings when I would hear sobbing in the darkness, the only sound above the far-off hiss of traffic. A miniature tent village arose on the grounds between the Wall and the nearby *Three Soldiers* statue. I visited the site often enough that I began to recognize the veterans camping there, and they became accustomed to my presence. I explained to them my own many-steps-removed experience of the war.

"I'm not a veteran," I said. "I was in school. I saw a lot of my friends go." Telling folks that I was a doctor always helped to break the ice. The resident veterans got to know my name and invited me into their tents—not right off, but I'd see them every week and eventually they came to trust me. We spoke about their experiences in the war. As I know from writing this book, the very act of recounting a memory can work toward healing.

It was summer. The yellow glow of lanterns lit the tents from the inside, setting the scene for so many tears, so many Bible readings, so many bull sessions. The veteran residents had brought in cots, and they had flags draped on the walls of their tents—the Stars and Stripes and POW/MIA flags. Vets came from all over the country, and some of them slept over for long visits.

What was I doing there? I had to know what these men—they were mostly men, though I knew many women served in the war—were thinking and feeling. I didn't know exactly why I felt an urgency to know them and understand what was in their hearts, but I did. We'd sit together inside those little tents that they had erected and talk. If I could, I wanted to share what they were telling me.

"Reflections on the Wall" took me a year to write. Many of the lyrics were based on sentiments I heard the vets express during those visits. At my own expense, working with Arthur Lisi, we recorded the song at Bias Studio, a local studio in Alexandria, Virginia.

From the North and the South
From the East and the West
From cities both big and small
From the rich and the poor, all colors they bore
Their names are there on the wall
They were bright young poets who would never write
Fathers who would never see their children grow tall
As old and as young as they'll ever be
Their names are there on the wall

Some friends who had heard "Reflections on the Wall" arranged for Arthur and me to meet with Jan C. Scruggs, the much-decorated, U.S. Army Purple Heart veteran who founded and led the nonprofit organization that raised the money for the memorial.

"I've got a song I wrote from talking to the guys," I told Scruggs. On a handheld tape recorder, I played the song that Arthur and I had recorded.

As the tape began to roll, I could see him wince inwardly. Visitors to the memorial were always coming in with all sorts of songs, poems, heartfelt letters, artwork, and eulogies. For some reason, teddy bear offerings proliferated at the foot of the wall even more than flowers. Pretty much every day, Park Service workers cleaned up whatever had been left, preserving the best of it, throwing the rest away.

Scruggs listened intently to "Reflections." Midway through, he held up one hand and covered his eyes with the other, overcome with emotion. Then he asked me if I would be willing to sing the song for the upcoming Memorial Day observation at the Wall, on May 27, 1987.

Performing "Reflections," standing poised above the smooth black granite slab inscribed with over 58,000 names, looking over the audience of veterans and their families, I experienced an intensity of emotion that burned away my ambivalence about the war. I only felt gratitude to the friends I had made, and that I could tell their stories in the lyrics of the song.

On the podium that day was a young U.S. senator from the state of Tennessee, Al Gore, a Vietnam veteran who would become vice president of the United States. After the performance, I was able to meet with many of the veterans in attendance, more than a few in tears after the song. Love mixed with grief in the mood of the afternoon.

★ ★ ★

The AIDS crisis raged during the mid-1980s, and fear and misinformation raged along with it. Anything to do with sex always elicited a prickly reaction in part of the populace, and bigotry against gay men figured in, too. I approached the situation purely from a health-care standpoint. Stigmatizing sufferers only interferes with an effective medical response to a disease, as I knew from the history of the bubonic plague, leprosy, and STDs.

The inaction at the top echelons of government infuriated me. I remember a bitter joke going around at the time. A congressional panel hears testimony about the crisis. "AIDS strikes heavily among gays and addicts," the witness testifies. The sleepy politicians remain unmoved. Then the witness adds, "It also affects men who visit prostitutes." Suddenly all the gray-haired senators and congressmen on the panel woke up, demanding that something had to be done about the epidemic.

It's the same old story, whereby nothing pierces the indifference of some individuals until it comes home to them. President Ronald Reagan never lifted a finger to address the contagion that swept the country, never even spoke the word "AIDS." Then Rock Hudson, a dear friend of both Ron and Nancy, died of the disease. Only then did the federal government begin to respond to the problem.

All the blame and ostracism floating around the country stirred me to action. I composed "We're All in This Together," probably the only song in the world ever written about a virus.

To combat misinformation, I carefully had laid out the facts in the lyrics as I understood them. People were dying all over the world, not only gay but straight men, IV drug users, women, children—even the unborn, who would come into the world infected. I knew the epidemic reached deeply into disenfranchised communities, especially the minority poor.

Like an alien from a distant place
It's entered our world
Bringing death, fear, suffering, and pain
To men, women, boys, and girls.
In every city, village, country, or town
Its presence is known.
For without regards to race, color, or creed
It strikes the old, the young, even the yet unborn.
It wages war against mankind
Entering the river of life called blood.
It spreads destruction not through how we hate
But rather through our need to love.
We're all in this together, together you and me
If one of us is a prisoner, then nobody's really free
We're all in this together, together we must stand
So come my brothers and my sisters it's time to lend a hand

Within the world of medicine, "We're All in This Together" struck a chord. Physicians, nurses, and health-care workers were on the front lines. They understood the stakes. For the U.S. audience, I did a version of the song in English. We tried to enlist a Spanish vocalist to sing it but couldn't find anyone. I learned some rudimentary Spanish and sang it myself. Through Arthur's contacts we were able to enlist a female Portuguese vocalist who recorded the Portuguese version for use in Brazil, a country that had been hit very hard by the virus. I was invited to perform the song at the Pan American Health Organization headquarters in Washington, DC.

Photographer Marty LaVor and I developed a poster to distribute in hospital and clinics. For the graphic, I enlisted an interracial couple that lived across the street from me. The kids in the family presented a whole color wheel of different skin tones, so we made a visual for the poster with all their hands, the hands of their parents, and my own hands. I started working with the Whitman-Walker Clinic in DC, which provided medical services for gay people. I traveled to Baltimore to work on a clean needle drive.

In the course of the initiatives surrounding "We're All in This Together," once in a while I fielded a predictable question from this or that reporter: "Are you gay?"

"No, I'm not," I would always respond. "I'm a doctor and a songwriter."

Lisi produced recordings of "Light Up the Night," "Reflections on the Wall," and "We're All in This Together." At the time I tried not to overestimate the impact these records would have and didn't fantasize about being up on stage at the Grammys anytime soon. Entry to Washington Metro transit cost 60¢ back then. Employing the traditional formula of keeping things in perspective, I told myself that with the recordings I could get a ride on the subway, as long as I had six dimes in my pocket.

It turned out my songs would do me a lot better than that.

★ ★ ★

During this period, my duo buddy Billy Pierce and I cut a sort of calling card record, a 45-rpm single that had Sam Cooke's "You Send Me" on one side and "Desperado" by the Eagles on the other. We sold the record to fans at our gigs, but I also thought I would use it to reach out to local clubs looking to book acts. So I had the single on hand one afternoon in 1983 when an opportunity dropped into my lap that started while I was listening to the radio driving home from the hospital.

"*Breakout!*" The announcer sounded like a carnival barker. "*Breakout!* A TV show that seeks the top talent from all over the District and Northern Virginia to pair with the decision makers in the Music City, Nashville, Tennessee! Washington to Nashville! Send in an audition tape to *Breakout!*"

That sort of business wasn't for me. I had no ambitions beyond the local area, the clubs, shows, and benefits that I was already doing and doing well with. Nashville could have been as far away as the Emerald City of Oz. I did plenty of down-home music in my act, but I did country my way, the soulfolk way, mixing in gospel, R&B, and folk, flavoring the blend with my own idiosyncratic style. Call it willow tree music.

What little I knew of Nashville summoned up a realm with a glorious past and a present that was in danger of losing its way. The town had a dark side as an avenue of broken dreams, a Hollywood-like land of sharks that preyed on wannabes. I didn't know that world, didn't particularly want to know it, and had never pursued knowing it. The country music I loved—Johnny Cash, Charley Pride, George Jones, Hank Williams, Loretta Lynn—was not the kind of stuff they were playing on country radio in those days.

Even as I scribbled down the address that the radio announcer gave, I had no expectation that anything would come of it. But I found myself in the same "nothing ventured, nothing gained" position as when I picked up that postcard calling for graduate school applications at the College of William & Mary. The act of sending in an audition tape would cost me the price of postage. I mailed in the Billy & Cleve single we had just pressed, along with some publicity stills of us performing, then thought no more of it.

Against all odds, the *Breakout!* TV show connection came through. I tried not to get too excited about the development. Billy and I would be taped performing for a show to air on a local community cable TV program in Nashville. We did three songs: Sam Cooke's "You Send Me," Harry Chapin's "Circle," and Bette Midler's "The Rose," written by Broadway and television actress Amanda McBroom.

The producer on the program sent a compliment my way, saying he booked us because we were unlike any other act on the show. "We don't have anybody doing strictly acoustic music."

"That's soulfolk," I said.

"Whatever it is, you stood out, and that's why we had you on."

Talking over the phone, the producer and I found common ground. Formerly a preacher, Moses Dillard was from North Carolina, an old soul and an old hand who had been around the music scene since forever. Involved over the years with gospel, R&B, and even disco, his credits ranged from session work as a guitarist at the Muscle Shoals Sound Studio in Alabama, to producing soul icon Al Green, singer-songwriter Peabo Bryson, and the classic duo of Sam & Dave.

We both had come from church backgrounds. The Black church wasn't an old boy network, it was the hallelujah network. Even though Dillard was now based in Nashville, he was not deep into the country music scene of the city, a fact that led me to think he might be a good fit with my genre-mashup approach, mixing folk, soul, gospel, and country.

"You should come to Nashville," Dillard told me. "You have any more material than the three songs?"

"We would like to come," I said. "I've always had in mind to record a full album, my songs and other people's, the kind of stuff Billy and I do on our gigs."

"If you're ever no-bullshit interested, you let me know," he said. "I'll be happy to help you produce that."

The free market being what it is, any number of "insiders" and "professionals" line up to help aspiring artists realize their dreams, record their demos, and become stars. For a price. In the country's major music centers of Los Angeles, New York City, and Nashville, you can't throw a rock without hitting one of these eager career boosters. Once folks heard I was a practicing doctor, a cardiologist, I could practically see the dollar signs lighting up in their eyes. I might have been a fairly small guy, but I was a lot taller standing on my wallet.

The business end of music had never engaged me much. I was always sort of loosey-goosey about it, but I thought I understood how the game was played. I had no issues with enlisting a seasoned ally to give my songs polish and depth. But whoever I hired, whatever outfit I worked with, they would have to give me a thing I absolutely required. The end result had to be a record that would make me hold up my head and be proud. Nothing slipshod or unprofessional. I watched my pennies and was never a spendthrift, but as long as I got what I wanted, I was happy to lay out the money.

Some folks buy fancy sports cars, or invest in blue chip stocks, or build fishing lodges in the Ozarks. Folks like me fund their passions, and my passion was music. I ponied up somewhere in the neighborhood of $8,000 to cut my first album. Invoices for session musicians and studio time came in and I would pay them. I bought airline tickets for Billy and me to fly to Nashville and rented accommodations for each of us.

And Moses Dillard proved true. We recorded at LSI Studio in Nashville in 1986. As the producer, Dillard brought in players and background vocalists. When he wanted an orchestral sound on a cut, he hired the Nashville String Machine, the town's favored chamber ensemble. *Timeless*, the album that came out of the sessions, still occupies a central place in my heart, like a mother's youngest baby or a father's first child.

Billy and I had a ball working on it. I found the recording studio to be one of my new favorite places in the world. I felt alive and electric there, with creative ideas and split-second inventions caroming off the walls like newly split atoms. Wearing headphones and standing in front of a microphone, I felt like I inhabited my true self, connecting with something basic and joyful. *This is me*, I reminded myself once again. *This is what I do.*

As rare as creative talent is, what might be rarer still are the kindred souls who recognize talent and reach out to foster it. Their names should be enshrined in a hall of fame of their own. Jim Stewart and Estelle Axton at Stax Records in Memphis, Berry Gordy at Motown in Detroit, Sam Phillips at Sun Records in Memphis, Owen Bradley and Chet Atkins in Nashville—all these figures had far-reaching legacies of fostering talent. John Hammond at Columbia Records recognized the genius of a raw folksinger named Bob Dylan, and discovered a roll call of other artists, too—Benny Goodman, Count Basie, Billie Holiday, Robert Johnson, Bessie Smith, Aretha Franklin, Pete Seeger, and Bruce Springsteen.

Moses Dillard acted in that role for me. Like his namesake, he led me out of the wilderness into the promised land. *Timeless* was in every sense a collaboration between the two of us. Moses and I just clicked. There's no other way to describe our friendship. Intuitively, without having to talk about it much, we seized upon the concept of presenting traditional music and adding in all the flavor of our culture, like spice in a gumbo. I saw him as Dr. Frankenstein, crowing out "It's alive! It's alive!" as each track came together.

"What if we had fiddles?" one of us would say to the other. "A gospel chorus in the background!" "A steel guitar!" We were channeling the kind of excitement that I imagine had bubbled up in Wolfgang Mozart's heart, two centuries before when he was composing symphonies: "Oh! If only we had clarinets. You have no idea of the effect of clarinets!" I stood in awe of Moses Dillard. Here was an artist who knew what he was doing in the studio. All the rest of us were just trespassers on his real estate.

During our time in Nashville, Billy and I laid down only basic guitars-and-vocals tracks. Moses feathered in the plumage later, adding tracks, guitar fills, harmonies. Jerry Jeff Walker's "Mister Bojangles"? Nobody did it the way we did. Shel Silverstein, the "A Boy Named Sue" songwriter and children's book author, wrote a poem called "Hey, Nelly, Nelly." Folksinger Judy Collins set it to music. When I heard her version, I imagined a whole different concept of the song, and that's what we put on *Timeless*.

Even my own songs breathed new life when put through the Moses Dillard flavorizer. I always remembered a patient from my time working in the ER at Greater Southeast, a sex worker who was trying to get her life straightened out. She had found the Lord, she said, and religion was going to be her path to freedom. I called the song I wrote about her "Freedom," and Dillard squeezed every ounce of drama out of it.

My song "Sarah" took me back to childhood, walking along country roads with my first love, how she and I had this precious time together and how our lives would soon change completely. Moses laid an opening flourish on "Sarah" that resembled a disco run from the showband the A-Strings. The arrangement should not have worked, but it did. Nobody was doing music like that.

I never intended *Timeless* for the Nashville market. Both Dillard and I knew that the tunes weren't something to appeal to commercial radio. We aimed for something simpler. I wanted a record we could sell at our Billy & Cleve performances, or place in the racks at Penguin Feathers, a chain of popular independent record shops in the DC area.

The homeboy-sourced creation turned into something of a hometown product. It takes a village, and sometimes the village is a hospital. For a cover graphic we recruited the husband of a patient who painted Western-themed art and had sold to galleries all over the country. Billy and I posed for him. Another patient of mine, Joe Holleman, a songwriter from Nashville who had moved to northern Virginia, helped me compose the liner notes for *Timeless*.

We had a great album of songs. We had a striking album cover. We just felt good about it all around. It didn't matter one bit that it wasn't going to go Top Ten with a bullet on the *Billboard* charts. The project wasn't designed for that.

Joe Holleman tweaked my rough draft of the liner notes, editing, revising, and transforming the original text. The result turned into what I felt was one of the most beautiful passages I have ever read, a statement straight from the soul, straight from the soulfolk:

> I have come to the music capital of the country to express musically what I have learned from listening to Mahalia Jackson, Hank Williams, Elvis Presley, Otis Redding, Sam Cooke, Bob Dylan, Gordon Lightfoot, the Beatles, and especially the ballads of the great Harry Chapin. I came to Nashville to sing my songs, to voice my hopes, to say the words I've heard along the roads and highways, to preserve images I've seen in faces everywhere, to help those in need slip the bonds of servitude and rout the imposters who shout against the winds of change. If one man abroad in a crowd is lonely, I want him to know I've been down that road. If one prisoner rails at the law's delay, I want him to know I've felt the insolence of office. Most especially do I want you to know I've loved and imagined and dreamed.

★ ★ ★

Though I can't speak for other species, I like to think human beings are gifted with two hearts, connected not by blood vessels, tissue, and nerves, but by spirit and soul. One heart is a muscle pump. The other heart partakes in that little shard of the godhead I was talking about, one that's embedded deep within us and which can't be diminished, no matter what wrong we may do.

One heart is concerned with the maintenance of physical life, the other with life's purpose and meaning. The first is what I dealt with every day in my cardiology practice. I plumbed its mysteries in med school and beyond, and I'm still a student of its intricacies. The second heart is what I reached for with my music. I first detected its faint rhythmic beat beneath the backyard willow tree in Jennings.

The physical heart will succumb to death, but the metaphysical one lives on to become part of the substance of the universe. I feel that long after my flesh and bone body has passed away, the music from my soul will live on. Pretty to think so, anyway.

After *Timeless*, I felt I needed to do more "second heart" music. In 1979 the first vote on making Martin Luther King Jr.'s birthday a national holiday failed in Congress. In response, the groundswell of public support in the Black community, fueled by grief and the need to honor a fallen hero, kept the political pressure on.

Frustrated that the effort seemed stalled, I fretted over the injustice of the situation, sometimes lying awake at night for hours. One evening in 1985, after lots of tossing and turning, I finally dropped off into a deep sleep. Then at 4:00 a.m. I snapped awake suddenly and completely. I realized I had a complete song in my head, lyrics and melody both. The act of creation rarely happens that way. Usually, the process is long and arduous.

"Martin" became one of the signature compositions of my life. The song arrived fully formed, as if it had been floating out there in the ether waiting for me. I simply woke up, grabbed my guitar, and sang. I didn't even feel like taking credit, since I served only as the medium for the message.

As soon as I recorded an initial work tape, I called Moses Dillard in Nashville, too excited to care that it was early in the morning there and I would wake him up.

"Moses, man, I just wrote a song, and I think it's *the* song!"

"Who is this?" he said groggily.

"It's the song, the song, the one everybody's been looking for! Stevie's 'Happy Birthday' anthem is one thing, man, but this is the one that's going to be sung by gospel choirs in churches."

"All right, all right," Dillard said a little grumpily. "You send it to me. I'm going back to sleep now, Cleve."

Moses called me up a few days later. "It's the song," he said simply, the first words out of his mouth. He and I made a date to record it in Nashville.

I started to perform the new tune immediately, adding another tribute to "The Ballad of Martin Luther King," the song that I had composed in the immediate aftermath of the assassination. "Martin" represented a different take.

You marched from Selma to Washington
Hand in hand for freedom's sake
With faith in God and hope in Man
A sleeping nation yet to wake
You were a soldier in the army of justice
Fighting a battle we all had to win
Where a man is judged on character and deeds
Not on his color of skin
We all love you Martin
You finally made us see
That our nation could never be strong
Until all God's people are free
We all love you Martin

As the years will come to pass
Your voice will sound like a mighty storm
Free at last, free at last
Thank God almighty
We are free at last

I sang "Martin" everywhere—during my Billy & Cleve gigs, at schools and at churches, sometimes with a full gospel chorus behind me. I performed in the rotunda at the U.S. Capitol, the bell-like space ringing out with the tune. The legislative bill to make MLK's birthday a federal holiday had been passed in 1983, and I worked with the Martin Luther King, Jr. Federal Holiday Commission to spread the song far and wide.

A sense of ownership did not enter into my feelings about "Martin." I essentially donated the song to the movement. I trembled as I performed the tribute in front of Mrs. Coretta Scott King at Freedom Plaza in Washington DC. I also sang the song at an "I Have a Dream" ceremony at the King Center in Atlanta. If the good Lord had seen fit to take me right after that particular concert, I would have gone willingly and died a happy man.

Living with, thinking about, and being inspired by Martin Luther King Jr.'s beliefs for as long as I knew his name, I had aligned myself both morally and politically with him, especially since my days at Southern University. He proposed a principle that I understood intuitively and embraced wholeheartedly: Addressing the moral conscience of a human being is the only real way to create lasting change in society. An appeal to conscience was what wound up ending slavery, what freed colonized countries from the imperial yoke, what forever bent the arc of history toward justice.

When I sang "Martin," I felt myself reaching out to connect with the second heart, the moral conscience, of every member of the audience.

CHAPTER 15

Love Light

"THIS IS THE REAL THING, DR. FRANCIS." I could hear the tension in the ER doctor's voice on the phone. "Get here ASAP."

My pager had buzzed in the wee hours of the morning, and I recognized the number as the Mount Vernon Hospital emergency room. A summons from an ER after midnight usually means life-or-death trouble. My cardiology practice always established our on-call schedule six months in advance, and so it was only chance that my name happened to come up that weekend.

I stayed on the phone as I dressed, careful to don suitable attire in the wake of that first-night-on-the-job incident when the hospital security guard alerted police to a "Black man in jeans" emerging from the radiology department. The ER physician gave me a quick rundown of the symptoms presented, which clearly indicated a myocardial infarction, "MI" for short.

"Wife reports patient is sweating profusely, with chest pain and shortness of breath," the ER doc said on the phone. "Patient is a heavy smoker with a history of respiratory conditions." He mentioned the man's name, Olaf Hall.

The nighttime streets were thankfully clear of traffic. I was minutes away. Well, Mr. Hall, I thought as I drove, you might want to take a look around the room. Because along with the nurses, physicians, and other hospital staffers present, you'll see Death standing at your bedside, too.

Examining the patient's EKG at the hospital, I could tell that the coronary artery supplying blood to the right side of his heart was occluded. We were not yet able to judge the extent of the occlusion, but a large, right-sided MI could result in massive heart failure. The artery in question also supplied blood to the organ's natural pacemaker, so any blockage there would require the insertion of a temporary pacemaker. Given his symptoms and high levels of anxiety, Hall's borderline low heart rate represented the emergency's only faintly positive sign.

In that era, the armamentarium of cardiac care did not yet include the full array of clot busters and stents available today. Nor were there any specialized cardiac care wings at Mount Vernon, as there were at other large hospitals. The main goal was to relieve pain and anxiety, treat any heart failure, and ward off lethal arrhythmias that could take the patient's life in an instant.

That night the clock ticked on toward 4:00 a.m. with only three of us—Olaf Hall, the nurse, and me—as the sole human beings present in the room. Luckily for Mr. Hall, the nurse on duty was Kathy Dibbens. I called her "the patient whisperer" for the compassionate, intuitive care she provided. She had trained and served in the military medical corps and could detect changes in a patient's condition even before any monitor could pick them up. She was one of the best nurses I had ever worked with in my career.

A fourth unholy figure stood waiting, too. The comedian W. C. Fields used to refer to death as "the fella in the bright nightgown." I never liked that guy, and dedicated my life to heading him off whenever he showed his ghostly face. After a few hours, Olaf Hall drifted off to sleep. I took it as a good sign.

"He might have turned the corner," I murmured to Kathy. We continued to keep a sharp eye on the patient's vitals.

I had spent many similar nights in Mount Vernon's coronary care unit. A feature of the rooms that I always treasured were the giant, east-facing windows. That night I kept silent watch to see if the patient would live or die. Outside the window, the dawn light stole up slowly on the far-off horizon. A new day began. When the sun rose fully, I knew that Olaf Hall would survive, and together we would witness the beauty of the scene outside the window.

Little did I know that Olaf's survival that night would be the beginning of a new chapter in my own life.

After stepping away to get coffee at the nurses' station, I came back to the room to greet a weak but awake patient. "Good morning, Doc," he said. "You look a little tired." We both smiled. A man who could summon a joke was a man who would be more likely to live. My patient was free of pain, breathing better, and his heart rate was where it needed to be.

I addressed him as "Mr. Hall," or "Olaf," and he told me that everyone knew him by his nickname, Pug. I guess anyone whose given name was Olaf deserved a nickname.

"I want to warn you, Doc," he said, after thanking me for taking care of him. "My older brother, John—my only brother—will be visiting, later today or tomorrow. He's taking the first flight he can find from Florida."

"Oh, that's fine, family visits are fine, no need to warn me, Mr. Hall."

"No, please, just call me 'Pug,' okay?" he said. "'Olaf' sounds like some old Swedish codger. And I do need to warn you to prepare yourself. Everybody calls my brother Big John, and it's not just because he's 250 pounds. You might want to lay in an extra oxygen supply, because he takes up all the air in the room."

"Fine, fine, don't worry, now," I said. Anxiety is the enemy in any heart attack recovery.

"You'll see what I'm talking about when you meet him."

Nothing Pug Hall could have said would have prepared me for his brother. I just happened to be on the unit making rounds the following morning when the doors of coronary care swung open and in walked Big John Hall from Boca Raton, Florida. He sported jet black hair swept up in an Elvis-style pompadour, a blue blazer, a pair of white cotton duck pants with a white patent leather belt, no socks, and white patent leather shoes to match the belt. The heavyweight gold chain hanging around his neck completed the ensemble, along with giant rings the size of quail eggs on several fingers of both hands.

"My name is Big John Hall," he announced to the ward nurse, his booming voice sounding like a clap on the back. "I'm here to see my baby brother and talk to the doctor who's taking care of him."

Elvis has entered the building. In the man's flamboyant Southern accent, and in his overlarge personality and style, I heard an echo of Jimmy Dean's hit song "Big Bad John."

I introduced myself and gave an account of what had transpired the previous night, giving him to understand that the patient's condition had stabilized. I told Big John that while I liked the general direction of things, his brother was not yet out of danger.

"But if the trend continues, Pug'll do fine," I said. "I can see him being discharged in a week or so." Bluff and gruff as Big John was, I saw tears spring into his eyes as we entered his younger brother's room together.

As a vital aspect of providing medical care, I always make it a point to get to know the patient as thoroughly as I can. Part of that includes getting to know their family, friends, even business associates—whoever was close enough to patients to visit them in hospital. It's not a question being nosy or intrusive, it's simply good medical practice. An arrogant or standoffish bedside manner can act as a detriment to healing.

To know more about Pug Hall, I also had to learn about John Hall and their relationship as brothers. They were the only two remaining members of their family.

During Pug's recovery, I saw John almost daily. A longtime professional musician, Big John Hall performed as the lead singer of an R&B quartet known as the Heartbeats. He was the only white member in a group where the other three members were Black. The Heartbeats toured on what was known as the Chitlin' Circuit—dancehalls, clubs, and small venues that catered mostly to Black audiences.

John and Pug Hall were from a dirt-poor area in coal country Kentucky. They had known a lot of Black families during childhood. Segregation breeds prejudice as surely as contaminated water breeds cholera. I could usually tell right away when a white person had grown up around Black people. We understood each other. Our exchanges were easy and relaxed.

Becoming acquainted with Big John was a two-way street, and during our conversations he found out all about me, too. We bonded over him giving me credit for saving Pug's life. The bond deepened when he heard of my lifelong passion for music, from a backyard willow tree in Louisiana to "Reflections on the Wall" and "Martin."

"You got something for me to listen to?" he asked. "Whyn't you bring me in a tape of yours?" His Kentucky accent remained very much in play, and he pronounced "yours" as "your'n."

The next day I gave him two cassettes, the "You Send Me/Desperado" single I recorded with Billy Pierce, and the *Timeless* album I did with Moses Dillard.

Big John examined the tape cassettes as if they held secrets. "Now, this here material ain't R&B, is it, Doc? I can judge the songs myself if they're R&B, but if they're something else I got other people I can get to listen to them."

"They are something else," I said.

"Yeah, I'll bet they're something else, Doc, because you are something else!" he said, laughing.

I thought no more of it. As his brother recovered, Big John and I parted as fast friends. I counseled Pug to quit smoking, and the two of them left me wishing that I had a brother in my life like Pug had Big John in his. I didn't realize it right away, but I soon came to understand that when you're friends with Big John, he will automatically make you part of his family.

He loved me for what I did for his little brother. Pug Hall lived for another twenty-five years after I first treated him. That was enough to put me in the good books of his brother forever. Big John called me up from Florida after listening to the music I gave him, bubbling over with plans for my career.

"You know Eddie Jones and the Young Bucks?" he asked. "I want to put you together with them, see if y'all can get a little soul thing going."

Eddie Jones and the Young Bucks were mainstays of the Washington, DC music scene. The band members came from the Southeast neighborhood in DC, the same underserved area where I had spent a year working in the emergency room. Big John set me up to do occasional guest gigs when the group played clubs around town. Strictly a soul singer, Jones showed himself to be a little skeptical about my forays into folk and country.

"We have a young man who I'm sure you're gonna like," Eddie Jones would announce to the audience, giving me my cue to come onstage and sing a few numbers. "He's got a tremendous voice and here's 'Clean Cleve Francis!'"

As I stepped up to the mic Eddie would mutter a word of warning to me. "Don't you dare yodel in here, ya hear me?"

I understood. We were playing Black clubs, and those kinds of audiences did not suffer fools. It was like talent night at the Apollo Theater in Harlem. No mercy. If audience members didn't like what you were doing, they'd hound you right off the stage, or get up and leave the club themselves.

Curbing any impulse to yodel, I would do Sam Cooke's "A Change Is Gonna Come." My smooth style represented a definite change of pace from Eddie Jones's soul shout. I was Johnny Mathis, while he was more Marvin Gaye or even Sam & Dave.

My time with Eddie Jones gave me a priceless education in lead singer basics. Jones taught me to be more observant of the band and its dynamics. Accustomed to performing my own music accompanied only by acoustic guitar, I had always controlled the pace of my sets, deciding when to start singing and when to stop. Softer-and-louder dynamics were also up to me.

Now as a lead singer with a band behind me, I had to come in at a specific point, and step back other times. I needed a telepathic connection with the players, to be able to signal them to repeat a verse or vamp a song. If for some reason I missed an intro, I had to wait for the entrance to "come around again." Eddie Jones ran a tight ship. The stage act had to be seamless, with no bumps or falters.

Jones also did me the enormous service of taking me around to little hole-in-the-wall record stores scattered all over DC. With a bottomless knowledge of soul, R&B, and the blues, he functioned as a musical historian. We became good friends, and on my days off we would search for songs together, seeking out obscure tracks on old albums that suited my range. We dug into the racks for fifties soul music, Johnny Ace records, Sam Cooke's raucous live recordings in front of Black audiences, early cuts from Bill Withers. Every weekend turned into a treasure hunt.

"Oh, yeah, yeah, yeah," Eddie would croon, fishing out a vinyl copy of "Steppin' Stone" by Little Mary Staten. "This is the stuff you need."

By hooking me up with Eddie Jones and by providing other opportunities that helped me expand my horizons, Big John Hall effectively transformed the way I approached music.

"You have to get out from behind the guitar, Cleve," he told me. "You've got to recognize what you are. You're a singer. You're a performer. You should be at the mic with a group behind you."

Going onstage as a lead singer was what Big John himself did with his band, the Heartbeats. I've noticed that a lot of advice folks give can be boiled down to three words: "Be like me." Big John wanted me to be like him. It's the kind of performing he knew and believed in. But I appreciated the man's spirit, enthusiasm, and support. And he turned out to be right.

As a sort of a graduation ceremony from the Big John School of Music, he brought me a couple thousand miles across the country to Coronado Island in San Diego. The Heartbeats had a gig in the ballroom of the landmark resort hotel there. Big John proposed calling me up onstage for a few songs as a featured singer.

A graduation ceremony or a trial by fire? I was nervous as hell. For my first professional appearance as a lead singer, I played to a packed ballroom of tourists and military personnel. The three-song setlist I did seared itself into my memory: Johnny Ace's "Never Let Me Go," a version of "Just the Two of Us," a Bill Withers song that got the audience up on their feet, dancing and mouthing the words, and finally, of course, Sam Cooke's "A Change Is Gonna Come."

If anyone ever happens to ask, I could truthfully report that I was reborn as an artist that night, in front of a ballroom audience with a yellow California moon shining on the waters of San Diego Bay.

★ ★ ★

New Orleans icon Allen Toussaint wrote a song that Bonnie Raitt made famous, called "What Is Success?"

> *Now what, what is success?*
> *I don't know, can you tell me?*
> *What, what is success?*
> *Is it do your own thing?*
> *Or to join the rest?*

Can you tell me? To a lot of people, success in the music profession means huge stadium and arena shows, chart-topping songs, maybe an acting career to go along with it.

I've been to Fan Fair in Nashville, I've performed at the Rotunda of the U.S. Capitol and atop the Vietnam Memorial Wall, and I can relate exactly where I found my sweetest definition of success. It wasn't where you would necessarily think, either.

In the late 1980s, while I was still under the wing of Arthur Lisi, Moses Dillard, and Big John Hall, I recognized that the songs in my repertoire could be grouped into two categories. One category contained numbers I had written myself, mostly cause-oriented compositions that I could play at gatherings of supporters. Those songs included "Martin," "Reflections on the Wall," and "We're All in This Together." They were designed for occasions when I would "play a concert for the other guy," as Woody Guthrie had said.

A second group of songs I performed were covers, tunes I liked and admired that were written by other people. They were still mine, in the sense that I would put my own distinctive soulfolk spin on them, but they were different from movement songs.

I disliked nothing more than a cover song that sounded identical to the original. Why even do a cover if all you could come up with was a carbon copy? Get distinctive, put your own individual stamp on the song. Jimi Hendrix's recording of Bob Dylan's "All Along the Watchtower," Whitney Houston's take on Dolly Parton's "I Will Always Love You," Aretha Franklin's reimagining of Otis Redding's "Respect"—those were the kind of covers I respected.

A performer has to know how to read the room. Performance venues that were perfect for a song like "Martin" wouldn't be suitable for the cover songs I was doing. The civil rights crowd would look at me cross-eyed if I trotted out "Honky Tonk Blues" by Hank Williams. I needed performance spaces where audiences would be receptive to my cover songs. I needed a place where I could cut loose with the occasional yodel.

I arranged to meet with the owner of the Birchmere Music Hall, one of the most prominent venues in the DC area. A well-known, prestigious club, the Birchmere represented something of a reach for me. Begun as a strip mall restaurant by Gary Oelze in 1966 and branching out into concerts in 1974, the venue grew, relocated, grew, and relocated again, enlarging from a two-hundred-seat capacity venue to three hundred and then five hundred. The music market of the Greater Washington metropolitan area ranks in the Top Ten in the whole country, and punches above its weight because of all the national media located here.

Media, sure, and Washington politicos, too.

> Bill Clinton came here a couple of times [Birchmere owner Gary Oelze told a radio interviewer]. Al Gore used to live up the street and was here all the time. One night as Gore was leaving the White House, Clinton asked where he was headed. Gore said, "To the Birchmere to hear Jerry Jeff Walker." Clinton said, "Hillary and I will go with you." The four of them showed up, then they came back to see Kim Richey.

The Birchmere was a top music venue in a nationally ranked music market, and it was additionally attractive to me because it was located on my home turf. If by chance I could shoehorn my way into the Birchmere, I would join musicians I admired who had previously appeared there, big names such as B. B. King, Merle Haggard, Aaron Neville, Ricky Skaggs, and John Prine. The Birchmere was one of Vince Gill's favorite venues. Mary Chapin Carpenter got her start there. Locally at least, the place represented the big leagues.

I met with Gary Oelze and his booking guy, Michael Jaworek. This was back when the Birchmere was still a three-hundred-seat hall. Could I fill a place that large? Phi Beta Kappa Hall on the William & Mary campus had been one thing. This was quite another.

"I've heard that you play around town," Oelze said. "The *Post* had some coverage, right?"

I nodded. He was probably referring to one of the "singing doctor" articles that seemed to be the only approach the media could come up with. Human beings sure do love their pigeonholes. They can stick a label on you and then they don't have to think any more about you.

"We liked the tape you sent along," Oelze said.

Jaworek looked dubious. Bookers conducted business according to a strict, cold-blooded calculus. It was all about "putting butts in the seats." Demonstrate you can do that and you're golden. Fail and you're gone. I wanted to assure Oelze and Jaworek that I had a following, wanted to tell them about performing at the Capitol and on the Mall. But I kept my mouth shut as the two of them put their heads together and mulled it over.

"Okay, we can give it a shot," Oelze finally said. He turned back to Jaworek and said, "Maybe his patients will come to see him."

Thus for the first time I played the celebrated Birchmere Music Hall in Alexandria, Virginia. Oelze had been correct, many of my patients and coworkers did come to see me for the first show. They brought along family and friends. The crowd was large enough that the skeptical Michael Jaworek invited me back. Each time I appeared the audience grew.

I loved the hall, loved the respectful crowd that came not to socialize but to hear music. The management took a stern attitude toward cross talk during the shows. Anyone who disrupted the performance would be warned once, then actually escorted out if the talking continued.

After appearing at the Birchmere several times, I slowly began to attract people who had never heard me sing before but had read about me in print media or seen me on TV. Over and over again, concert after concert, I proved myself capable of putting butts in the seats. I became a featured regular from 1987 on, appearing twice a year, every six months or so. I watched my audiences grow bigger and become more mixed, both racially and with young and old faces in the crowd.

Birchmere turned out to be a watershed, and soon enough it became the only place I was playing. Work pressures limited the number of concerts I performed there, but we always played to a packed house.

Big John Hall had helped me to discover my sweet spot, my natural métier, my true musical self. I transformed from something resembling a folksinger, or a singer-songwriter, and turned into a lead singer and performer. I went onstage with the Young Bucks behind me, playing music written out by Arthur Lisi. Another time I had the Bucks try to play country, Cleve Francis style. The experiment failed.

Even when playing the R&B numbers on the setlist, the Young Bucks weren't a perfect fit with my style. I did better when Big John put me in as lead singer backed by the Heavy Country Band, a popular, seasoned act from the DC area. The musicians in the group all had day jobs—a contractor, a master electrician, and an air conditioning technician from Sears. But Heavy Country backed the Black country and rockabilly singer Big Al Downing on tour, and the group had been knocking on Nashville's doors for years.

As their named implied, the Heavy Country Band definitely had a country sound and a country brand. Founder Joey Martin and other members of the group did great when they stayed within the classic country repertoire. They could be real barn burners, for example, doing Hank Williams (I yodeled some). But Heavy Country didn't sound exactly right on the other material I wanted to do, folksongs, Harry Chapin numbers, and the beautiful fifties R&B nuggets Eddie Jones helped me retrieve from the dusty racks of obscure used record stores.

"If you want something done right . . ." I heard the echo of Mary Francis in my ear. I needed to build my own back-up group and develop my own sound. Helped by word of mouth and press coverage, I had been selling out the Birchmere every time I appeared. Gary Oelze paid me a percentage of the gate, which meant I was pulling down five or six thousand dollars per show. That in turn meant I could pay musicians above and beyond what they usually received on gigs—$300 or $400 a night, as opposed to normal survival wages of $25 or $50 per show.

I wanted to develop my own band. I wanted musicians who could be flexible, who remained uncommitted to any specific genre. It didn't happen right away, but over the years I got what I wanted. I hired a jazz violinist and a jazz lead guitarist, a pair of folk-country rhythm guitarists, and a trio of background vocalists experienced in gospel.

In truth, I went wild. I brought in a full percussion section, which meant both a drummer *and* a percussionist. Harmonica. Flute. Saxophone. The U.S. military had a bluegrass band to entertain the troops, and I recruited a banjo player there. Keyboard. A steel guitar *and* a dobro. I found a fifteen-year-old cello prodigy from a local high school. He stood six five and played with me for years.

It wasn't just a backing band. It was a freakin' mini orchestra. The Birchmere eventually had to extend the stage to fit us all on.

And man, did we woodshed. I had an unfinished basement in my house, and we were able to fit a dozen musicians down there. Neighbors could tell I had a concert coming up because the block would be parked thick with the players' cars. We practiced one o'clock to five on weekend afternoons, staggering the various sections coming in to rehearse at various times.

After that, after the band would leave, I would practice with a tape of what we had just rehearsed, singing the whole setlist as if I had the entire band behind me. I never simply just memorized songs—I had to have them down cold. So I went through all the numbers one by one, painstakingly performing the set, doing each song twenty or thirty times, until I had the lyrics and melodies permanently imprinted on my brain.

The Birchmere treated artists like royalty. As was the case with a lot of clubs, every musician and crew member got a menu from which to choose their dinners, on the house. The club had a washer and dryer in the dressing room for bands that were on the road. Everyone on the staff was cool, friendly, and professional, and every aspect of the facility was top drawer—sound, lighting, seating, everything.

I never ate before a show. The kitchen would save my food for after the second set. My preshow routine included a single glass of merlot, and I would usually drink only half. Say my prayers, meditate, run to the restroom, do some vocal warm-ups, and I was ready to go.

One of my favorite movies is *Local Hero*, with Burt Lancaster. That was me. I was a local artist, killing it on my home turf, pretty much uninterested in pushing my performance career elsewhere. Why would I want more? I can't tell you what a comfortable home Gary Oelze had made the hall. Heading into the Birchmere felt like slipping into a warm bath. I was doing the best music of my life. The kudos I received, applause, the cheers, the ovations, all of it indicated the solid connection I had forged with the audience.

I can hear that song "What Is Success" playing in my head. Tell me what—what?!—what is success? I asked myself the question back then, and I ask it again now. Here is what success meant for me back then, and I guess what it still means for me today. All the music I made and all the causes I had supported had come together. I had become one of the top regional acts in northern Virginia. Locally, at least, no one could possibly ask for more than to be a lead act at the Birchmere Music Hall. But . . .

"Hello?" came the voice over the phone. "This is Jack Gale from Playback Records in Miami. Is this Cleve Francis? I got your contact information from a gentleman I think you know by the name of Big John."

★ ★ ★

Jack Gale took part in the shadow sector of the music industry that I had encountered before. Dozens upon dozens, probably thousands of producers and studio engineers would record an artist's songs for a fee, with uneven results. These outfits catered to the unsigned and unknown, professionals who were "between comebacks," as they say, or semiprofessionals with day jobs, as well as amateurs and out-and-out wannabes. These artists populated the fringes of the music world. For those on the inside, they were like children with their faces pressed to the glass of the candy store window, on the outside looking in.

I didn't kid myself. I understood my status as an outsider. Waylon Jennings has a song, "Too Dumb for New York City, Too Ugly for LA." I was neither ugly nor dumb, but I was content with my role as a local artist, a big fish in a small pond, selling out the Birchmere several times a year.

Meanwhile, in my twin roles as both a doctor and a musician, folks were always buttonholing me, tugging on my sleeve, wanting to sell me something. I stuck to my hard-and-fast rule. As long as I got what I wanted, I would enter into a collaborative relationship with anyone who would serve my purposes. Mary Francis did not raise foolish children, so of course I vetted the hell out of people with whom I worked.

Jack Gale had cut his teeth as a radio announcer and a DJ. Originally from Baltimore, he had one of the great radio voices, a big, deep, basso profundo tone. Most importantly, Jack Gale loved what I was doing.

"Big John physically drove your tapes over to my house," he told me on the phone. "Didn't use the mail as most normal people do, just showed up on my doorstep and rang the bell. I could not believe it. I mean, that's dedication. That's a man who believes in you and your music."

Gale explained that he produced records for a lot of different artists, mostly country singers who were not on major labels but needed merchandise to sell at their shows. He mentioned recently pressing an album for, yes, Waylon Jennings.

Selling music directly to fans could be a financially viable strategy, going the DIY route, cutting out the massive expense involved in a big-label recording. At the merch table in the concert hall lobby, alongside T-shirts, posters, and ball caps, vinyl records and CDs put cash directly in the pockets of the artist, no middleman involved.

As far as pay-for-play outfits went, Gale's Playback Records was near the top rung of the ladder. I checked it out—professional and reliable, the label put out a polished product. The company's formal name was Playback Records Nashville since Gale specialized in country. Because my backing band now featured steel guitar and banjo, I had begun to feel more and more comfortable with a country sound.

"I love your voice," Gale told me on the phone. "I'd sure like to get together with you and collaborate on a recording."

"You have a studio you use down there in Miami?" I asked.

"Oh, I record in Nashville," he said.

Sold.

With Big John sitting in to observe the sessions, and Jack Gale marshaling a crew of crackerjack studio musicians, we recorded an album. The ten-track collection, released in 1990 as *Last Call for Love*, featured some covers and a few of my own songs. In catalog listings the release got classified as "rock, folk, country" (and for some reason "world" was thrown in there, too). But to me *Last Call* was country all the way—my own distinctive, personal take on country.

We rerecorded my song "Moonlight Lover," which I had already recorded with Moses Dillard for my second album, *Timeless*. I always thought of "Moonlight" as my stab at writing straight-ahead country. Jack Gale approached the cut very differently from the version on *Timeless*. The same tune on *Last Call* lost its folk vibe entirely, turning out to be more upbeat, in the style of rockabilly country. I took the lesson in how different producers can deliver a song that seems almost unrecognizable when compared to other versions. We also recorded a country-flavored cover of Brook Benton's "Endlessly," one of my all-time favorite songs from one of my all-time favorite singers.

Some cuts on the *Last Call* album Gale chose himself. "I've got this midtempo number called 'Love Light,'" he said. "The last person to record was Glen Campbell, on the B-side of 'Rhinestone Cowboy.' I'll send it to you, see what you think."

The first time I heard "Love Light," I didn't take to it. I couldn't feel the emotional hook to the song. Besides, "Rhinestone" had been a humongous hit, which meant plenty of folks had already heard the B-side tune. I told Gale I would take on a pass on recording the song.

"You've got to trust me here," he insisted. "Your voice would do really well for this number. It'd fit right in on your album. I classify it as something in the neighborhood of gospel-soul-country."

After we recorded the song, Gale didn't want to stop there. "You know, Cleve," he said, getting all honey voiced, "it would be wonderful if we had a video of 'Love Light.' I wouldn't be interested in producing one myself, but I can put you with somebody who would do a bang-up job."

Gale knew a Miami filmmaker named David Jean Schweitzer who wanted to get into making country music videos. A new cable channel, MTV, had kicked off back on August 1, 1981, and it revolutionized music promotion with its heavy use of music videos. From then on, every record label had to have a video version of their releases. Budgets ballooned into the millions. The mania spilled over into other genres besides pop and rock. There were even music videos created for classical releases.

The trend had cooled somewhat as the 1990s wore on and would change again with the advent of the internet, but at the time we recorded *Last Call for Love*, videos were still a going thing. Videos had become especially popular in country music, complementing the storytelling flavor of the songs.

CMT, Country Music Television, launched on March 5, 1983, at 6:19 p.m., going live two days before its major competitor, TNN, The Nashville Network. The two cable channels would go head-to-head for several years, until TNN's parent company, Gaylord Entertainment, bought CMT in 1991 for $35 million. Meanwhile CMT built a viewership that ran into millions of American households.

Did I need a video of "Love Light"? Did I even *want* a music video of "Love Light"? I was a Washington-area artist. What was I going to do, show it on the local community cable channel?

Then again, *some people at my age buy fancy sports cars* . . . I was a single man with few family obligations. From working my tail off at Mount Vernon Cardiology Associates, I had the coin. If I wanted to have a music video done for one of my songs, who was around to object? I wondered just how much such a production might cost. I went out and actually priced a Maserati just for the comparison. If I could fund a music video for less, I thought, then I might consider it. A music video came in cheaper by a whisker.

"I've got a lot of friends in the movie business," David Schweitzer told me when I contacted him. "These are professional people who are doing major movies right now."

Yes, yes, David, I said to myself, wanting him to get to the point. *How much would it cost, this oh-so-professional video creation?* I waited for him to get around to giving me a quote. He hemmed and hawed a little more, then came out with it.

"If you can give me, you know, $25,000, I can get a lot of this stuff done by these really qualified people," he said. I could almost hear him gulp over the phone, proposing such an outlandish amount. Then he said it again. "I'll need at least $25,000."

I went all in. I said "yes" mainly as sort of a lark, as something of a goof, really. I know, a $25,000 goof sounds absurd. Spending an amount like that represented a wild-ass thing to do, for sure. But I had the money. What else was I going to spend it on? I told myself I was interested in the creative process of matching moving images to music. *Some people my age in my income bracket go on round-the-world cruises.*

We filmed the project in the Fort Lauderdale area. David and I worked up a three-minute family drama that was probably one of the first integrated videos in country music. We ran the whole color spectrum, casting an aging Black couple, two puppy-love white kids, and a glamorous young white couple with young children.

We needed to cast a woman who would play the character of the wife. At the time, I was dating an elementary school principal from Alexandria, Bernice Johnson.

"How would you like to be on camera?" I asked. "A free trip to Florida. You'll have an incredibly handsome leading man to play opposite you."

Bernice laughed, I laughed, and eventually she came around to saying she would. David Schweitzer really came through. He had access to top-flight production facilities—lighting, hair, makeup, everything.

David shot me on a soundstage singing "Love Light." In the minidrama I played two roles, the father and the son, an older Cleve Francis and a younger one. The makeup folks on the crew did a magical job aging me. David used special colorization effects on the finished product. The result looked superb, fresh, and like nothing else in the world of country music videos at the time.

When I screened "Love Light: The Video," I realized David Schweitzer had managed to make a $25,000 budget look like $100,000. The music and the drama worked off each other so well that the film packed an emotional punch. The video displayed Jack Gale's production of the song to great effect. You've heard of country music described as "three chords and the truth"? This video was three minutes and the truth.

It had been almost a year since *Last Call for Love* had dropped. Jack Gale had sent me a box filled with unsold albums, along with all of the promotional items we had put together for the release.

"The record is probably over, Cleve," Gale told me when I called him up. "And you know, we gave it a good shot."

Playback Records did not have access to the kind of country radio stations that could break big records. Gale's label also dealt with a musical charting system printed in a magazine called *Cashbox*. That magazine didn't have the industry standard charts, which were published by *Billboard*, and *Cashbox*'s charts had less impact on what decisions were made at radio stations. And as an album release, *Last Call* had seen its last call.

Now what? I had a music video from a dead album and no outlet on which to show it. Does a film exist if no one sees it? I was over the moon about David's film creation. As a vehicle for the song, the video could not have done a better job. When Jack Gale first pitched it to me, why had I not seen the possibilities of "Love Light" right away?

How goes the idiom? In for a dime, in for a dollar. Or, actually, in for twenty-five thousand dollars. I had already gone pretty far down the path of crazy with this project. Why not go all the way? I booked a flight to Nashville and showed up at CMT headquarters, having sent a copy of David's music video as a calling card.

"I wonder if I could see Stan Hitchcock," I asked the receptionist-guardian woman at the front desk, naming the president of CMT. In a measure of the down-home atmosphere at times on display in Nashville, after only a short wait I was ushered into Hitchcock's presence.

When I walked in, Hitchcock rose to his feet and grabbed my hand. He had a full head of hair, a salt-and-pepper beard, and a great welcoming smile. He wore horn-rimmed glasses. He looked like what he was, a business executive.

"Cleve Francis!" he exclaimed, leading me to a comfortable club chair. "Can I get you anything? Coffee? A Coke?" In the South, any carbonated beverage was a "Coke," including everything from orange pop and ginger ale to Coca-Cola itself.

My mouth was dry but I didn't want to ask for water. I wondered what was going on. What was Stan Hitchcock so excited about? I doubted whether the "Love Light" video had even made it to his desk yet. More likely, I thought, the videotape had been lost in the CMT mailroom, or thrown away. The channel must receive dozens of submissions every week.

Hitchcock sat down, not at his desk but in a chair right beside me. "Normally, normally," he began, repeating the word for emphasis. "Normally CMT was created to display artists that have been signed to major labels."

My heart sank as he went on. "We don't work with anything designed by amateurs because we can't depend on the quality. The office gets tapes submitted by mail all the time. The quality can be as low as somebody shooting these things with camcorders, you know?"

He was crushing me with bad news. Was he telling me that he thought David and I had created an amateur production? I wanted to tell him that the "Love Light" video was shot on a state-of-the-art 35-mm movie camera, the kind they use in feature filmmaking.

"No, we can't give slots away on our channel just willy-nilly. We don't let amateurs do it because the quality is just not there."

Right, Mr. Hitchcock, sir, you've already said that, sir, I thought to myself.

"But this video, your video!"—he actually clapped his hands together—"your video of 'Love Light' is of a similar quality, or even above—yes, sure, *above*—above the quality that we are getting from the major labels."

I laughed with relief. In fact, I almost cried with relief.

"Well, we are going to play it," Hitchcock said. "It's a good song, and it tells such a good story, we just *have* to play it. And as I said, the quality of it is above our standards."

Yay, David Jean Schweitzer, I thought. CMT put the "Love Light" video in heavy rotation. It played on the channel eight to ten times a day. Suddenly I was getting beamed into millions of homes across America. How CMT ranked videos in those days was straight out of the stone age, hand-tabulating how many viewers called in or wrote with requests for a song. Hitchcock called me to say his own kids were staying up at night to watch the video.

Back home, I had CMT on the TV all day long. I monitored the channel's chart of its most popular videos, witnessing ours climbing up, up, and up. We hit the Top Ten, with my humble song listed alongside videos from Garth Brooks, Vince Gill, and Reba McEntire.

Jack Gale had been pleased with the video but expressed pessimism about its staying power.

"It'll no doubt go good for two weeks, then it'll fade away," he predicted.

That didn't happen. "Love Light" outlasted all the videos that debuted when it did. When our entry hit CMT's Top Ten, I started to be recognized in the street. Media outlets requested interviews. My patients excitedly told me, "I saw you on TV!" Appearing on television—the marker for success in modern American culture.

And the phone lines lit up. I had gotten messages before with news that would change my life. The packet from the admissions office informing me that I had been accepted at Southern University. The notice from the *Breakout!* TV program, saying that Billy and I were invited to go on the air for the show. Or, more recently, the call from Jack Gale, telling me he wanted us to record an album together.

All doctors get bombarded with cold calls, and I got my share of those, too, mostly from pharmaceutical representatives and financial investors wanting to tell me about this or that exciting opportunity coming my way. A good office staff will screen incoming calls to filter out unnecessary ones. At work on a busy afternoon, I had just come out of the examining room and needed to make notes on the patient I had just seen. As I sat down at my desk, my office manager, Karen Daniel, buzzed me.

"There's a Ray Pillow on the phone," she said.

"What about?" I didn't immediately recognize the name.

"He said he's calling from Nashville, so I thought you might want to take this one."

Ray Pillow. Wasn't there a "Pillow" who was a member of the Grand Ole Opry? Back in 1966, he had a song that charted, "I'll Take the Dog," a duet with Jean Shepard (now a member of the Country Music Hall of Fame).

"Did he ask for Dr. Francis?" I asked.

I knew the difference between medical calls and music calls. My professional stage name was Cleve Francis. If the voice on the other end of the line asked for "Dr. Francis," it meant hospitals and patients. I punched the blinking white square that indicated a call on the line.

"Hello?"

"My name is Ray Pillow. Am I speaking to Cleve Francis?"

"Yes?"

"I work A&R at Capitol Records. Mr. Jimmy Bowen would like to meet with you."

The skin of my scalp prickled. It was all coming at me too fast. A&R I knew to be short for "artists and repertoire," company representatives in charge of finding and developing new acts at a record label.

"I'm sorry," I said. "Who is Jimmy Bowen?"

"Jimmy Bowen is the president of Capitol Records Nashville."

CHAPTER 16

Nashville Calling

THE DAY-TO-DAY ROUTINE at the office carried me forward for the rest of the afternoon. I saw patients and listened to hearts, trying not to feel unsettled by the call from Capitol Records. I resembled those poor souls in Japanese samurai movies, sliced open by a sword but for the moment still standing. I went through the motions. Just under the surface, though, an inner battle raged.

"Wow, wow, wow" fought it out with other, more unexpected responses: "no, no, no" and "why now? why now? why now?" I was elated, but also afraid of what could happen next.

Ray Pillow had requested that I give him possible open dates for me to fly out to Nashville. He said that his office would handle the travel arrangements.

All right, I counseled myself. Are you going insane here? Anyone in their right mind would be over the moon to field a summons from a Nashville label chief. So what was this "no, no, no" voice squawking in my brain?

Label presidents make the final decisions about who gets signed and who doesn't. I rooted out articles in the Nashville press to get all the information I could on Ray Pillow's boss.

James Albert Bowen was then in his early fifties. He had scored a #14 pop hit at age nineteen with a teen pop song, "I'm Sticking with You." Then he jumped over to the other side of the recording studio's glass window and became an in-house producer for Reprise Records in Los Angeles, working with Frank Sinatra and his Rat Pack brothers Sammy Davis Jr. and Dean Martin, among others. Bowen moved to Nashville in 1977 and subsequently worked as the Nashville chief of several major labels, eventually taking top posts at MGM, Elektra/Asylum, Warner Bros., and MCA before heading Capitol Records Nashville. Over the years, he had produced a stellar lineup of major artists, including George Strait, Reba McEntire, Hank Williams Jr., and Waylon Jennings. Luckily, Garth Brooks was already on Capitol when Bowen became president of the Nashville division in late 1989. During Bowen's time at Capitol, Brooks developed into a superstar, eventually becoming one of the top-selling artists of all time.

The more I dug into what had been written about Bowen, the more I marveled at the arc of his life. An article named him as "an agent for change" in country music. Born in Santa Rita, New Mexico, he long identified as "Texas dirt country." His father gave him his first guitar when he was five. He was playing with a country band at a roadhouse bar while he was still in grade school.

"We would play behind chicken wire and fencing," he told an interviewer from the outlet *CanvasRebel*. "There was always a brawl before the night was over. I was actually too young to be in the bar, but if you played in the band, you could play but you had to leave and go outside during the break. I got paid $10 a night. I was the richest fourth grader I knew."

Here was a producer and music executive with a performer's soul. I kept reading descriptive words such as "mercurial," "passionate," and "artist-oriented."

At the moment he was producing a country album for Andy Williams. I liked the incredible spread of the man's experience, and I was especially impressed with that "agent of change" tag that had been applied to him. Anyone taking me on in Nashville, I thought, would have to be willing to swim against the prevailing currents in country music.

The voice on the phone hadn't been pranking me. Bowen was the real deal, and Capitol was, too, one of the top record labels—scratch that, Capitol was *the* top label in Nashville. So I'll ask again, doctor dude, what's with the "no, no, no" business? Why ask why now? Are you serious? How about "it's about time!"

Only later would I find out what triggered the call. Bowen had just come home from playing golf. Walking through his den, he heard "Love Light" playing on CMT. Liking the voice, he looked up to see a Black singer. He stopped in his tracks, listening to the rest of the song. He then picked up the phone and called Ray Pillow.

"Ray? I want you to locate a singer named Cleve Francis and set up a meeting." Bowen had to spell the name, since the A&R chief at Capitol Records wasn't familiar with it.

I was forty-six years old, more than halfway home, age-wise, judging by the biblical life span of three score and ten. I had inhabited a lot of roles in my life, some more major than others. Dutiful Son. The Little Preacher. Willow Tree Troubadour. Medicine Man.

Years of study and years as a research scientist contributed to my present focus on the art of healing. If I counted the years beginning when Mary Francis bought me my first guitar, I had spent even more time as a singer, songwriter, and musician. Medicine and music had equal weight in my personality and sense of self.

Now I was set. Finished. Fully realized. I had the Birchmere as a prime performance outlet. I was the founder, director, and chief partner in a thriving cardiology practice. I had realized every dream that Mary Francis had ever imagined for me, and then some.

Was I going to disrupt that carefully balanced existence for a vault into the unknown? Did I want to offer myself up to the dog-eat-dog world of Nashville? No, no, no. I refused to do it. I'd take the meeting, sure, politely thank the agent of change for his interest, and treat the visit to Music City as if it were a trip to Disney World. Golly gosh, ain't this wonderful? Well, time to get back to real life.

As Ray Pillow had promised, FedEx delivered a roundtrip ticket to Nashville along with accommodations at the Loews Vanderbilt Plaza Hotel on Broadway. When I landed at Nashville International, a uniformed driver held up a card with my name on it. He grabbed my bags and led me to a white limousine waiting at curbside.

"Would you like refreshments, Mr. Francis?" he asked after I got settled in the back. "We've got a full bar."

I chose a Coke. I tried to act nonchalant. Had I ridden in a stretch limousine before? I think I would have remembered. Was it too much of a rube move to converse with the driver? I found out his name was Milton. He was from Chicago. I sat back and shut up.

From the airport we headed toward downtown Nashville on I-40. For the third time in my life, I watched the Nashville skyline rise into view. In 1985 I had recorded *Timeless* and "Martin" there with Moses Dillard, and in 1990 *Last Call for Love* with Jack Gale. Somehow the view looked different through the window of a fancy limousine.

Whoa, there, pardner. Don't let it go to your head. I thought of "Living for the City," that 1973 Stevie Wonder hit about a greenhorn hitting the Big Apple, right before he gets taken advantage of and winds up in prison. "Wow! New York City! Just like I pictured it. Skyscrapers and everything!"

At the Loews Vanderbilt Plaza, Capitol Records had arranged a full suite for me. I would soon learn that Jimmy Bowen always went first class. I felt like someone had just given me the keys to the Music City playground.

"I'll give you time to get settled in," Milton said. "I'll be back in a couple of hours to take you to Mr. Bowen's home. Just come on down and I'll be waiting out here in the front drive."

★ ★ ★

Catching my breath in my room, I counted up all my contacts in Nashville. It wasn't a long list. Moses Dillard, of course, but he was unavailable. But I also knew Tony Hamrick, whom I had just met the previous year. He acted as road manager for a band that played Zed's Restaurant in Alexandria, and he recognized me from the "Love Light" video on CMT. The two of us got to talking right there in Zed's. He had asked if I had management and a publicist.

"No, man, I'm just local," I said. "I really didn't realize what was going to happen with the video. I didn't think it would blow up like it has."

"Well, it's all over CMT, that's for sure," he said. "If you're ever in Nashville and need introductions to anyone, look me up and I'll hook you up."

Understandably a little jittery about the meeting with the Capitol Records honchos, I reached out to Tony. He met me at the hotel and Milton drove us out to Bowen's together.

Jimmy Bowen lived a few miles from downtown, on Franklin Road. His large, modern, Southern-style manor house, situated high on a hill, featured a down-home front porch that looked out on several wooded acres. Milton didn't need directions. He had been to the place numerous times before. A pair of immense, showy iron gates swung open to allow the limousine entrance to the property and the drive up to the top of the hill.

We were greeted first by Ray Pillow. Friendly, craggy-faced, with swept-up graying hair, everything about the fiftysomething Pillow screamed Nashville veteran. Ray arrived in the Music City in 1961 as a winner in the Pet Milk Talent Contest. *Billboard* magazine named him most promising male country artist in 1966. A member of the Grand Ole Opry since then, he charted eighteen times with songs like "Thank You, Ma'am" and "Reconsider Me."

But offstage Pillow was always into the business side of music, too, starting his own label, Sycamore Records, before becoming Jimmy Bowen's right-hand man at Capitol.

Since Pillow had been born in Lynchburg, we bonded about sharing common ground in Virginia. He guided Tony and me into the big-as-a-barn kitchen area of the house.

Bowen came in from the back of the house, wearing his usual velour warm-up suit and trademark newsboy cap. Wire-rimmed aviator glasses anchored by a chain dropped to his chest whenever he took them off, which he did often. He and I shook hands.

"I'm Jimmy Bowen," he said, and I couldn't help thinking of the Man in Black greeting his audiences with "I'm Johnny Cash."

I introduced myself and Tony. "My wingman," I said.

Bowen held a copy of the Playback Records album that Jack Gale had produced, *Last Call for Love*. I noticed red markings and scribbled words all over the sleeve of the album cover. As an icebreaker Bowen ran through all the songs one by one, saying what he liked and what he didn't. He mentioned "Love Light" as his favorite.

He paused, gazing down at the album notes. Then he threw me a minor league curveball. "So who the hell are you, man?"

The question caught me off guard. I didn't know what to say—I mean, how do you respond when someone asks you that? Do I answer in professional or personal terms, or perhaps metaphysically? "I am a humble human being, walking the face of the earth in search of three chords and the truth." Something like that.

"I'm a cardiologist," I said instead.

"That's *your* problem," Bowen said, whip quickly.

I laughed, Bowen laughed, and Ray Pillow laughed. Consider the ice broken.

"I'd like to offer you a record contract, Cleve," Bowen said.

Wow, wow, wow, no, no, no, why now, Lord Jesus? why now? why now?

Bowen understood that my head was swimming. "You don't have to decide right away. Capitol will send you the contract. I would produce the first album. Ray here will help you search for songs. He'll be my lead with the project."

He asked if I had a manager. Right at the moment, I didn't think mentioning Arthur Lisi's name would cut it. "You'll need to find one," Bowen said, "but it's not crucial to do it soon."

"There'll be time for that," Ray Pillow assured me.

"I know some folks," Tony said.

"The contract will be for three albums, with a yearly review and options to renew or not."

Bowen's voice sounded far away. I heard a strange buzzing in my ears. This was what I always wanted, right? Right? Your dream come true? Then another thought flew in out of nowhere. Why didn't you offer me a contract ten, fifteen, twenty years ago? I would have snapped it up in an instant then.

Bowen talked, I listened. He explained that he had spun *Last Call for Love* multiple times, gauging the range and timbre of my voice. "Cleve, you might be the first Black man since Charley Pride in possession of a natural country singing voice."

Giving me a reality check, he added that I wasn't the first Black artist to come down the pike recently, attempting to sing country songs. "But you can always hear how they modify their R&B or pop sound to make it fit," he said. "Your voice is just naturally suited for the genre."

It was time to introduce into country music a non-nasal vocal style, he said, "a deeper, soulful voice."

Yes, I thought, citing singers in my mind who served as my own favorite role models, like Johnny Mathis and Nat King Cole.

"Nat King Cole is an example," Bowen added. I smiled.

Ray Pillow pitched in. "We don't want you to feel that you have to wear a big Stetson hat or any of the costumes worn by country artists."

"That's right," Bowen said. "Jeans and boots and a casual look will do. You just have to deliver the music. Meeting you now, I know you have your head screwed on straight and will be able to handle yourself with the press and the public."

He fell silent. Ray Pillow gave me a raised eyebrow look and asked me if I had questions. I told him and Bowen that I owed them both a whole boatload of gratitude.

"It's just a lot to take in," I said, rising to my feet.

Bowen held up his hand. I sat back down.

"This is important," he said. "This thing won't be decided by us, this question of whether you make it or not. I don't know and can't control 'the Redneck Factor.' That's what I call it, 'the Redneck Factor.'"

Everyone present knew what he was talking about. I glanced over at Tony, the only bro in the room who could possibly qualify as a redneck. Where I grew up, "redneck" wasn't an insult, just a description. Tony and I occupied opposite ends of the political spectrum. But I had never caught a whiff of prejudice in my dealings with him.

"I can only hope that radio will accept you," Bowen said. "We have a great promotions team, and I can assure you that they'll do everything they can to make it happen."

He rose to his feet then. I stood up and we all shook hands.

"I feel that it's time for a change," the agent of change said.

The meeting lasted nearly an hour. Milton drove Tony and me back to the hotel. The two of us went to dinner at a nearby restaurant. The street was alive with young people, but somehow the vibe still resembled a friendly small town. I loved it. I imagined myself living there, taking up residence in Music City, becoming a Nashville star surrounded by ace Nashville cat musicians who would blow the socks off anyone who heard us.

The flight back to National Airport in Washington, DC took less than two hours. As we landed I had a feeling of coming back down to earth. Northern Virginia. Here was my life, I thought. Here was home. This was me.

What was I going to do?

★ ★ ★

In some sense, this is all false drama. If you've read the first pages of this account of my life, you already know the path I chose. But putting myself in my shoes back then, returning from Nashville to Alexandria, in my own house and at my own medical practice, there was nothing false about being torn between two worlds. The dilemma felt very real.

Human beings are homebodies. We like our comfort. Beginning in middle age, settled into our lives and careers, we tend to hang up a "do not disturb" sign on our safe and secure existences. I estimated the chances of Nashville working out at less than fifty-fifty.

So I did what a lot of folks do when they don't know what to do. I asked my mother. With her lifelong love and encouragement, Mary Francis had put me where I was then.

We spoke about the positives and negatives of the situation. Then she said, "You have to make me a promise, Butch."

"What, Mama?" For some reason, I felt as though I was about to break into tears.

"Promise Mama that you will not let those people rob you of all you've built in your life. If you decide to go to Nashville and things are not going the way you want them to go, be brave enough to come back to your practice."

I polled the populace, too, everyone I knew, everyone who knew me. The patients I spoke to, some of whom I had known and treated for over a decade, surprised me with a near-unanimous response. "You only live once." "I love you as my doctor, but get out there and find out what this is all about." "I'll be okay, Doc, don't worry."

Several patients told me of their own "lost chances," when because of family responsibilities they had given up a dream they loved. I heard stories of regret, of abandoning art, writing, or playing a musical instrument. "If you don't do this, you'll always wonder what could have happened."

Still, I sulked. I had done everything that had been asked of me, hadn't I? Worked my tail off to get where I was. Took care of my siblings, bought my mother a house. I felt like Job questioning God. What else do you want from me?

I had the contract in hand. "Be careful what you wish for," folks say, but I had not really wished for such an outlandish gift, did not have the chutzpah to even imagine it happening. How could I leave a practice of fifteen years in order to devote my life to music? How could I trade one for the other?

Medicine was the one of the great professions in the world. What would people say about me if I simply turned my back on it? They would ask tough questions. Were you ever really serious about being a physician? How can you abandon all the people who entrust their lives to you?

I summoned the five partners at Mount Vernon Cardiology Associates to a business meeting, careful to have our attorney present. I had founded the group and served as president and CEO. The partners said they wanted me to remain the president of the corporation.

"If I do this," I said, "I'll remain in contact with the firm for major decisions. I will not draw a salary."

"I'm afraid your leaving will put the practice at risk," said one of the partners.

The attorney immediately weighed in. "The only one at risk is Dr. Francis," he said. "The rest of you will have to work harder or hire another associate. But you will all benefit from seeing his patients."

The lawyer then added a kicker that I found difficult to choke down, considering I was the one who founded the practice. "The associates are under no obligation to take Dr. Francis back into the practice if and when he decides to return." I felt as though I was burning my bridges behind me.

When in doubt, talk to Moses Dillard. It was a rule of thumb that served me well ever since I'd met the man. I believe Moses had been born into the world already a wise old soul. Then he just got older and wiser as time when on. I called him and laid out the situation.

He went silent on the other end of the line. "Mose?" I said. "You still there?"

"Brother, I know you must be tired, but it appears that you are one mission short," he said finally. "You know you don't have a choice, right? History has landed on you."

"History," I muttered.

"You don't realize what's happened? There is no Black man on the face of the earth that has this deal. Not one. You remember the last time anybody who looked like us was signed? That was Charley Pride and the year was 1965. Almost thirty years ago. Three decades."

"I know how long it's been," I said petulantly. "But I'm too old. If I was in my twenties or even in my thirties, that'd be different, but I'm forty-six, Mose. Nashville is a young man's game."

"Moses my namesake was an old man when he led the children of Israel out of bondage in Egypt."

I gave a bitter laugh. You know you're in trouble when folks start to go all biblical on you.

"You have to go, Cleve," Moses said. "There is nobody else here. You have to hold this spot. You weren't given all these talents for nothing."

On a pretty early spring evening, still mulling things over, I took a long walk along the George Washington Parkway. I was with Marty LaVor, a congressional staffer and professional photographer and my best friend back then. I had met him at the Mount Vernon Racquet Club, where Marty demonstrated his high velocity serve and mean backhand. Later he served as my personal photographer, traveling to clubs and concerts where I performed, providing photos for press coverage.

During that springtime walk beside the Potomac River, we could see historic Fort Washington across the water, where the conspirators who helped John Wilkes Booth's assassination plot had been hanged after the Civil War. Marty urged me to take up the Nashville challenge. We went through a checklist of positives. I had no family constraints. I was single and as young as I would ever be. Money wasn't a problem. In other words, I was a free agent. Then Marty said something that made me think.

"As far as I know, the history of country music is not exactly well stocked with folks who look like you. That's the reality, right? Have you ever looked into it?"

I knew what Marty said to be true in a general sense, but did I know the details? Before committing to a career in country music, I needed to find out what I was getting myself into. I dove into research at the Sherwood Hall Regional Library, located right across the street from the hospital. The forbidden Carnegie Library in Jennings had shut me out, a situation that had always rankled. Now I had a library card that granted me full access.

Dipping into the stacks and consulting staffers, I went through the same motions as two decades before, when I plumbed the history of people of color in folk music. Now I went through the same research routine with country.

CHAPTER 17

A Secret History

WHEN DID COUNTRY MUSIC START? Recently, researchers discovered a wax cylinder in Pennsylvania containing what they have suggested is the oldest recorded country song. Sung by Louis Vasnier, a Black man from New Orleans, the track "Thompson's Old Gray Mule" was laid down in 1891. What do you know about that?

Most people trace country music's beginnings back to when it still carried the label "hillbilly" and emerged from the American South and West. As a business, country music began in the early 1920s, with landmark recordings by Eck Robertson, Fiddlin' John Carson, and Vernon Dalhart, among others. But in the minds of many folks, the 1927 recording sessions conducted by talent scout Ralph Peer in the mountain town of Bristol, Tennessee, mark "the Big Bang of Country Music."

Prominent in the Bristol sessions were the Carter Family—A. P., Sara, and Maybelle—who went on to become a kind of founding family of country music. Maybelle Carter was the mother of June Carter, who became the wife of Johnny Cash. I had a vague notion of the importance of the Bristol recordings, but until I dug deeper I had never before encountered the name Lesley Riddle.

Nicknamed "Esley," Lesley Riddle began working with A. P. Carter around late 1928 or early 1929 helping the Carter Family leader find songs to record. A guitarist and multi-instrumentalist from Tennessee, Riddle joined A. P. in searching the mountain valleys of his home state, southwestern Virginia, and western North Carolina, going into churches, farms, village squares, and dance halls.

When the two song catchers would encounter someone with a good song, A. P. would write down the lyrics, while Esley would memorize the tune. Returning to the Carter Family home in Poor Valley, Virginia, they would share the melodies and words with Sara and Maybelle. Some of the songs were so ancient no one knew their provenance. I learned that Esley Riddle was a Black man, and he had been there at the beginning.

In the course of my research, I kept turning up names and stories, such as Rufus "Tee Tot" Payne, the Alabama street musician who mentored Hank Williams, and DeFord Bailey, a harmonica genius who was one of the early stars of the Grand Ole Opry. Of course, Charley Pride stood as a country icon, but there were others who had been unknown to me, like Stoney Edwards, O. B. McClinton, Virginia Kirby, Howdy Glenn, La Melle Prince, Ruby Falls, and G. Hawl Jones.

Cross-fertilization ran throughout the whole country music tradition. In 1930, jazz great Louis Armstrong recorded with the man known as "the Father of Country Music," Jimmie Rodgers, another discovery of the Bristol sessions. Bluesman Howlin' Wolf patterned his trademark yowl after the yodel of Jimmie Rodgers.

Arnold Shultz, the son of a formerly enslaved man from Kentucky, put the blues in bluegrass by teaching bluegrass icon Bill Monroe everything he knew about the blues. Top-selling 1930s and '40s country star Bob Wills and his band, the Texas Playboys, mixed Black jazz and blues, Mexican mariachi music, and big band swing with country music, creating a rich blend known as western swing.

I knew Ray Charles's 1962 album *Modern Sounds in Country and Western Music* practically by heart, though it came out when I was a teen and I didn't discover it until later. Two other singers from R&B who released groundbreaking country recordings were Linda Martell, with her album *Color Me Country* in 1970, and Tina Turner, whose first album as a solo act, released in 1974, was *Tina Turns the Country On!*

Lenora Ross, signed to RCA in 1975, was (as far as I could discover) the first Black female country singer signed to a major label. The Pointer Sisters won a Grammy in 1974 for Best Country Vocal Performance by a Duo or Group with their song "Fairytale."

Charley Pride had been a trailblazer, but he had been a lonely one, for years one of the few Black artists signed to a major label in Nashville (in the 1970s, Stoney Edwards and Big Al Downing joined him in that small club), and one of only three Black members of the Grand Ole Opry to this day. Born in sharecropper's shack in Sledge, Mississippi, Pride came out of the same Jim Crow environment as I did. When he hit the country charts in the mid-1960s, the civil rights movement gripped America in general and the South in particular.

Recalling his childhood in a TV interview, Charley Pride shared some early words of wisdom from his father. "My dad used to say, 'Now, "Pride," you just think about the name itself. Whatever you want to try to do, do it good.'"

As I had followed Mary Francis's prescription for success, Pride followed his daddy's. For Pride, the proof was indisputable: twenty-nine #1 singles on the *Billboard* country chart, Entertainer of the Year at the 1971 Country Music Association Awards, a Grammy for Best Country Vocal Performance in 1972 for an album with the hit single "Kiss an Angel Good Mornin'."

We stand on the shoulders of giants, and Pride was the giant I was aspiring to follow. When I visited Nashville for the Bowen meeting I had seen a funny bumper sticker: "What would Ernest Tubb do?" a variation on the more common "What would Jesus do?" I posed a different question: What would Charley Pride do?

I thought about the velvet-voiced forerunner, and considered what a towering figure he was. From my research I knew he hadn't stood alone. Country music was American music, which meant it varied as much as the nation did. Music possessed no race. To call some of it "white" or "Black" ignored its true, wonderfully unbounded nature.

Familiarizing myself with the stakes a bit more, I needed to decide. Was I in or out? Another thought surfaced, about an incident I had with another Charlie when I was sixteen years old. One day I had been cleaning the office of Charlie Holston, my employer and my family's patron, while he small-talked with a friend.

I worked silently while the two men jawed about the big news of the day, James Meredith enrolling in Ole Miss, the formerly strictly and proudly segregated university in Oxford, Mississippi. Out of nowhere, Holston turned and asked me a loaded question.

"So, Butch, what d'ya think about that business, this Meredith boy integrating Ole Miss?" The two white men looked at me. Holston had pronounced the word "business" as "bid-ness" and "integrating" as a three-syllable sneer. I knew I should have answered with noncommittal politeness, but something inside of me rebelled.

"Somebody has to do it!" I exclaimed.

My cheekiness was not rewarded. Holston immediately fired me from doing yard work and performing odd jobs for him. He hired me back after a month, and I like to think that somewhere in that prejudiced, hidebound, hard-hearted soul of his, he might have seen the truth in my remark.

Forty years later, I finally concluded that the same sentiment applied to me about going to Nashville.

Somebody has to do it.

I FedEx'd the signed contract back to Capitol Records.

★ ★ ★

I loved my new life, I loved the music I was making, and good glory I absolutely loved Nashville, Tennessee. Like the Land of Oz or Hollywood, the place lived in fantasy far beyond its physical boundaries. Music Row was a street of dreams, or actually a whole neighborhood of dreams, filled with famous landmarks, label offices, radio stations, and recording studios catering to the music business. Yet when I arrived the town felt unpretentious and real, down-home, unhurried, and countrified.

Back in 1954, the piano-playing producer and Nashville pioneer Owen Bradley and his brother Harold opened the first major studio in the area of town soon to be dubbed Record Row. Back then a rather down-at-the-heels residential district and only later renamed Music Row, this hallowed ground has since grown to become the most consequential music-making neighborhood in the world.

Sited between Wedgewood Avenue and Demonbreun Street along 16th through 19th Avenues—known as Music Square East and Music Square West, respectively—this two-hundred-acre patch of real estate is where the majority of the best-known country music of the past seventy years has been recorded, published, and marketed. Some songs are also created there, ground up, soup to nuts, from lyrics and melodies to polished commercial tracks.

Don't come to Music Row expecting live music—Bobby's Idle Hour Tavern is the exception that proves the rule—since most of the picking and grinning goes on "Behind Closed Doors" as Charlie Rich's hit would have it. Some of the humble residential buildings hide state-of-the-art recording studios. When I hit town, Capitol Records was located at 1111 16th Avenue South, with an imposing façade of stone and wood. We rarely went there, since it seemed a realm of bean counters and lawyers.

Nashville as a whole was simply a friendly place, with lots of smiles, birdsong, and sunshine. Somehow it pulled off the trick of being a big city with a small-town vibe. I wandered Hillsboro Village, a booming neighborhood a few blocks west of Music Row. The streets were filled with stores, bars, and clubs. Little shop-filled streets led off from the main drag. Music City struck me as welcoming, not overwhelming.

I enjoyed the throngs of happy young people enjoying themselves, many of them students from nearby Vanderbilt University. I felt years younger myself just being there. I hit the venerable Ernest Tubb Record Shop on Broadway and found for sale there my Playback Records album, *Last Call for Love*. The weather resembled the heat of Jennings, reminding me of home. I was back in the South, or at least farther south than Alexandria, anyway.

The first time I had visited seven years before, when I was working with Moses Dillard on *Timeless*, I got myself all duded up for a walk downtown. I wore what I thought was the required Nashville fashion, ostrich-skin boots, Western-style shirt, a big old cowboy hat that balanced atop my head.

As soon as I ventured into the streets, I realized I had it all wrong. Everybody else in the neighborhood dressed casually and normally, wearing T-shirts and khakis or jeans, while I looked like a clown. I knew better this time around. Bowen had ruled out the cowboy look for me.

Nothing but the best for Jimmy Bowen's artists. Whenever I was in town, Capitol Records put me up at Union Station Hotel, the opulent former train station and proud old landmark. At first, because I thought I could balance music and my medical practice without cheating on either one, I traveled to Nashville in a series of surgical, three-day lightning visits. My time there was all work and no play.

Capitol set up the flights, overnighted the airline tickets to the cardiology office, reserved my rental car, and booked the hotel. I would finish work on Friday, catch an hour-and-a-half flight on American Airlines to Nashville, arrive at six or seven-thirty, and check into my room. Sunday afternoon I would turn around and zip back home. I piled up the frequent flyer miles.

At times I felt as though history was stalking me. When I attended the 1992 Academy of Country Music Awards in Los Angeles on April 29, I enjoyed the show, hosted by Clint Black, Lorrie Morgan, and Travis Tritt. Garth Brooks took home the awards for Entertainer of the Year and Male Vocalist of the Year. The man was a phenomenon. No one deserved it more.

But outside the Universal Amphitheatre in Universal City, the world was in chaos, with half of Los Angeles in riot mode. The community was reacting furiously to the not-guilty verdict for the LAPD officers caught on video beating Rodney King. News of what was happening outside spread through the protected enclave of Universal City. I saw fear registering on people's faces in the audience. I had my own private thoughts: unrest in another dome.

Back in Nashville, Bowen wanted to go, go, go. He insisted the first Cleve Francis release on Capitol Records had to drop by the end of the year. This was a crazy expectation and a near impossible schedule. But Bowen felt we had to capitalize on the popularity of the "Love Light" video.

First order of the day was choosing songs for the new album. Ray Pillow and I spent all day every Saturday of every one of my weekend visits for a month making the rounds of music publishers. There were dozens upon dozens, probably hundreds of publishing companies in town, just like there were hundreds upon hundreds, probably thousands of songwriters.

Out of that huge abundance we had to ferret out a dozen blockbuster singles, a collection of million-selling gold-record hits. Short of that, we searched for twelve songs that would suit my voice and would pass muster with Jimmy Bowen.

Pillow and I traipsed around Music Row and listened to a dozen or more songs in one music publisher's office after another. We'd put our heads together and choose our favorites. "Listen, can you send us a tape of just these three?" Ray Pillow would say, and then we'd be on to the next stop, the next office, the next publisher's thousand-song catalog. Ray Pillow would also do song-catching rounds during the week.

Later Saturday night or on Sunday morning we'd be ready to pass through the iron gates of Bowen's estate to audition the couple dozen possibles for him. The listening session resembled an audience with the Pope. No other sounds were allowed to distract from the matter at hand. Television off, radio off, AC off. Bowen cocked his recliner back and lay there like Buddha, eyes closed, newsboy cap down low, mind in a total Zen focus.

"This one's called 'I Carry Your Heart with Me,'" Pillow would say. Sometimes Bowen didn't even want to hear the title, and sometimes he'd wave the song off after hearing only a couple of notes. I marveled at his confidence. "Best ears in the business," Pillow whispered to me. It was a good sign when Bowen deigned to listen to a song all the way to the end.

"Put that one on hold," he would say. The practice of putting a hold on songs represented a complicated sort of calculus. The publisher agreed to take the song out of circulation, reserving it for an artist's exclusive use. That meant an act could depend on having access to the material, but it also meant a risk for the songwriters, since their work would essentially be in limbo.

Early on in his career, Garth Brooks placed a song on hold for a year and a half before he was able to release it, his hit "Friends in Low Places" by songwriters Earl Bud Lee and Dewayne Blackwell. "Putting that kind of faith into an unknown artist is unheard of," Brooks stated in the CD liner notes to his album collection, *The Hits*. "Thanks Dewayne and Bud for believing in me."

During our initial listening sessions, one song appealed to all of us, Bowen, Ray, and me, and wound up giving the upcoming album its title. The veteran songwriters Bob McDill (now a member of the Country Music Hall of Fame) and Paul Harrison composed a love song that echoed my exuberant mood about being in Nashville. "Tourist in Paradise" described me to a T in those days. When Nashville turns on the juice, it can indeed be a kind of paradise that cannot be duplicated anywhere else.

Jimmy Bowen had just renamed the label, from Capitol Nashville to Liberty Records. "What, like Freedom Records wasn't available?" I teased him. "Free At Last Records?" Bowen laughed. He really did seek to change an environment that was famously resistant to it. Folks usually went ahead and called it Capitol anyway.

Occasionally the universe beamed out an "Earth-to-Cleve" message, a sobering, return-to-base reality check. After spending the afternoon song-catching at a number of music publishers, Ray Pillow dropped me off at the hotel. He told me he'd pick me up later for a trip out to the Opry.

At the appointed time I stood waiting for him in front of the Union Station Hotel. The grand old rockpile turned golden in the sunset. My second home, I mused. Only in America could a Black man be standing where I was, a cardiologist with a major label record contract, preparing to head out to Opryland. Affection for my country and affection for my hotel merged into a warm, sentimental soup.

A fob of car keys sailed through the air and I instinctively raised my hand and caught them to keep from getting hit in the face. I had been too busy marveling and musing to notice that a white guy had driven up in a fancy sports coupe. He had tossed his car keys in my direction. In his eyes, I was a valet waiting to park his ride.

"Oh, no," I said, "I'm a guest at the hotel."

A stricken look crossed his face. He apologized profusely for the mistake. Although I didn't have any particular uniform on, I was dressed up for the Opry, wearing my brand-new Justin boots.

The dude kept saying he was sorry. "Well, you know, I'm from Washington, DC," I told him. "Back there you might have lost your car if you'd have done that." We both chuckled.

A beat later, Ray showed up. I recounted what had happened. Ray Pillow was always a jokester, and the two of us belly laughed all the way to the Opry.

The knife-sharp comedian Paul Mooney used to have a funny-bitter riff about "the Negro moment"—when society reminded a Black person of his status in society. Didn't matter how prominent, even if you were Michael Jackson or Martin Luther King Jr., America was always happy to provide you with a Negro moment, though Mooney of course used the full-blown N-word.

"I'm not Black, I'm O. J.," Orenthal James Simpson used to say, before his arrest and trial told him just exactly who he was. Also relevant here is the sad old joke: "What do you call a Black man with a PhD?" What do you do to a Black cardiologist with a major label contract standing in front of the Union Station Hotel? You toss him your keys.

Even though my "only in America" moment had turned into a Paul Mooney–style "Negro moment," I felt not a twinge of anger or disgust. I steadied myself with the wisdom of Mary Francis, who always counseled me to try not to take such incidents to heart, because if I did, I would be controlled by the ignorant attitudes of others.

"You have to be self-contained," she told me. "You have to know who you are. People outside might not know who you are. They'll make assumptions. You never mind them, Butch."

Personal dignity is a tiny diamond in the middle of the soul that cannot be stolen from you or tarnished in any way. It's important to know who you are, so that you can develop immunity to whatever negativity comes your way. It's on them, it's not on you. I knew I would never be able to convince every man on the street of my self-worth. As far as I'm concerned, it's his loss.

Besides, in the next few days we were headed into a recording studio, one of my favorite places on the planet. By that point I had recorded eight singles, from "Follow Me" to "Martin," and three ten-track albums, *Follow Me*, *Timeless*, and *Last Call for Love*.

So it wasn't my first rodeo. But it was my first Grand Championship rodeo. I had never been inside a "real" recording studio with 24-track capabilities. One revolution Jimmy Bowen had accomplished during his time as a Nashville record executive was modernizing the recording process, dragging not only every label he worked at but all of Music Row kicking and screaming into the digital age. For my projects, Bowen rented studios by the week, and we had 24/7 access during that time.

For the *Tourist in Paradise* sessions, that meant the renowned Emerald Sound Studio, founded by hit songwriters Even Stevens and David Malloy, at 1033 16th Avenue South, in the heart of Music Row. Working with Stevens and Malloy, Eddie Rabbit kicked off the long line of artists who used the studio, recording "I Love a Rainy Night" there in 1980. After that came the deluge, including Johnny Cash, George Strait, and Alabama on the country music side of things, and Foreigner, Lynyrd Skynyrd, and Olivia Newton-John in rock and pop. I took to calling the place "Emerald City," in a nod to the wonderful world of Oz.

Laying down tracks represented only the first step in the recording process, but it was the sexiest one. Studio musicians arrived from all over, not only from right next door in Nashville, but from New York and LA, too. The concept of "Nashville cats" had been kicking around forever before

John Sebastian and the Lovin' Spoonful immortalized the term in their song "Nashville Cats."

We had the legendary Paul Franklin on steel guitar and dobro, bassist Leland Sklar and drummer Carlos Vega making up the rhythm section, celebrated session man Reggie Young on guitar, John Jarvis on keyboards, and Lisa Silver on fiddle. I stood in awe of these musicians. They listened a single time to the original demo track and in a matter of minutes they were playing as if they had known the song all their lives.

I didn't know if I could pull my own weight among such gods, but I tried my best, laying down preliminary vocal tracks. These had to be strong because the musicians fed off the energy of the lead singer. It took only two days to do ten tracks, winnowed down from the dozens of candidates that Ray Pillow, Jimmy Bowen, and I had picked out after weeks of song-catching and catalog sifting. We then did the final lead vocal sessions, with me enclosed in a sound booth wearing headphones, positioned in front of a high-end microphone shielded by a circular pop screen.

I preferred recording in the evenings, when my vocal cords had been limbered up during the day. I followed the yellow brick road and usually showed up at Emerald City around seven or eight o'clock.

My customary glass of merlot stood ready. A bag of throat lozenges and water were also handy. A lyric sheet rested on a music stand, for reference should Jimmy Bowen want to cite a specific passage. I sang each cut five or six times, occasionally more. Bowen or Bob Bullock, the recording engineer, stopped the process when I mispronounced a word or had a lapse in concentration. Three songs per session was normally my limit, after which I needed a rest.

Once in while Bowen asked me to come to the control room and we'd listen to a track together. "I need some more here," he'd say, or "cool it down right there." After long nights of trial and error, the words I wanted to hear from him eventually arrived: "I think we got this one" or "this one is in the bag," and "let's go on to the next song."

Of course, the long road to releasing a record didn't actually end there. Next came overdubbing, adding instruments or background vocals to this or that cut, then mixing, combining the separately recorded tracks into one smooth audio file. Days of intense, exhausting work on the part of Bowen and Bob Bullock followed, overseeing the final mixing and mastering of the tracks. Meanwhile I was having the time of my life, skipping off to shoot music videos, not only in Nashville but in Houston, Miami, and New York City.

With the advent of CDs, the glory days of vinyl albums were gone, when stoned teenagers mooned over the intricacies of the cover to *Sgt. Pepper's*

Lonely Hearts Club Band, looking for hidden meanings. But graphics were still part of the overall CD package. *Tourist* featured a photograph of yours truly, bearded and smiling, standing against a purple backdrop wearing a blousy, maroon shirt printed with the leaf pattern of an Amur maple tree.

Weeks of work as spring passed into summer. Thousands of dollars spent—I actually didn't want to know how much. (Ray Pillow later told me Capitol Records spent over a quarter million dollars on the album, all in, which was about major-label average for the time.) Dozens of people contributed their labor and creativity, from Nashville cats to songwriters, producers, recording engineers, A&R staff, and music publishers. Art director teams pitched in, as well as designer, photographer, videographer, and promotion and marketing teams, distribution networks, record store clerks, all the way to the folks who cleaned the studios at the Emerald City of Oz.

At last I held it my hands, the long-awaited first Cleve Francis CD on Capitol Records, *Tourist in Paradise*. To reach this point—from beneath the weeping willow in Jennings to being a genuine country recording artist—had taken more than thirty-seven years.

The cuts included a new version of "Love Light," "You Do My Heart Good" by songwriters Mike Lantrip and Tom Paden, "Tourist in Paradise" by Bob McDill, "The Tip of My Fingers" by Bill Anderson, and "How Can I Hold You" by the songwriting team of Billy Dean, Chris Waters, and Tom Shapiro. The album ended with a big ballad called "Those Were the Days, These Are the Nights," which might have been more suitable for a group such as Foreigner.

Events during the release of one of the singles would be a reminder of what a thin racial line we were walking. Bowen and the team had decided on three singles. One would be a rerecorded version of "Love Light," to take advantage of the exposure from the music video. The second single was to be "You Do My Heart Good," and we had not yet decided on the third, with the choice being a toss-up between "The Tip of My Fingers" and the title cut, "Tourist in Paradise."

Due to a mix-up with the song-holding process, "The Tip of My Fingers" was placed on hold for both Steve Wariner and me. Wariner got the green light to proceed. His version scored #3 on the *Billboard* country charts.

As a result, my producing team decided that "Tourist in Paradise" would be the third single release from my first album. With all the usual promotional factors in place, we proceeded to film the music video. The video portrayed me as a traveling vaudeville act who carried an entire party in a suitcase.

As the song played on the soundtrack, I would walk out in front of the audience, bow, and then open the magic suitcase. Out would come a full band as well as folks from all walks of life, jumping and dancing to the music. At the end of the song, they would all climb back into the suitcase, I would close it, bow, and walk off stage. I remember our thinking at the time that—because the scenes included a whole cast of different characters, including children—viewers would naturally recall the "Love Light" video.

When Bowen saw the video, he exploded. He yelled at everybody involved and immediately fired the video production company. He felt that the video portrayed me as Stepin Fetchit, a subservient character played by Black vaudeville star Lincoln Perry in the 1920s and '30s. The character embodied all the ugly racial stereotypes of the day, playing prejudice for laughs.

Bowen felt that the video would get us crucified in the press and that Black media outlets would react especially strongly. As the only Black man on a major country music label at the time, I would be singled out and derided for participating in such a tone-deaf charade. "What were they thinking?" would be the common reaction.

During Bowen's tirade, I looked around at the faces of people he was dressing down. I could tell that Bowen and I were the only ones who knew who in the hell Stepin Fetchit was. Privately, in my own mind, I took my share of the blame. I had been so intensely involved in the video project that the negative social implications had totally gone over my head.

We settled on releasing "How Can I Hold You," a song that had already been released on an album by Billy Dean. We hired an entirely new production company and made a new video for the album's release.

Despite the video's popularity on CMT, the reissue of "Love Light" only reached #52 on the *Billboard* Hot Country Songs chart. "You Do My Heart Good" did better, but still peaked at #47, while "How Can I Hold You" trended the wrong way, reaching only #74.

The album itself really moved—right into the cutout bin. My first foray into big-time country music wasn't the debut Jimmy Bowen and Capitol Records had hoped for. There were reasons for that, and the biggest one I never saw coming.

CHAPTER 18

Turn Your Radio On

WHAT HAPPENED? It actually wasn't true that my first album on Capitol/ Liberty was a complete failure. Not at all. Those music videos produced to accompany the singles, the ones I had a ball appearing in, flitting around like a bird to locations all over America? I shot music videos in Miami, Fort Lauderdale, Houston, Nashville, and New York City. They all went into heavy rotation on both the country music cable channels, Country Music Television (CMT) and The Nashville Network (TNN).

Music video saturation and press coverage clearly helped elevate my public profile. If being a star means getting recognized when you walk down the street, or that people want your autograph, then I was becoming a star. Maybe not A-list, but not D-list either, instead sitting comfortably in the B-list ranks. It made me wonder if what folks did all day was sit around watching CMT or TNN.

The local weekly newspapers started to track my movements around town in their gossip pages. I was in the mix.

"Capitol Record's new talent Cleve Francis seen eating Neapolitan at Arturo's Tuesday evening . . . "

A comical misdial also got me boldface notice in *The Tennessean*, the town's newspaper of record. A friend gave me her number, but I must have misdialed, because a strange voice answered. The exchange went like this:

THE GUV'NOR: *Hello, this is the governor's mansion.*
ME (LIGHTLY, THINKING IT WAS A JOKE): *So are you the governor?*
THE GUV'NOR: *Yes, I am. How did you get this number?*
ME: *I don't know. I was calling somebody else.*
THE GUV'NOR: *To whom am I speaking?*

ME: *Cleve Francis. I'm an artist on Liberty Records.*
THE GUV'NOR: *This is Governor Ned McWherter and you've called my private number.*

We wound up speaking for quite some time. Gov. McWherter told me of his humble background (sharecropper's son, shoe salesman, beer wholesaler), and I told him about mine. Among other subjects, we discussed the great distances that tour bus drivers were forced to drive and the question of how long a driver legally could drive a bus without parking it to rest. Both road safety and the tour schedule had to be considered.

"I was thinking there should be a rule we would have to hire two drivers," I suggested. I had often thought the Danny Morels of the tour bus world were grievously and dangerously overscheduled.

"Of course I strongly support the music industry," he said. "I don't have to tell you how crucial it is to Nashville and the state of Tennessee. I'll look into this tour driver business."

Meaningful changes in tour bus regulations were eventually put in place. Did my offhand comment lead to relief for road-weary drivers? I'd like to think so. Gov. McWherter signed off by saying that while I might call him any time, I was most definitely not to give his phone number to anyone else.

A very cordial conversation, all told. My PR team passed on the anecdote to *The Tennessean*, so it went public the next day. I made sure not to reveal the governor's secret phone number.

Some of all this was by design. Capitol assigned an amazing woman named Bonnie Taggert to act as my publicity representative. If Bonnie had ever run for mayor in Nashville, she would have won in a landslide, because it seemed to me that she knew every single person in town. I first grasped the success of her publicity push when she took me out to breakfast early on in our business relationship.

We went to the Pancake Pantry, one of the places in Nashville well known for being frequented by music folks, and especially famous because so many country stars often showed up there. This was not a tourist attraction but an iconic Nashville breakfast restaurant where music industry hopefuls and those who had already made it shared the same space for a Southern breakfast. They didn't come to sign autographs or to get their pictures taken. They came to eat pancakes, sausage, grits, and eggs.

As we walked in, Bonnie looked across the busy restaurant. "That's Garth over there," she said.

You have to understand that in those days Nashville was Garth Brooks's town (still is, in many ways). He was the supernova not only in country music but in the entertainment scene as a whole, outselling even the Beatles in their heyday. His concerts were spectacular events. There sat the biggest star in the world in Pancake Pantry with his wife and child, fans and industry figures lining up to say hello.

When we slid into our booth, I made sure I sat with my back to him, because I didn't want to be staring at the guy or have Brooks think I was assuming a connection just because we were labelmates. Cool Cat Cleve, that's me, paying no attention at all to the eight-hundred-pound gorilla in the room. I certainly wasn't going to go over and make an overture. Celebrity culture can turn ordinary folks squirrelly, and I didn't want to fall victim. Luckily, this was before cellphone cameras came in big, so he didn't have to be subjected to constant fan selfies.

Bonnie sat across from me, and while we glanced at the menu, she looked up and said, "Someone is here to meet you." I turned and Garth Brooks stood beside me, holding his baby child in his arms.

"Cleve, my name is Garth," he said.

"I know who you are," said Cool Cat Cleve. I stood up, we shook hands, and I made a goo-goo face at his child.

"I just want to wish you all the luck in the world," Brooks said. "I like your music and know you're going to do really well with it."

We exchanged a few more pleasantries. I reached over and made a show of finger-shaking the baby's tiny hand. Then he went back to his table. I sat down to my breakfast. Bonnie had a grin on her face like the cat who swallowed the canary.

"That was good, Cleve," she said. "That was very good."

Bonnie Taggert served as my ambassador to Music City. She introduced me to Chet Atkins, a superb guitar virtuoso, yes, but also a towering figure in shaping modern country music as a whole while serving as the Nashville head of RCA Records and one of the label's key producers from 1957 to 1973. He signed Charley Pride to RCA and blazed the trail for Pride to enter into the upper echelons of Nashville stardom. At our meeting, Atkins and I had a long talk about his experiences working with Pride.

Bonnie set me up with local media to help boost my name recognition in town. A key placement was with Ralph Emery, known as the Johnny Carson of country music. He might as well have been called "Mr. Nashville" due to his near-constant presence as a country music disc jockey and radio and television host since the 1960s. Bonnie arranged for a slot on Emery's TNN cable show, *Nashville Now*.

"Be on your toes, Cleve," she warned me beforehand. "You'll be taped in front of a live audience, and Ralph can be a little sharp-tongued. Let's just say he doesn't suffer fools gladly."

"I got you," I said. "Thou shall not be a fool."

I recalled a story about Emery from 1968, when the Byrds—then working on recording their pioneering country-rock album *Sweetheart of the Rodeo* in Nashville—appeared on both the Grand Ole Opry and Emery's fabled WSM radio program. The group's foray into country-rock did not sit well with some audience members at the Opry—Roger McGuinn, Gram Parsons, and company were heckled—or with radio host Ralph Emery.

When McGuinn and Parsons visited Emery on his radio show, hoping he would play their new country-rock single, the Bob Dylan song "You Ain't Goin' Nowhere," Emery flatly told them no. He considered the song rock & roll, and he wouldn't play it on his country radio show. No one wanted to be on the wrong side of the "prickly protector of program purity" as one newspaper article described Emery.

I was getting good at being spontaneous while doing interviews, so I wasn't too worried. I learned the cardinal rule of not staring into the camera lens, and instead concentrated on interacting with the host or interviewer. The cameras would take whatever angle was necessary, and my job was to pretend they weren't even there.

Early in the afternoon of the *Nashville Now* appearance, I went through makeup and did a run-through with the band. As the show went live—or actually, as it went live-to-tape—Ralph Emery came out to introduce me on camera. After my performance of "Love Light," I crossed to the interview desk, where the host shook my hand. I sat down in the guest seat across from him.

"Well, what should I call you?" Emery asked. "Should I say 'Cleve,' or should I call you 'Dr. Francis?'" It was the same old "country doctor" routine I encountered everywhere.

"It depends," I said. "Do you have insurance?"

Ralph laughed, the audience broke up, and I suddenly found myself in the good graces of the dean of Nashville media. For a second number, I sang my country version of Brook Benton's "Endlessly." A great fan of Benton, Emery had hosted the singer on his show. He really liked my version and went on to invite me to appear multiple times over the years I spent in Nashville.

I was in the mix in town. In connection with the musician's union, I worked with the great Porter Wagoner on, yes, a health insurance committee. Wagoner, now a member of the Country Music Hall of Fame, also assisted in promoting my ideas on Black artists in country music on shows he hosted.

The problem was, the issue was, the fundamental quandary was—none of that helped move records. All the media appearances, all the autographs

I signed, all the mentions in the monthly *Music City News* tabloid, all the "hey-how-are-you's" that came my way from Nashville royalty, it was like icing that had no cake underneath. With *Tourist in Paradise*, I learned a bedrock-basic lesson.

Nothing matters if country radio won't play your music.

★ ★ ★

Tourist in Paradise was released in March 1992. I had never witnessed anything like Liberty's radio outreach effort, which spanned the entire country.

I held the mistaken assumption that with the tracks in the can, my work was done. In the months between cutting the album and its release, I learned a hard lesson in the obligations of a recording artist. I don't think I've ever worked so hard, and that's coming from a kid who did manual labor under the boiling Louisiana sun.

For three months, going out two weeks at a time, my radio promotion team and I divided into four groups, made the rounds of every single country radio station in the known universe—at least it felt that way.

Bill Catino, Capitol's head of radio promotion, and his running buddy, Sam Cerami, put me through the paces. The tour was grueling, but it was also golden. These two Italian guys did everything top shelf, top drawer, top quality. That included always flying first class, a new experience for me.

Bill and Sam loved food. They always favored the absolute best places to dine in every town we visited, including the world-class restaurant scenes in New York and San Francisco. I didn't know jack about Italian food, and for sure didn't understand that there was something called a formal "meal structure." I learned on that tour. The servers brought out huge trays and I dug in, thinking this was the entire meal, when it was just the antipasto. The food just kept coming, the *primo*, the *secondo*. I was already full and the kitchen still laid it on. I thought, where am I going put all this?

Also on my promotions team in charge of the Northeast region was Terry Stevens, who had been a big-time radio personality on Chicago's WKQX. As we traveled the country through the frigid temperatures in the heart of winter, Terry told me more than I ever wanted to know about the music business. The inside story, as Terry presented it, wasn't all that pretty. It's like what they always say about the legal profession and sausages: You never want to peek behind the curtain and watch how it actually gets done.

During my radio tour I was still living in Alexandria, and Capitol/Liberty organized the entire business—flights, hotels, meals, a per diem for incidentals, everything. Back home in Alexandria I'd get FedEx'd a stack of airline tickets thick as a checkbook. Off I'd jet, meeting up with Bill and Sam at this Hilton or that Hyatt Regency. It was dizzying, like "if this is Tuesday, it must be Tampa." We'd check in, then operate out of the hotel as our home base, renting a car to hit every radio station within driving distance.

The whole purpose of the extravaganza was to introduce me to station owners, programming directors, and DJs. Often Bill and Sam would throw listening parties, renting out a suite in the best hotel in the area. They'd invite the radio people to come and stay overnight, with the label providing the rooms. First we'd wine and dine the folks at the hotel restaurant. Afterwards we'd all adjourn to a "listening suite," where my album would be playing on the sound system. There were hors d'oeuvres and an open bar. I would work the room, making the meet-and-greet rounds, talking to people from different radio stations.

I found myself in a constant state of stunned amazement at the level of luxury. And these tours went on *all the time*, year in and year out, with the whole lineup of Capitol artists. Nobody thought anything of it, as though it were simply standard industry practice.

It was beautiful. It was also exhausting. After the dinner, the listening party, and being "on" for the schmoozefest, I'd stagger up to my room and collapse, falling into bed sometimes fully dressed. The label put me up in the finest, most elaborate luxury suites available. I barely experienced them. The next morning I would rise, but I wouldn't necessarily shine. We'd have to make a 6:00 a.m. flight and do it all over again somewhere else.

On this initial radio tour I first encountered the downside to being characterized as "the singing cardiologist." That was always the hook, in every media appearance, every article, every interview. The country doctor. I couldn't shake the categorization no matter how I tried.

Bonnie and the Capitol PR team piled on. They sent out a small blue plastic doctor bag to all the country radio stations. Included was a plastic stethoscope, a toy microscope, a pair of beach slippers, a plastic bag filled with sand and seashells, and a suitcase ID tag, everything emblazoned with the words "Tourist in Paradise." The "Love Light" single had a medical prescription form from Capitol, signed by me with instructions to play four times a day.

I couldn't deny that the country doctor concept served me well in getting television appearances and mentions in the press. It's an example of the "man bites dog" rule of thumb in the news business. A country singer wasn't news. Neither was a doctor. But a country singer who was also a doctor? Bring on the cameras and set up the microphones! I learned on that radio tour that being pigeonholed also had a negative side.

"So you're a cardiologist, am I right?" I remember a radio DJ in Kansas City, early on in the tour, asking me that question. "Why in hell would you want to be a country singer when you get to do doctoring?"

He was just a kid, in his late twenties, shaggy hair falling in his eyes. We weren't on air or anything, just talking in the shabby, claustrophobic confines of his sound booth. I had been questioned along these lines before, of course, but something in the kid's tone struck me. I thought, here is a DJ making, what? Five hundred a week, tops? I come along with all my privilege and major label standing, the celebrated country doctor, and how is he going to react? I heard the resentment behind his words.

We made a stop at a radio station in North Carolina once, where a program director adopted a slightly different tack. "I can't play your record because it's out of tune," he informed us.

What in the world? Jimmy Bowen, recording engineer Bob Bullock, Ray Pillow, some of the finest ears in the music business—they were going to let an out-of-tune record hit the bricks? Mixing, mastering, listening to the songs hundreds of times before they would ever allow an album to be pressed?

"What do you mean by that, sir?" Bill Catino asked, a man who had been more than several times around the block, too. He took offense.

"Yeah, you know, I can't play this," the program director said. "Send me something that's correctly recorded, then I can consider it."

The album had been recorded just fine. Superbly, in fact. He was just reaching for a reason not to play it. Maybe the "country doctor" label had proved its poison once again. Bill, Sam, and I left the station shaking our heads.

But there was nothing for it. I wasn't getting the spins I needed to break through. Media exposure wasn't the issue. *People* magazine ran an article. *The Today Show* on NBC had me on. *Music Row* magazine named "Love Light" Independent Music Video of the Year. Ralph Emery laughed at my joke.

Didn't matter. None of it mattered. Country radio acted as the gatekeeper, and the door might as well have been welded shut. The situation is different now, when songs break over the internet. Back then a single ironclad metric ruled the market. You had to go through radio to get to #1, to get the Country Music Association Awards or the Academy of Country Music Awards, to get on major tours, to play the great venues around the country, to make people aware of your songs and sell records. There was simply no way around it.

★ ★ ★

The situation with country radio didn't really hit home until I mulled it over later. But the brutal schedule of 1992's radio station tour accomplished one positive result. My idea of being able simultaneously to do music and medicine fell by the wayside. An emergency consult at Mount Vernon Hospital sealed the deal, the one where I missed Buddy's heart murmur on a first listen. I decided I could not in good conscience risk failing my patients.

So I pulled up stakes and moved to Nashville, essentially pushing my chips to the center of the table and going all in. Nineteen ninety-three was going to be my year to shine, I was sure of it.

The alternative to splitting my time between music and medicine was . . . having a blast on a concert tour. Being on the bus, playing gigs for audiences who loved my music, with Liberty Records on scheduling, promoting, and paying for the whole shebang. All I had to do was get up onstage and sing my heart out.

The label knew I had a built-in fan base in the Washington, DC area, so that's where they sent us first. The Washington Area Music Association held an annual event called "Crosstown Jam" and that year WAMA asked me to host. Next we hit Blackie's House of Beef in Springfield, Virginia, and a couple days later did a concert at my alma mater, the Medical College of Virginia. After we taped a TNN program called *Path to Stardom*, we traveled cross-country to Chicago for a show at a club called Synergy.

Ocean City, Maryland, Springfest '93. The Spring Fair in Greenville, South Carolina. The City Festival in Fuquay-Varina, North Carolina, a club called Long Branch in Raleigh, North Carolina, then a sold-out show at my home club, the Birchmere Music Hall. I flew out to LA for the ACM Awards, flew back for a concert in Chesapeake, Virginia, and then did a fairgrounds concert in Owensboro, Kentucky.

If it's difficult reading a full paragraph of tour dates, think how hard it might be to hit one location after another. And I know what you're thinking. Blackie's House of Beef? This wasn't a stadium tour, this wasn't even a concert hall tour, this was entry-level gigging, setting the foundation for a fan base, building it brick by brick. The dates might not have all been pretty, but they sure were fun.

At one time or another I opened for top acts, including Ricky Van Shelton, Ronnie Milsap, and Doug Stone. One stop on the tour even peaked into legend territory. At the Chesapeake summer outdoor concert series, I opened for Charley Pride. As far as I know, that kind of all-Black lineup had never occurred before in professional country music. The stage manager took me over to Pride's trailer before the show. We introduced ourselves to each other and shook hands.

"Yeah, well, best of luck out there," he said. I found him to be polite, reserved, and strangely remote. No fist-bump "hey, brother!" from him. By that time he had been in the business for almost two decades. I guess he had seen it all, because that's how he came off, not tired, just disinterested. Meanwhile I was experiencing one of the peak moments of my life. Me! In Charley Pride's trailer! I had to hold myself back from asking for an autograph.

The one-two punch of Nashville's Fan Fair (audience: 25,000) and Alabama's June Jam (75,000) represented the midsummer pinnacle of the tour, the only time we did indeed play to stadium-sized crowds.

For the June 1993 Fan Fair, the band and I met at the Shoney's parking lot, the same way we did for all our long, cross-country bus trips. The trip to the Nashville Fairgrounds lasted only a half hour, but the whole town seemed to have taken on a circus atmosphere. Folks lined the streets and roadways, heading to the show, many of them geared up with merch from their favorite artists.

Our driver arrived early in the loading area so the musicians could get to the stage for a sound check. We were parked behind the grandstand. As the band members climbed out to head for the stage, I stayed behind. I wanted to take a moment alone to say my prayers, go through some vocal warm-ups, but most of all savor the journey that had led me there.

Described not quite accurately in the press as "country music's Woodstock," Fan Fair brought together enthusiastic audiences and top acts for four feel-good days of concerts, special events, and autograph signings. The annual summer blowout resembled nothing else on the entertainment scene. Rock and pop might have had big summer festivals like Lollapalooza. What distinguished Fan Fair was the personal warmth it brought to the sometimes hard-knuckle world of the music business.

From the first Fan Fair in 1972, the emphasis always remained on face-to-face interactions between stars and their followers. After appearing in concert, musicians adjourned to booths set up in the fairground exhibition halls, where they would greet fans, sign autographs, and pose for photos. Fan Fair was part love fest and part gathering of the tribes, a chance for the audience to celebrate country music. Most importantly, fans could recognize how they were an essential part of the equation.

The love and loyalty flowed both ways. Fans waited hours for a chance to have a brief meeting with their idols. The artists demonstrated a similar degree of commitment. Garth Brooks once stayed in his Fan Fair booth signing autographs for over twenty-three hours without a break. Many artists had huge fan bases, and the lines at some of the booths stretched football-fields long.

I had attended the previous Fan Fair, but only as an observer. That was the year, 1992, when Garth Brooks became the dominant force of nature on the entire music scene. I witnessed him not only bringing down the house, but also dismantling the house, packing it away, and storing it for safekeeping. This time around I would be the one to open the 1993 Capitol Records edition of the event.

The band left me alone on the bus, careful to give me the time to get dressed and prepare for the performance. The bus driver was elsewhere. I thought over all the places I had performed, this gig being by far the largest audience to date. I've always been nervous before shows. I've concluded that this is a good thing, since I never wanted to be overconfident.

I did my vocal warm-up drills. Keeping the vocal cords happy forms part of the regimen of most singers, or at least those who want extended careers. Vanderbilt University Hospital had a whole clinic dedicated to treating musicians with throat issues. The rules were simple: no cigarettes, no hard liquor, control the air flow to the cords.

Filtering in from the grandstand outside came the dull hiss and roar of crowd noise, sounding tinny coming through the aluminum walls of the tour bus. I said a short prayer, after which I sipped my usual half glass of merlot. After having been shown how on the sets of multiple music videos, I could do my own makeup.

For a stage costume I chose the same short black jacket that I used in my promo photos for the "Love Light" video, the slick $1,500 number with a constellation of rhinestones on the lapel. Black slacks, black T-shirt. As footwear I slipped into the only product deal I ever entered, black Justin Western boots the company had furnished. The beautiful, durable kicks had served me well my whole time in Nashville.

The bus sound system played the three songs I would perform, "Love Light," "How Can I Hold You," and "You Do My Heart Good." All had been filmed as music videos and were in rotation on CMT, popular with the fans who were responsible for my being at Fan Fair in the first place.

Tony Hamrick rapped on the bus door and swung it open, standing on the pavement below. "Showtime, Bud," he said.

I followed behind Tony's six-foot-plus frame as we weaved through a path lined by backstage techies, photographers, TV cameras, and folks from the hospitality tents who wanted to see me perform. Tony handed me off to my manager, Clarence Spalding, who stood next to Bonnie Taggert, my publicist.

"Kick ass," Bonnie murmured to me, giving my shoulder a squeeze. Clarence shook my hand and said, "Go get 'em." I heard the stage announcer speaking about me and "Love Light," the song by which most people knew me. Applause swelled from the audience even before the announcer finished his intro.

"Capitol Records recording artist, Cleve Francis!"

The band launched into the intro to "Love Light" and I trotted onstage, smiling wide and greeting the crowd with both arms raised. I walked up front, took the cordless mic off the stand, and began singing "Love Light." The audience members knew the words, and thousands of voices sang along with me. Hearing that, feeling connected with America, with humanity, with the whole wide universe, moved me like nothing else in the world. I closed with "You Do My Heart Good." As I bowed myself offstage, twenty-five thousand people stood and applauded in unison.

Backstage, a cluster of reporters and photographers closed around me in what felt like a chaotic rugby scrum. I tried to keep my balance, physically and emotionally, amid the crush of attention.

The Nashville Network conducted an interview. "Your appearance today represents a historic moment in country music," the interviewer proclaimed breathlessly.

None of it seemed real. Besides, I had a meet-and-greet booth to get to. I extricated myself from the media crowd and followed Clarence Spalding to the fairground fieldhouse. Staffing the booth were Alfred and Judy Mitchell, close Maryland friends since my Singer's Studio days. I had looked out to see their beaming faces at almost every show I performed in the Washington, DC area. Along with my fan club president, Sandy Heuerman, they had driven the ten-hour trip to Nashville.

A long line of fans waited for me. For two and a half hours, I signed autographs and stood beside folks for snapshots. Many of those present brought copies of my first CD for me to sign, and photos they had taken when I performed in their hometowns.

I was euphoric.

The band and I took a long weekend off to decompress. Tennessee could be almost impossibly beautiful in early June, when the magnolia trees were in full bloom and fragrant breezes blew down from the surrounding hills. I tried to assure myself that this moment wasn't the happiest I had ever been, before concluding that yes, in fact, it was.

★ ★ ★

At another *Nashville Now* show taped that year, an instance of serendipity happened that I'll take with me to the grave. My old music professor at

Southern University, Dr. Huel Perkins, the man who "discovered" me, if anyone could say they had done so, gave me a call.

"I'm going to be in Nashville soon, traveling for the National Endowment for the Humanities," he said. "I wondered if you would be in town, or what your schedule is going to be like."

Normally at that point in time my tour schedule took me hither and yon, wherever the Capitol Records winds blew. But on the date Dr. Perkins gave me our space-time coordinates just happened to mesh. "It's great," I said. "I'm actually going to be on TV one of the nights you're here, and in the afternoon I'm taping the show. I'd be honored if you would be my guest."

Dr. Perkins and I had been in touch, not constantly, but here and there ever since I left Louisiana. He had gone on to do great things, compiling a stellar professional CV: an appointment as the director of education programming at the National Endowment for the Humanities, a long tenure at Louisiana State University as vice chancellor for academic affairs, named to the board of advisors for the Fulbright foreign scholarship program. He was always in the business of helping people realize their dreams.

Almost four decades after Dr. Perkins changed my life at Southern, I'd be seeing him in the flesh again for the first time. I want you to think back to all the folks that inspired you—relatives, teachers, mentors, coworkers, even bosses or superior officers in the military. How great it would be if you could reconnect with them after years apart, in order to demonstrate to them how their influence helped shape the person you've become. That's what Doc's visit meant for me.

I picked him up from his hotel, and we drove out to Opryland together. After all those years he still looked like a damned teenager. I had forgotten how impressive his physical presence could be. Part of it was that at six three he stood taller than pretty much any other person in the room. Doc Perkins gave off a bigger-than-life vibe, not only in my opinion, but to other people, too. He had a great laugh. "So handsome but so married," his female students would sigh.

We reminisced while driving crosstown to the Opry. "Cleveland," he said. "You've come a long way, boy." Even back at Southern, he would call me "boy" sometimes, but somehow the word sounded different than when, say, Charlie Holston used it.

"Well, I never imagined this," I said.

"Neither did I," he said. "I wished you well pursuing medicine, and here you are in Nashville. Did the medical thing, too. A twofer! I remember you sitting in my office on that damned stool I had, picking at a Sears & Roebuck guitar!"

I knew that Doc Perkins had had aspirations of his own. When he graduated from Northwestern, he wanted to be a conductor of orchestras, a position at the top of the food chain in the classical music world. Perkins died of a heart attack in 2013 without achieving that dream, but his heart would be gladdened to know that other Black musicians have broken through in the classical world. For example, Jonathon Heyward is the music director for the Baltimore Symphony Orchestra, Kwamé Ryan conducts the Charlotte Symphony Orchestra, and Thomas Wilkins is the principal conductor for the Hollywood Bowl Orchestra.

As we drove through town, I pictured Doc standing, baton raised, up in front of a philharmonic somewhere. He would have done great, but those doors had been closed to him. Our loss. Instead I took him to the *Nashville Now* show, sat him in the first row of the audience, and had Ralph Emery call him out as an honored guest.

After Fan Fair and June Jam, the tour the band and I were on picked up where it left off. Coyote Joe's in Charlotte, North Carolina, Silver Moon Music Barn in Buena Vista, Georgia, then back up the Eastern Seaboard to Merriweather Post Pavilion in Columbia, Maryland. Officially, Capitol Records promoted the campaign as *The Walkin' Tour*, not because we would travel from venue to venue on foot, but after the name of the second album I did for the label.

The other major change for me was that my original manager, Clarence Spalding, left after managing me for a year to take on a rising act, Brooks & Dunn. My new manager was Steve Small, a mild-mannered and well-connected Nashville insider.

Walkin' dropped in May 1993, and this time around Jimmy Bowen brought in one of country music's greatest and most seasoned producers, Jerry Crutchfield, to join as his coproducer. Here was the Nashville gold-standard triple threat, a musician-songwriter-producer, with platinum and multiplatinum spangling his resume just like the country stars with whom he worked: Tanya Tucker, Anne Murray, Tammy Wynette, Glen Campbell, Lee Greenwood, and many more. Crutchfield produced Greenwood's signature song, "God Bless the U.S.A."

Tall, bearded, and raspy-voiced, Jerry's trademark phrase in the recording studio was, "C'mon, let's listen down." Crutchfield and I got on well because among other elements of his background he was a great devotee of gospel music. The Little Preacher in me responded well to his arrangements and style of production. Ray Pillow and I went through a similar song-catching routine as we had on *Tourist*. Jerry Crutchfield's super-successful songwriting brother, Jan, contributed two tracks, "If You'll Stop Hurting Me," and "Heartaches on Parade."

While I was out on the road, having the time of my life with the boys on the bus, the album was slowly withering on the vine. Capitol released the album's singles, the title track, by songwriters Tim Nichols and William Robinson, and "I Won't Let You Walk Away," by Keith Follesé, Adrienne Follesé, and Chuck Jones. Neither charted.

It made for an odd disconnect, the euphoria of being on the road while in the meantime the album we were touring behind was turning out to be a wet firecracker.

On July 4, 1994, I opened a show for Doug Stone, the country music singer-songwriter just then coming off a brilliant run of one platinum and three gold albums. The venue was Fort Belvoir, an army base (and former slave-labor plantation) next door to George Washington's historic Mount Vernon home.

In the audience that day was my stepfather, Pete Francis.

A quarter century had passed since I helped my mother and two young sisters flee this man's clutches and move to Williamsburg. I had seen him a few times in the intervening years. Once when I visited Jennings I drove him to the dentist because his teeth were pretty bad, paying the bill for him. I didn't think of him all that often.

Mary Francis and the rest of the family agreed that Pete Francis should be allowed to meet his grandchildren, my sisters' kids, whom he had never seen. He spent a week in the area, staying at different houses, including my mother's. It was all very cordial and peaceful. He pronounced himself happy to see his children and get to know their kids.

It was only a coincidence I was performing in the area, so he was able to attend the one show of mine he would ever see. Standing in front of the mic, I glanced over at him a few times, standing in the VIP section stage right. He wore a straw-colored Western-style hat. I wondered what might be going through his mind seeing me on stage. His expression was hard for me to read, but he appeared proud.

I felt a faint sense of sorrow for the two of us. We just couldn't make it work. I guess he had his own demons bedeviling him. The opposite of love is not hate but indifference. I realized that's what I felt for Pete Francis, my childhood tormentor. Not love, not hate, just . . . nothing. Like seeing an acquaintance from long ago. That day of the Fort Belvoir concert would be the last time I would see my stepfather alive.

The tour ended on a strange and somewhat unsettling note. The 50th Annual National Peanut Festival ran for ten days every autumn in Dothan, Alabama. The event definitely wasn't peanuts as far as crowd size went, attracting 200,000 people every year.

George Washington Carver kicked off the very first peanut festival in

Dothan with a speech in 1938. The brilliant agricultural scientist more or less saved the South from the boll weevil and soil exhaustion by diversifying into cash crops and introducing peanut farming as a going concern. We used to call them goobers back where I came from. Mary Francis used to serve them up boiled.

That year the event organizers invited me to appear in concert and named me "Guest Grand Marshal" for the day. The weather that morning came in overcast and windy, and the November temperature had already turned chilly. Since Dothan lay only a short distance from his home in Georgia, Tony had arrived in town the night before. The band and I came by tour bus from Nashville, showing up on the morning of the concert.

"Follow me," Tony said as soon as he entered the bus, practically growling out the two words and nothing else. The big guy served as my director of security, and the tone of command he used meant I wasn't going to ask any questions. He led me off the bus, across a parking lot crowded with people and vehicles, and into a hotel attached to a nearby golf club. We went straight to Room 224, and he left me there with a warning not to open the door to anybody but him. I locked myself in and waited. What fresh hell might this be?

Folks around Nashville were always curious, asking me all the time if I ever encountered discrimination while on tour, wanting to know if there had been any name-calling, heckling, or booing. I almost exclusively toured in the Deep South, so I suppose the question seems natural. But I replied with all truthfulness that never once had any incidents happened during the whole time I was out on the road.

Most people who came to my shows knew exactly who I was. They had heard the music or seen the videos. Audience members attended without ulterior motives, simply because they wanted to see me perform. They brought their children and their children's grandparents along. They held CDs for me to sign, applauded and cheered and sang along with the songs. Long lines of fans greeted me after the shows.

So what was this? I could not have gotten any deeper in the Deep South than Dothan, Alabama.

A police captain returned with Tony. "We don't want you to feel overly concerned, Mr. Francis. It's just that a few of our officers had a little dustup yesterday with some knuckleheads, I guess you would describe them as skinheads."

"They just want to make sure you're safe and everyone's safe and no one makes any trouble," Tony said.

"Is it serious?" I asked. I wasn't alarmed, I wasn't afraid, I wasn't anything. I just wanted to know what was going on.

"There was some concern that these idiots might retaliate by causing physical harm to you during the parade," the captain said. "I mean, to you as Guest Grand Marshal."

"It'll be fine," Tony assured me quietly. "You know I'm there for you."

I looked at Tony, looked at the captain, and shrugged. "Let's go," I said, and we walked out the door to lead the parade.

That day the Guest Grand Marshal of the Peanut Festival waved and smiled at the crowd, standing in a bubble-topped white limousine. I traveled the entire two-and-a-half-mile parade route, starting out on Main Street, the town's east-west thoroughfare also known as Route 84. Below me in the back of the limo sat Tony Hamrick. Alongside him was an armed police detective.

The temperature had dropped enough that on-air TV reporters wore stylish fur jackets provided by a local high-profile area businessman and Mercedes-Benz dealer. A nearby Burger King stocked the backstage green room with sausage biscuits. A good down-home time was had by all. Other than peanuts, nothing happened.

After my concert, I rode in the bus back to Nashville, feeling the chill in the air in more ways than one. I was two albums in on my three-album deal with Capitol/Liberty. Lots to show for it in terms of buzz, not much in terms of record sales. A metaphor rose in my mind, the Apollo 13 astronauts returning from the moon in 1970, an explosion on their craft, their oxygen supply leaking down to zero. Commander Jim Lovell and pilots Jack Swigert and Fred Haise somehow made it back home.

I felt like in some ways I was limping back to Earth, too. As the weather turned colder that winter of 1993, I wasn't quite sure about my future in Nashville. I didn't think Jimmy Bowen would spring for the third album in the deal. If I was honest, I wasn't sure myself that I wanted to do another one.

I don't like bitterness of any kind. I don't like it in myself, and I don't like to be around other people poisoned by it. I remember getting cornered by a hapless failed songwriter at an album release party that year. He complained on and on about how he wasn't getting any breaks, how Nashville had crushed his dreams.

"You know what I call this place?" he asked me. "'Nashvile,' because it is, it's vile." I got away from him as soon as I could. Every once in a while you can see a similar lost soul wandering the streets of Music Row like the Ancient Mariner. Bitterness is the psychological equivalent of castor oil. It tastes awful, and it doesn't help much.

Rumors about me swirled around Nashville. One was that I had paid Jimmy Bowen and Capitol a million dollars to sign me. Sometimes folks think doctors are made of gold, but that idea was pure fantasy, an insult to me and to Bowen. Other rumors insinuated that Jimmy was in trouble at the label and was on his way out. That one proved true, since he left Capitol in 1995, the same year I would depart from Nashville.

If I was going to stay in Music City for another go-round, it wouldn't be for the minuscule chance of hitting the superstar jackpot. Evidently, it wouldn't be for record sales, either. It wouldn't be because I was too damned mulish to know when to call it quits. I heard the echo of Mary Francis's wisdom. "Be brave enough to come back home."

Clinging by my fingernails, I had to find another purpose to keep hanging around in Nashville. As I gazed around at the landscape of country music, I believed I knew what that new purpose had to be.

CHAPTER 19

Know When to Fold 'Em

IT'S SIMPLY HUMAN NATURE not to want good things to end. My time in Nashville seemed golden to me. Everywhere I went I met good folks with whom I enjoyed spending time, shooting the breeze, making music, laughing and joking like people do when they're happy.

In town my social life revolved around Bonnie and Joe Taggert, Ray Pillow and his circle, and my producer Jerry Crutchfield. Also in the mix was my new manager Steve Small. This core group of Nashville pals had extensive networks of friends themselves, who provided me with a wide-ranging group of acquaintances. I spent a lot of time on the road touring, but Nashville was my home base. The small apartment I rented meant I could retreat if I had to, though the whole scene was right nearby, from the recording studios and music publishers of Music Row to the clubs, restaurants, and bars of Broadway and Hillsboro Village.

Steve Small was well known and well respected in Nashville, not to mention very well connected, and he was always eager to use those connections to further my career.

"Do you golf?" he asked me, early on in our manager-artist relationship.

I told him that no, my cardiology practice barely left me time to cram in a bowl of cereal in the morning, much less a four-hour session on the links. My physical exercise had been confined to tennis. I well understood that golf fever gripped Nashville and all of Tennessee. Steve emphasized how good playing a round or two would be for solidifying business relationships and how great it was at forging friendships.

Bonnie Taggert's husband Joe happened to be a PGA-level golf pro who took me in hand. I dug into books and videos. The culture that has grown up around the game felt familiar to me—wild enthusiasm for the game mixed with the rueful understanding that perfection was impossible. I learned to temper my expectations for success, remembering a line I had come across in my reading: "You hit a ball as far as you can, and if you can find it the same day, you've won."

My game progressed to the point that I could join in on one of Nashville's premier charity events, the "Vinny" pro-am golf tournament founded by country great Vince Gill. Just being on the same course as champions John Daly and Payne Stewart lent a magical vibe to the event.

And golf was a gift that kept on giving. I had the opportunity to appear as a celebrity golfer in events across the country, including several tournaments sponsored by the American Heart Association. I also assisted Vince Gill in a local Nashville event aimed at introducing young kids to the game, broadcast on local television.

Golf wasn't the only game in town, either. At a celebrity softball game, I was approached by the great George Jones (yet another future Country Music Hall of Famer), who told me that he really loved the way I sang "Love Light." He told me that his label was trying to get him to do a cover of it, but he said no because he wanted it to be my song.

I had begun collecting allies and autographs. Ray Pillow made a point of taking me around backstage at the Grand Ole Opry, introducing me to country royalty: Roy Acuff, Little Jimmy Dickens, and—my favorite comic genius—the great Minnie Pearl. All three of them were already at that time members of the Country Music Hall of Fame.

But as 1994 slid into 1995, it was hard to miss the signs that my time in town was ending. I looked in the mirror every morning and tried to convince myself to face the facts. When artists fall off the charts in Music City, bit by bit they turn invisible.

I had received an early hint of what was happening the year before, when the single "Walkin'" failed to break into *Billboard* magazine's Hot Country Singles chart.

Tony pulled me aside. "I think we're done, Bud."

"What are you talking about, man?" I asked, surprised. "We're just getting started. We haven't even been out on tour yet!"

"Right, and I know, I know," he said. "I just want to tell you the truth. But country radio is telling you something right now with 'Walkin,' which is a damned good song. But it isn't charting. Basically, if you want to leave your practice behind to go out on tour and everything, well, you can do that. But you're pretty much done."

A strong dose of the cold, hard truth. Even though I heard Tony's words, I was also the son of Mary Francis, who taught me never, ever to give up easy.

"You're serious?"

"Yeah, because I know something about the industry. You've been out there, like, two years with 'Love Light.' So far country radio done turned its back on three singles from the first CD. Now one of your strongest songs, 'Walkin,' is being rejected. Might be time to stick a fork in it, Bud, because it's done."

My mind struggled. I could not, would not accept what Tony was telling me.

"You might be right," I said. "I'm just not at the point to stop."

We went through with the *Walkin'* tour and I had a fantastic summer. How could I quit? How could it be over when I was Guest Grand Marshal of the National Peanut Festival?

One of the biggest hits in country music also served as a wonderful example of everyday folk wisdom dished up in a song lyric. Don Schlitz wrote "The Gambler," and Kenny Rogers made it famous. I'll be damned if those words don't go through the minds of people all over the world whenever they're faced with hard choices.

You've got to know when to hold 'em
Know when to fold 'em
Know when to walk away
And know when to run

Coming back to Nashville after the tour, I watched Tony's doom scenario slowly becoming a reality. Despite the efforts of my promotions team and the reaction of the fans on the tour, all of the singles released from the *Walkin'* album flatlined. I braced myself, expecting any minute to get a call from Jimmy Bowen with the news that Capitol wouldn't pick up the option for a third album. Instead, he surprised me by approving the project.

"We just need to hook you up with a different producer," Bowen said.

At that point, I could have bowed out graciously. What stopped me was the thought of leaving behind a legacy, a body of work in Nashville that would prove I was more than just a minor blip on the radar. Other Black artists could take heart about what I had achieved. A three-album major label run could not be easily dismissed.

This time Bowen assigned Robert Byrne to the project. Though Byrne had a full head of white hair and a salt-and-pepper beard, he actually was younger than any other producer with whom I worked. He had learned his craft as a songwriter and producer in Muscle Shoals under the tutelage of the great Rick Hall at FAME Studios. I felt a huge blast of positive energy when he came on board. Byrne strongly felt that as a songwriter and with his contacts around Nashville, he could deliver that one crucial track I would need to have a real impact on the charts. He owned his own home studio, and we recorded the album there.

You've Got Me Now dropped on August 23, 1994. Byrne had various soundproof rooms in his house, and I recorded many of the tracks in one or another of those rooms. For one of the singles, "Love or the Lack Thereof," Vince Gill, a good friend of Byrne's and a friend of my publicist Bonnie Taggert, came over to the house and sang background vocals. Because of the line-dancing craze that was going on around the country, Bowen believed this would be the first single from the album.

Despite a slick video, "Love or the Lack Thereof" failed to chart.

Byrne himself wrote the album's title song, "You've Got Me Now," a beautiful country ballad that somehow seemed to describe the situation that I was in. Without me even realizing it, the titles of my three Capitol/Liberty albums reflected my status in Nashville. The first year in town I was a tourist in paradise, the next year I was walkin', and by the third year the music business had got me and was gently guiding me to the exit.

Through one of my contacts from the days of Moses Dillard, Rev. Nelson Wilson, we reached out to pop star Patti Austin to cut a duet with me of a Mike Reid song, "We Fell in Love Anyway." Capitol released the song as the second single from the album, accompanied by a wonderful video shot against the backdrop of New York City.

What's the definition of insanity that folks always talk about? Doing the same thing over and over and expecting a different result. We all understood that the song would probably not chart. I wanted it on my CD simply because I was elated to record with Austin, one of the strongest Black female voices on the planet.

By that time the promotions team at the label appeared less and less enthusiastic. They took longer to return my calls and provided no more promotional swag like the plastic doctor's bag that had gone out with the first album. I continued to make TV and media appearances, but I was just marking time. The tour gigs became less frequent. My band turned restless, with key members peeling off to tour with other artists. My keyboard player, Mark Jordan, took a job with Bonnie Raitt.

One of the last concerts on the final tour turned out to be one of the strangest. I knew it was an evil omen when I walked out of Shoney's restaurant and saw parked in the lot the tour bus Tony had nicknamed the Brown Bear. It had come to this. You know your position in the Nashville pecking order has dropped when you board the lumbering, ancient vehicle, realizing that it was yours only because no other artist would be caught dead in it.

We were happy to be doing a gig, any gig. Even though the venue was in his home state of Georgia, Tony had never heard of the place, an outdoor concert venue deep in the sticks of Putnam County. When the driver pulled the Brown Bear into the place, it was if we had entered an alternate reality.

A giant multicolored Egyptian temple sat in the middle of the meadow where the stage was set up. We had entered TamaRe, the compound of a quasi-religious group led by a charismatic leader. Born in Boston as Dwight D. York, he went by a lot of names, some of them trademarked and one that came equipped with longitude and latitude coordinates. The list of the man's monikers ran long:

> Dr. Malachi Z. York-El, H. E. Dr. Malachi Kobina Yorke™, Imperial Grand Potentate Noble: Rev. Dr. Malachi Z. York 33°/720°, Consul General: Dr. Malachi Z. York ©™, Grand Al Mufti "Divan" Noble Rev. Dr. Malichi Z. York-El, As Sayyid Al Imaam Issa Al Haadi Al Mahdi, Irie I Sayyid Al Mumbra Issa El Haajidi Tundi, the Divine and Noble Blackthello

The regal, white-bearded figure who approached us didn't introduce himself to us by any of those names. "I am Ben of York," he said, trailing behind him a retinue of colorfully clad courtiers.

TamaRe proved to be a seriously strange realm. The United Nuwaubian Nation of Moors, a Black nationalist sect that followed a religion created by Ben of York, combined elements of ancient Egyptian beliefs, UFO lore, and random conspiracy theories. Among his many roles, York saw himself as a great artist, singing and recording music, also under a dizzying array of names, labels, and groups. "Jackie and the Starlights" was one of the straightest.

Despite all expectations, the concert went off better than any other on the tour. The audience of several hundred Black Nuwaubians knew all my songs and sang the lyrics along with me. York's daughter took the stage and sang a country number. I thought I had died and gone to heaven. Finally, I sang before a Black audience who loved country music.

(TamaRe was a far different experience from my appearance before a Black audience in San Antonio, Texas, in 1993. I was hired by the venue to perform at the National Black Events Planners Convention. Before I could finish my third song, every member of the audience had walked out. Every single one! What I was doing wasn't Black music to them. I felt totally humiliated and embarrassed.)

Ten years after the TamaRe concert, I was disabused of any notion that the Nuwaubian compound in the Georgia outback was heaven, coming to realize the place was instead a version of hell. A federal court convicted Dwight D. York of multiple child molestation and RICO charges, resulting in a prison sentence of 135 years. He resides to this day in a maximum-security prison in Colorado.

★ ★ ★

I had been in tough spots before in my life, but the last year I spent in Nashville began with what felt like my lowest point. All the work, all the energy, all the folks pitching in to help me—had it just been wasted time? With gigs drying up I had a lot of time on my hands. I had been on the receiving end of a thorough education in the days and ways of the Nashville country music scene. I began to dwell on what it meant.

"I like your voice," Jimmy Bowen had told me, during that first meeting around his kitchen table. "You're like Charley Pride, you know, because neither of you sound like Black singers."

He meant it as a compliment, and I tried not to take offense. How can anyone be upset at being compared to Charley Pride? Bowen's comment represented an admission of a reality that in some sense I already knew. Any participation by Black artists in country music required an almost complete act of sanitation, a scrubbing away of any hint of vocal "Blackness."

Charley's first record was released without a photograph. Only after his voice had won over the public did his picture surface. Even then, he recollected showing up at concerts and walking out on stage, saying he could hear a pin drop when the audience realized that he was that singular rarity, a Black country singer. Charley Pride had been held up as the paragon he was, but he also served usefully as the sole symbol of Nashville's full acceptance of people of color.

Back then country music functioned as a dome as surely as Jennings, Louisiana, as surely as the medical schools in the nation. Black folks weren't alone in experiencing Nashville that way. The great country star of the 1950s, Kitty Wells, had to break through the industry's stubborn resistance to female singers. A common rule for country DJs at the time dictated never cuing up back-to-back female singers, because women didn't sell ads or records. Johnny Rodriguez served as the Charley Pride of Latino country artists, one of the pioneers in a realm where few others gained acceptance.

Pondering my fortunes, I formulated a basic premise. We are all born with the voices we have. When I released "Martin," I heard responses that made for a classic double bind. It seemed my voice sounded too white for Black radio and too Black for white radio. I felt no anger about the characterization, just puzzlement and frustration.

My vocal style arose from listening and loving the music of Sam Cooke, Johnny Mathis, Nat King Cole, and Brook Benton. I thought of the singers

I modeled myself on. None employed the Black dialects of the South, the voices of the blues, field hollers, and work chants—and early country music.

Sam Cooke was born in Clarksdale, Mississippi ("Ground Zero of the Blues"), but his family moved to Chicago when he was two years old. Benton came from South Carolina but he, too, moved north. Texas-born Mathis relocated to San Francisco at age five. Nathaniel Adams Coles, later Nat King Cole, spent his childhood in his home state of Alabama. Then the Coles family moved to Chicago, where Nat attended the same high school that Sam Cooke enrolled in years later.

All four of my vocalist idols were products of the Great Migration. The Black community changed during the period when they were coming up. The beginning of a middle-class culture had developed. How did a "Black voice" sound? There was no one answer to that question, since the sound could be as smooth as Mathis or as rough as Screamin' Jay Hawkins. The preconceived notion of a Black voice had become seriously outdated, even though Jimmy Bowen had embraced the concept as late as the 1990s.

When I finally thought I understood the true scope of the situation, I purposefully tried to remain cool-headed and logical. Anger is a natural human emotion, but it rarely makes change. I first learned that lesson from Mary Francis, a truth later reinforced by Gandhi and King. Country music had simply persisted with a leftover, wholly antiquated belief. Times had changed, but the establishment hadn't.

Strictly in business terms, it made no sense. A healthy percentage of the Black population in America listened to country. Millions were there to be made from this slice of the demographic pie. Here I thought y'all were capitalists at Capitol. What was stopping you?

Art is impossible to sanitize, homogenize, or pasteurize. Creativity is like matter in the universe, an amount that can't be added to or destroyed, but is simply transformed into different states. Removing the rhythms, voices, and sounds of the African cultural influence cannot be done, and not just in country but in any form of American music.

After all this pondering I experienced what a professor of mine used to call "a blinding glimpse of the obvious." On a cool evening on the cusp of spring, I happened to be walking along Broadway near the Ryman Auditorium. The wise words of Moses Dillard surfaced in my memory.

Actually, he had voiced something of a challenge. Back when we were working on *Timeless*, Moses had taken me on a field trip to the Ryman. In those days you could walk right into the place, savoring the great hall, the old-fashioned wooden seating, the numberless ghosts of the past. The Grand Ole Opry put on its first shows at the Ryman, and some stubborn traditionalists maintained that country had never been the same since the Opry moved across town to Opryland.

"Only two Black acts ever in history appeared on that stage," Dillard told me, shaking his finger at the front of the auditorium. "That would be DeFord Bailey and Charley Pride. You play your cards right, Cleve, you have a good chance to be the third one up there."

It was a powerful statement, and it hit me hard. It was only later that I found out that a few other Black acts had appeared on the Opry: Bobby Hebb in the 1950s with Roy Acuff's band, Linda Martell in 1969, the Pointer Sisters in 1974, James Brown in 1979. But you get the point. Black artists on the stage of the Grand Ole Opry were few and far between.

I guess I hadn't played my cards right, because although I had indeed appeared at the Grand Ole Opry, I never got the chance to play the Ryman Auditorium. At that moment, standing on Fifth Avenue North in front of the fabled Mother Church of Country Music I knew what I had to do.

Until then I had been relatively quiet about my insights into the country music scene, concentrating on doing everything possible to break through. But I had come to understand that however much talent I might possess, it was not going to do the trick, because the voice came along with a Black skin.

Going forward, I decided, I would work for change. I embraced the idea of "good trouble," that John Lewis, the civil rights leader and congressman, put forward. "Get in good trouble, necessary trouble," he said, "Help redeem the soul of America." Just replace "America" with "country music" in that quote, and you'd have my mission impossible. For my last year in Nashville, I would make it my goal to figure out how to move the needle, inviting more Black artists and Black audiences to join the country music family.

To lampoon the old "Got milk?" dairy industry advertising campaign, I would say instead "Got MLK?" Martin Luther King Jr. always managed to accomplish change by appealing to the moral conscience of society. Rather than bow out quietly, I would use my remaining time as an active major label artist to appeal to the moral conscience of music industry folks. I'd tug on the sleeves of every contact I had made, buttonhole label executives, producers, and media folks, and reach out to any superstar I could.

Moving the needle. I didn't know where the expression originated, but I always thought in terms of the old-fashioned, predigital input displays on a recording studio mixing board. The needle had been stuck near zero for way too long, throughout the early years, onward through Charley Pride and the era of the civil rights movement, through Ray Charles and *Modern Sounds in Country and Western*, and through the rise of the Black middle class. Jimmy Bowen, the agent of change, had tried. The needle had not really budged.

A common conception, largely unspoken but deeply embedded in the public consciousness, was that country music was created by and for white folks. The idea filtered into every aspect of the music business, resulting in an odd, skewed picture. It looked like a small number of handsome, almost identical white cowboys dominated the country music airwaves and the nation's concert stages. Two or three female singers also figured in. I know it's more complicated than that, but sometimes that's how it felt back then. No room at the top.

The typecasting cycle had been going on for decades. I heard an echo of the stereotype myself voiced by fans I met out on the road. I'll always remember a young Black kid who came up to me after a concert in Maryland.

"Love your voice, brother," he said. "But I can't figure why you're fooling with country music. That stuff's for rednecks!"

Advertising powers commercial radio. It's different now, with various ad-free subscription services. But the radio public represented the sweet spot, the coveted music buyer. The formula reflected the preconceptions and biases of the people in the business.

How could it be otherwise? With all respect to the late, great Charley Pride, it was as though the country music industry had shook the music tree and only a lone Black man who could sing country music fell out. Thus the marketing efforts in the genre included a single Black man and no Black women.

I wondered a lot about Pride, how he probably walked a tightrope during his time as a star. Could he have turned advocate as Harry Belafonte had done, vocally and publicly supporting the civil rights movement? What kind of message was he getting from the Nashville establishment? *Watch what you say, because we will not take kindly to any form of criticism from you.* We've seen just how vicious blowback can be. Just ask the Dixie Chicks.

The pernicious "for white folks only" idea had to be pulled up by the roots, because it wasn't going to go away by itself. I had no reason to abide by any code of silence. I could not be blocked from exposure on country radio any more than I already had been. This was 1995, and I could and would go public with my opinions and experiences. As Kris Kristofferson wrote and Janis Joplin sang, "Freedom's just another word for nothing left to lose."

Nobody came right out and said it, but I knew what some folks were thinking. The country music status quo was not at fault. It was me. I was to blame. If I wanted to move the ding-dang needle so much, I should have released some hits. In one of his films Woody Allen takes advice from a group of visiting space aliens. "Do you want to make the world better?" the little green men ask him. "Make funnier movies!" Want to change Nashville for Black artists? Make hit records!

What can anyone do with that sort of generalized input? I had done the best I could with the resources I had. I loved the songs Ray Pillow and I found. The material had passed muster with Jimmy Bowen, the agent of change, a man who possessed some of the best ears in the business.

I began talking to anyone who would listen about the situation of people of color in country music. I consulted with Rev. Nelson Wilson, a professor at American Baptist Theological Seminary, to whom Moses had introduced me. I met with Prof. Charles K. Wolfe of Middle Tennessee State University at Murfreesboro, an author, music historian, and biographer of Lead Belly. He judged the structure of the country music industry to be "inherently flawed," and urged a campaign for change.

Dome busting begins with an idea, a moral stance. That's how it happened with the abolition movement in this country, and that's how it happened with dismantling Jim Crow. I beat the bushes of the country music establishment, searching for those who believed in the idea that all people deserve a fair shake and an equal chance. Once formulated, a moral proposition such as that never fades. Swelling like a stream of water, it grows more and more powerful and begins to eat away at the foundations of the dome.

I knew that there were people who believed the posture of the industry toward people of color was inherently flawed. The look on the faces of especially the young people I met when I came to Nashville told me that. There were other agents of change besides Jimmy Bowen, powerful and prominent Music City figures such as producer Tony Brown and Atlantic Records exec Rick Blackburn.

The real breakthrough came when I spoke to Jim Ed Norman, president of Warner Bros. Nashville. I had met him earlier, when I sang on a children's album released on the Warner label and he produced the song I contributed. Norman was well aware of the issue of diversity in country music. He recommended that I speak to a Black woman from New York he had mentored, MaryAnne Howland, a marketing specialist who had recently moved to Nashville.

For our organizational meetings, Jim Ed provided use of the boardroom at Warner Bros. He also enlisted the assistance of Gail Hamilton, manager of Take Six, a Black vocal group that Jim Ed had signed. That's how networking happened, Wilson to Wolfe to Norman to Howland to

Hamilton. Tinkers to Evers to Chance. By the time we pulled together a first organizational meeting in the boardroom at Warner, twenty people showed up.

I opened the discussion by talking about the need for an umbrella trade organization, an entity to bring together Black artists and others working in country music. Adopting the name Black Country Music Association (BCMA), we put our heads together and dreamed big. Ideas ricocheted around the boardroom. We imagined a personnel resource for newcomers, a place where lists of music venues could be accessed, networking events where connections with music executives could be forged, a tour of Black acts.

What would have helped me when I had hit town three years before? I spoke about the willow tree in my backyard growing up. "That's what our group could represent for newcomers to Nashville, a sanctuary and a place for artists to develop their craft." I thought back to Rev. Collins and the help he gave to a young stranger new to Williamsburg, making me welcome and providing a safe haven.

Figuring into the BCMA mandate would be a push to educate both the Black and white public about the role that Black America had played in the nation's homegrown music of the soil, a sound that arose from a whole chorus of different voices. Some of those Black voices were writing songs that white artists turned into massive hits, numbers that helped transform the musical landscape of America.

To pick just one example out of many, rock & roll pioneer Otis Blackwell helped write Jerry Lee Lewis's barn burner "Great Balls of Fire" as well as cornerstone songs of Elvis Presley's early career, including "Don't Be Cruel," "All Shook Up," and "Return to Sender." Presley reportedly patterned his vocal interpretations after Blackwell's original demo recordings.

Blackwell also cowrote the torch song standard "Fever," which chanteuse Peggy Lee made popular but which was covered by nearly everyone, from Presley and Madonna to Michael Bublé, Bob Dylan, and Beyoncé. Songs don't know the skin color of their creators.

The country music idiom remains wide open for Black songwriters. During the period I was working on the BCMA in Nashville, songwriter Alice Randall cowrote "XXX's and OOO's (An American Girl)," a #1 country hit for Trisha Yearwood. The narrative style of the genre can yield fresh ways of expression, material rising directly from the Black experience. Lift every voice and sing, indeed. Beyond songwriting and performance, the music industry needed people of color to be involved in all of its aspects, including production, publishing, videography, and media. The BCMA had its work cut out for it.

The group selected me to be the first president of the BCMA. Accepting the position, I emphasized the need to seek private or institutional money to fund the effort. Without support, the group would exist only in the excited minds and grand plans of a few participants.

For my first official act, I traveled to Philadelphia for a conference of Black pop musicians, where I accepted an award on behalf of the country music pioneer DeFord Bailey. After sitting next to the great saxophonist Grover Washington Jr. at the banquet, I rose to give a brief account of Bailey's life. The evening represented the first time country music was included in the group's programming. I later visited the DeFord Bailey's gravesite and passed the award on to his son.

Back in Nashville, Rev. Wilson and I arranged a tour of the Country Music Hall of Fame and Museum. There we found a receptive audience that supported the idea of enlarging the range of artists involved in the field. Not only an accredited museum, the organization also reissues historic recordings, publishes books on country music, and holds an annual event inducting new members to the Hall of Fame. We wound up our visit by meeting the some of the museum's top executives, including CEO Bill Ivey, Deputy Director Kyle Young, and staff.

"You know, we get very few Black visitors to the Hall," said Ivey.

I coughed into my hand. "There's no reason for Black visitors to come," I said. I had just toured the museum, where the displays highlighted only two Black artists, DeFord Bailey and Charley Pride.

"Let me show you something," said one of the staffers. He led Rev. Wilson and me to the museum's basement, where a huge array of file cabinets held documents related to country music. Stored neatly away in hanging files were folders of material on every artist, every event, every relevant media mention.

The staffer opened a file cabinet and pointed out the files listed under "Black Artists." Bulging folder after bulging folder contained press clippings and concert reviews. I was astonished. I noticed that my name had already been added to the file. Laid out for me and Rev. Wilson was the entire history and impressive scope of an aspect of the music that had rarely been mentioned, much less celebrated.

The Country Music Hall of Fame and Museum has been described as the "Smithsonian of Country Music," and those files represented evidence for that claim. A stab of sadness hit me as I examined the dusty evidence of past lives, people who had thrown themselves against Fortress Nashville, only to wind up in the hanging file. I didn't have to mention that the material needed to be organized and displayed among the exhibits upstairs in the museum. That would soon happen.

In our humble way, the Black Country Music Association began to move the needle. A subsequent meeting at the Hall of Fame spurred the museum to compile and issue the 1998 anthology *From Where I Stand: The Black Experience in Country Music*, a three-CD box set showcasing the music of Black country artists through the decades. I'm proud to say that in 2024 the box set was updated and reissued, expanded to four CDs.

Out of our initial efforts grew a campaign in the music media. TNN provided me with a "bully pulpit" to discuss the matter at hand on national cable. I wrote opinion pieces for *Music Row* magazine and *Billboard*. Here's a quote from one:

> Country music is enjoying its biggest boom ever and has spent millions to attract new fans, even reaching out to Europe and the Far East. Yet the industry neglects a potentially large market at home. Recent Simmons marketing surveys reveal that a quarter of African American adults in major markets listen to country radio.

Hit 'em with hard-and-fast numbers, I always think, hit 'em in their pocketbooks. Let's see, one quarter out of a total of forty million Black Americans? That meant an untapped market of ten million consumers was essentially being discounted and ignored. If appealing to the moral conscience didn't do it, appeal to the profit motive. What could be more American than that?

★ ★ ★

The road gigs not only kept drying up, they began to blow away, too. Bus rides that formerly were so much fun now turned painful and pitiful because we were traveling such long distances to get to the gigs. One of our last shows sealed the deal for me.

My booking agency set up a concert for us at a racetrack in upstate New York. Unfortunately, the organizers neglected to stop the races for the performance. Funny cars continued drag racing down the track, engines roaring, tires smoking and squealing. No one, not even the band, could hear the music.

I continued to lose my core group of musicians. The guys had to take jobs with other groups to make a living. Tony and I found ourselves traveling with new musicians whom we did not know. The sets suffered. I had already lost my keyboard player to Bonnie Raitt. Now Waylon Jennings scooped up my bass player. I consoled myself thinking that once upon a time I had been able to attract world-class musicians.

History continued to stalk me. For months I was dogged with news of the O. J. Simpson trial, then saturating the media. Everything seemed off, everything seemed to go wrong. The Brown Bear broke down on a roadside in Alabama. Tony and the driver had to open the transmission housing, rotate by hand the filthy, oil-fouled entrails of the gear box, and get us back on the road that way.

Let's see, I was thinking to myself. Might the universe be trying to tell me something?

You've got to know when to hold 'em
Know when to fold 'em
Know when to walk away
And know when to run

Well, I wasn't going to leave town on a run or anything, but I decided to return to medicine. Some had suggested that I remain in Nashville to keep my hand in the music business. I also could have stayed and worked in Music City as a cardiologist. But I decided to go back home to Virginia, as I had promised my mother ("Promise Mama that you will not let those people rob you of all you've built," she had said to me). My whole professional life, family, and friends were there.

I phoned Bruce Tinker, the first partner I had taken on at the cardiology practice I founded. I wasn't sure what the response would be from the group. According to the contractual agreement we had approved, Mount Vernon Cardiology Associates was under no obligation to take me back.

"Cleve!" Dr. Tinker greeted me over the phone. I felt a nostalgic twinge just hearing his voice. "You called at a good time," he told me. "The doctor we hired in your place just resigned. She decided to practice internal medicine instead of cardiology because it was less stressful."

Good news. The development struck me as similar to other times in my life, ones that indicated the hand of the Lord at work or simply a quirk of good fortune. I explained that before I saw any patients, I would need a few general review courses to catch up after my three-year absence.

Dr. Tinker and I talked it over. Given the accelerating pace of medical innovation, three years might as well have been a century. There had been many advances in both medical and surgical treatment of cardiac diseases. And yet I was surprised how good it felt, diving back into a world I had known so well for so long.

"The practice will be happy to welcome you back," Dr. Tinker said, signing off.

My time in Nashville staggered to a close. Tony and I cleaned up my little Music Row apartment so I could get my deposit back. We rented a U-Haul to carry everything I had accumulated over the time I had been in town. I returned the rental furniture. With me driving my Lincoln Town Car and Tony in the U-Haul, we set a course back to Alexandria.

The blind fiddler Dick Burnett published a popular number in 1913 called "Farewell Song," which eventually became the folk, country, and bluegrass standard known as "Man of Constant Sorrow." One line struck a sour refrain: "If I know'd how bad you'd treat me I never would have come."

Truthfully I didn't feel that way at all. I felt no ill will or resentment. I had been given a great gift. From start to finish, I had an absolute ball. As the Nashville skyline receded in the rearview mirror, more in tune with my feelings was a line from (once again) Bob Dylan: "I've got nothing but affection for all those who've sailed with me."

Riding together in convoy, Tony Hamrick and I headed east on I-40. Mt. Juliet, Lebanon, Cookeville, and Crossville. Just past Knoxville, we picked up I-81 north toward Washington, DC. A new producer at the NPR radio station in Nashville had recently invited me to come in for an interview. It aired on the day we drove back. As the radio signal faded and the Appalachian Mountains rose in front of me, I listened to myself talking about being a country artist. It seemed surreal.

After making sure I was safe and sound back in Alexandria, Tony flew to his own home in Georgia and retired from the business. We remain friends to this day.

Returning home to family, old friends, and neighbors, I formulated an easy answer to their "how are you?" questions. "Well traveled but still intact," I'd say. Mary Francis pronounced herself happy that I had kept my promise to her of not losing all that I had gained.

The day I stepped back into the offices of Mount Vernon Cardiology Associates, Karen Daniel was there to greet me with a smile and hug. I had started the practice fifteen years earlier with her as office manager. She had restored my diplomas and medical certificates to the wall of my old office, adding in framed articles about my music career that she had collected from *People* magazine, *USA Today*, and *The Washington Post*.

"Welcome back, Dr. Francis," she said. I realized no one had called me that recently.

"Thank you, and thanks for these," I said, gesturing at the vase of flowers Karen had placed on a corner of my desk. She gave me the same warm smile she'd given me just three years earlier, when she buzzed to inform me of a call from Ray Pillow.

"Well, I'll leave you alone to get settled in," she said. "Give a call if you need anything."

For a long beat, I sat and gazed at the walls hung with souvenirs from a life in music and medicine. I had learned the intimate connection between touring and doctoring. Every patient encounter is like a song, with a beginning, a chorus, and a bridge, a complete story in and of itself, lived in major and minor chords.

I recalled being onstage in the UK, standing alone with my guitar to do an encore of "Amazing Grace." *Here I am,* I thought back then, *singing the same song that I learned an ocean away under our backyard weeping willow in Jennings.* All the sweeter that the world's most cherished hymn was written by a former slave ship captain who reformed and became a dedicated abolitionist.

What a fantastic journey I had been on, I thought. You can go home again, but you won't be the same person as when you left. I had become a more polished performer, stood on stages across the country and in Europe and the Caribbean, entered the magical realm of the Music City. Had I busted open the dome of Nashville? Maybe only a little. A crack for others to pry apart further, until the whole dome would be dismantled, falling as completely as the walls of Jericho.

"Brother, I know you must be tired, but it appears that you are one mission short," Moses Dillard had said to me back when.

In pocket billiards as in chess, the best players think two or three moves ahead. Minnesota Fats always knew where his cue ball would come to rest after sinking the called ball in the pocket. His first shot would set up his next shot, and the next and then the next, and in that way Fats would run the table.

Looking over my life, it seems wondrous to me how things played out. I can see that Jefferson Davis High School in Jennings set up Southern University in Baton Rouge, and Southern University set up the College of William & Mary. Taking an advanced biology degree at W&M put me in a position for entry into the Medical College of Virginia.

Or to put it another way, that backyard willow tree set me up for Dr. Huel Perkins, who set me up for Moses Dillard, who set me up for Jimmy Bowen and Nashville. Music melded into science, which gave me medicine. Medicine allowed me music. Was I always thinking two or three moves ahead? I'm not sure I can claim any high level of cleverness, but somehow that's how it all happened. Never leave your cue ball on the felt without a shot.

I returned home with my two hearts still intact, one physical, one spiritual. I had undertaken the classic hero's journey, familiar from mythology, entering a strange realm and coming back with wisdom to share with the community.

My next gig would be as a cardiologist across the street at Mount Vernon Hospital. I wanted to believe I had lit a fire that was not about to go out. My story was not a cautionary tale but one of inspiration. Music remained central in my life, and the Birchmere would continue to be my home stage.

I'd always try to serve as a mentor to young artists. I would never stop advocating for change both inside and outside of the music industry. I'd keep on channeling the Little Preacher in my life, have him yell from the rooftops about social justice.

"The enemy is fear," Gandhi said. "We think it is hate, but it really is fear."

I remember the first day I entered Mount Vernon Hospital after my Nashville sojourn. The morning was sunny and mild. I would return to the same medical community of doctors, nurses, administrators, custodians, and engineers that had given me a standing ovation when I departed three years before.

Wearing a starched white lab coat stitched with the name "Cleveland Francis MD," I left the offices of Mount Vernon Cardiology Associates. I crossed the street to enter the hospital without fanfare and without the company of my wingman Tony Hamrick. A page on the intercom system greeted me soon after I entered.

"Dr. Francis, please call the Emergency Room." A sixty-three-year-old female patient, a lifelong smoker who still refused to quit, had presented with chest pains that morning. I headed over to the same ER where four years ago I had been summoned to see Pug Hall. Entering, I made my way to the patient's curtained bedside and introduced myself to her and her family.

"Good morning," I said. "I'm Dr. Francis."

END

Afterword

Where Are They Now?

Moses Dillard continued to mentor young musicians and promote Black participation in Nashville until his unexpected death from a heart attack in 1991, at age forty-five.

James Albert "Jimmy" Bowen left Capitol/Liberty in 1995. He lives in Colorado with his wife, Ginger.

Victor Armand Liguori, professor of sociology at the College of William & Mary, environmentalist, mentor, unofficial music manager, partner in talks spiritual and profound, died on December 7, 2020.

Arthur Lisi, musical director, arranger, producer, musician par excellence, continues to teach and work in the northern Virginia area.

Tony Hamrick lives on in happy retirement in Georgia, where an evil-looking gent with a gold fiddle recently tried to hire him on as a road manager.

Dr. Bruce Tinker retired after a distinguished career at Mount Vernon Cardiology Associates, and we remain close friends to this day.

Herbert Raymond "Ray" Pillow died on March 26, 2023, after spending fifty years as a member of the Grand Ole Opry.

Dr. Huel Perkins passed away on April 15, 2013, five years after he and Thelma celebrated their sixtieth wedding anniversary.

Pastor David Collins, who gave this Louisiana kid a safe place to land at Williamsburg's First Baptist Church, passed away at his home in Roanoke, Virginia, on August 22, 1970.

Dr. Nelson Wilson, a Nashville-area minister at Burns Springs Church of Christ for three decades, died on May 12, 2021.

The Black Country Music Association continues under the leadership of President Frankie Staton, promoting showcases in Nashville of Black country musicians from across the country. As president emeritus of the BCMA, I continue to provide administrative and financial support to the organization and I've performed at many of the showcases.

Mary Francis (née Bower) died in Williamsburg, Virginia, on April 26, 2022.

Cleveland "Pete" Francis Sr. died on November 25, 2017.

Landry Joseph "London" White died in Jennings, Louisiana, on October 18, 2013.

My five sisters . . .

Fayester Foucard (née Francis) graduated from Southern University, earning a BA in music. The oldest of my sisters, though she is two years younger than me, Faye went on to teach music at the elementary and high school level.

Lois Marie Broussard (née Francis) became a critical care nurse practitioner and the mother of two sons.

Nancy Carol Wells (née Francis) graduated from Shenandoah Conservatory of Music and played flute, guitar, and cello. She became a music therapist and had two children. She died on February 13, 2012, of pancreatic cancer.

Elizabeth Francis graduated from Virginia Commonwealth University and became a physical therapist. She later earned a PhD from Old Dominion University in Virginia.

Barbara Gilmore (née Francis) went to Louisiana State University and graduated with a major in music. She had two children, with her son becoming an engineer and her daughter earning a PhD in immunology.

My loyal dog Jack faithfully accompanied me during my formative years, living a full and happy life before passing peacefully, my best friend to the last.

After returning to Virginia from Nashville, I assumed my former role as president and CEO of Mount Vernon Cardiology Associates. Following the original model of inclusion, with a multicultural and multiracial range of personnel, the group added five more members and took its place among the leading cardiology practices in northern Virginia. I was elected president of the medical staff at Inova Mount Vernon Hospital (1996–1998) and president of the systemwide Inova Medical Affairs Council (1998–2000), representing physicians in the entire Inova network. I worked as a staff cardiologist for Inova Schar Heart and Vascular, retiring from clinical practice in 2021. Afterward, the organization requested that I join the administration, becoming the diversity advisor and a member of the Inova Inclusion Council. I developed the "Dream Big" program, which is aimed at inspiring underprivileged students to pursue opportunities in health care.

In 2018, I received the Pioneer Award from Inova Schar Heart and Vascular for service in the field of cardiology in the community of northern Virginia.

In 2021, I received the first annual Hazelhurst Award from the National Museum of African American Music in Nashville for my pioneering work on inclusion of people of color in the country music industry. My image and song "Walkin'" became part of the music section of the African American Museum of History and Culture on the National Mall in Washington, DC.

In 2023, an exhibit in Nashville's Country Music Hall of Fame and Museum featured my involvement in country music and the Black Country Music Association. I also received a 2022 "Icon" award from the Black Opry organization. My media experience includes network appearances on ABC, CBS, NBC, TNN, and CNN, as well as guest spots on TV programs such as *Larry King Live*, *The Today Show*, *Good Morning America*, *CBS This Morning*, and *The Statler Brothers Show*, with radio features on NPR, Voice of America, and the Grand Ole Opry on station WSM. I've appeared on stages from Nashville to the UK: Fan Fair (now CMA Fest) in Nashville, June Jam in Fort Payne, Alabama, and concerts in Morecambe, England, and Millport, Scotland.

In 2024, I was invited to deliver the open convocation address to start the academic year at the College of William & Mary. I joined a long list of prominent speakers who also had been given this honor, including poet and writer Maya Angelou and U.S. Congressman John Lewis.

Acknowledgments

A SPECIAL THANKS goes out to my lovely wife, Hardeep Francis, who not only spent a year archiving all my articles, videos, tapes, and notes, but who also served as a sounding board and provided vital input that allowed me to complete this book. Much gratitude goes to my dear friend, author Gil Reavill, for his advice and assistance in bringing my odyssey to the page. I'm immensely grateful also to the late Bill Ivey, who wrote such an eloquent foreword only a few months before his passing.

I owe an additional debt to the many good people who helped me along the way in my life, my work, and in the writing of this memoir. The team members at the Country Music Hall of Fame and Museum shepherded the project through to completion in ways that always made me feel I was in excellent hands. They include Paul Kingsbury (without whom this book would never have happened), Allison Moorer, Michael Gray, Jeremy Rush, and Kyle Young. Thanks also to the University of Illinois Press for their support and input.

After the "Love Light" video became popular, I received a call from a retired Lutheran church secretary by the name of Sandy Heuerman, who volunteered to serve as my fan club president. With her people skills and organizational expertise, Sandy became an invaluable ally, serving as my secretary and international fan club president well into the 2000s, when she retired.

Much gratitude to my "Nashville Cats" band: Bryan Cumming (rhythm guitar, sax, and background vocals), Monte Causey (background vocals), Dino Zimmerman (lead guitar), Mark Jordan (keyboards), Terry Wendt (steel guitar), John R. Crowder (bass), and Michael Clark/Billy West (drums).

I also want to give a shoutout to my band from the Birchmere era, including Myron Prosser, one of the best fiddle players in the business, Bruce Middle, a lead guitarist, two folk-country rhythm guitarists named John Georgiou and Mark Walters, background vocalists Darci Vanderhoff, and Steven Lisi, and bass players Jim Boberg and Bryan Fox, who played with the band at different times. I had a full-fledged rhythm and percussion section: drummer Eric Northern and percussionists Larry Boddie, Tony Duncanson, and Sam Turner. With me also were a steel guitar and dobro player, Casey O'Neal, and a fifteen-year-old cello prodigy, David Bendahan, the son of a nurse I worked with. Harmonica players included Roger Hart and Gary Green, and on flute and saxophone I had Terry Thompson, Davey Yarborough, and Robert Holmes. The U.S. military had a bluegrass band to entertain the troops, and from that outfit I recruited a master banjo player, Keith Arnesen. Of course, Arthur Lisi was heavily involved, working as my band director and providing keyboards. This was the full-bodied lineup for the thirty-song recording in 2007 credited to "Cleve Francis and Friends," entitled *Story Time: Live at the Birchmere.*

Many others helped me along the way in my life, my music, and my work. They include Melton Alfred, Kathleen Barry, Archer and Viola Baskerville, Dr. Andrew Besch, Jimmy Bowen, Dr. Douglas Ray Breaux, Ella Breaux, Sidney Briscoe, Dr. Garnet Brooks, Lois Broussard, Bob Bullock, Robert Byrne, Bill Catino, Sam Cerami, Charlie Chase, Katherine F. Clark, Dr. Lawrence Clarke, Rev. David Collins, Charles Cook, Lorrianne Crook, Jerry Crutchfield, Karen and Jack Daniel, Moses Dillard, the Early Birds of the Mount Vernon Racquet Club, Ralph Emery, Tina Eshleman, Fayester Francis, Nancy Francis, Holly G. of the Black Opry, Jack Gale, Dr. Mark Gallini, David Gapp, Barbara Gilmore, Gale Hamilton, Tony Hamrick, Katie Haas, Precious Hatchet, Charles and Marjorie Holston, MaryAnne Howland, Bernice Johnson, Betty Johnson, Eddie Jones, Nita Jones, Michael Jaworek, Eugene Krizek, Joan and Marty LaVor, Dr. C. W. Lee, Dr. Victor Liguori, Vicky Liguori, Arthur and Nancy Lisi, Amanda Martinez, Janice McZeal, Steve Moore, Dr. Jason Morda, Dr. Minh Ngo, Jim Ed Norman, Gary Oelze, Morgolis Oxendine, Dr. Huel Perkins, Huel Albert Perkins, Mrs. Thelma Perkins, Billy Pierce, Dr. Donald Ray Pierre, Ray Pillow, Dr. Narian Rajan, Dr. Gorman Redding, Bertel Reder, Ron Rogers, Steve and Patti Rosenberg, Dr. Arnold Rosenblatt, Dr. Michael Royfe, Steve Rupp, David J. Schweitzer, John Knox Singleton, Beckie Sipe, Steve and Laura Small, Clarence Spalding, Gail Spight, Frankie Staton, Terry Stevens, Dr. John Sunew, Juanita Thibeaux, James Threalkill, Dr. Bruce Tinker, Pam Tinker, Dr. John Titius, Lorna Totman, Daisey Voigt, Gloria

Wank, Nancy Carrol Wells, Janie West, Dr. Leslie Williams, Elizabeth Wilson, Rev. Nelson Wilson, Ron Wynn, Dan Zagami, Jean Zimmerman, Brian Zinsmeister.

And finally, I want to send out a very special thank you to all the fans of my music who entrusted me with their hearts and to all the patients who entrusted me with their lives.

Discography and Videography

1967 "The Willow Tree"/"It's Got to Get Better" (45-rpm single)
My first recording, done while I was a student at the College of William & Mary.

1968 *Follow Me* (vinyl LP)
Funded by Victor Liguori and fans, the album included many originals and covers of songs popular at the time of its release.

1982 "Light Up the Night"
This song was written for the "Lights of Love" ceremony at Mount Vernon Hospital in Alexandria, Virginia.

1983 "You Send Me"/"Desperado" (45-rpm single)
Recorded with folk/blues guitarist Billy Pierce, the self-produced single served as an audition demo for Moses Dillard and the *Break Out!* cable program.

1985 "Martin" (45-rpm single)
Produced professionally by Moses Dillard in his Nashville studio.

1985 *Timeless* (LP)
Produced in Nashville by Moses Dillard and me as a prime example of my soulfolk sound at its best. Contains several originals.

1987 "We're All in This Together"
This song was written for AIDS education. Video available on YouTube.

1987 "Reflections on the Wall"
A tribute to Vietnam veterans. Video available on YouTube.

1990 *Last Call for Love* (LP)
Produced by Jack Gale on Playback Records Nashville. Included "Love Light," "Traveling Man," and "Endlessly."

1992 *Tourist in Paradise* (CD album)
My first release from Capitol/Liberty, produced by Jimmy Bowen and me. Included a rerecording of "Love Light," released as a single, as was "You Do My Heart Good" and "How Can I Hold You"

1993 *Walkin'* (CD album)
Produced by Jerry Crutchfield and Jimmy Bowen. Included classic country and contemporary tunes from various songwriters.

1994 *You've Got Me Now* (CD album)
Produced by Robert Byrne. Included a duet with Patti Austin.

2007 *Cleve Francis and Friends—Story Time: Live at the Birchmere* (CD album)
Produced by Arthur Lisi and me, featuring a twelve-piece band recorded live at the Birchmere Music Hall in Alexandria, Virginia. Liner notes by author Kwame Alexander.

2023 *Beyond the Willow Tree* (LP)
A vinyl double album released by Forager Records. Contains all of the original material from *Follow Me* (1968), plus additional never-released acoustic tracks.

Music Videos

Year	Video	Director
1990	"Love Light"	D. J. Schweitzer
1992	"You Do My Heart Good"	Bill Young
	"Walkin'"	Sara Nichols
1993	"I Won't Let You Walk Away"	Joanne Gardner
1994	"Love or the Lack Thereof"	L. J. Kreussling
	"We Fell in Love Anyway" (with Patti Austin)	Dominic Orlando

Credits

"Circle"
Words and music by Harry Chapin © 1972 (renewed). All Rights Reserved. Used by permission from the Harry Chapin Foundation.

"Fixin' to Die Rag"
Words and music by Joe McDonald © 1965 (renewed 1993) by Alkatraz Corner Music Co. Reprinted by permission of Alkatraz Corner Music Co.

"Abraham, Martin and John"
Words and music by Dick Holler © 1968 Stonehenge Music (BMI) administered by Wixen Music Publishing, Inc. All Rights Reserved. Used by permission.

"Hey, Porter"
Words and music by John R. Cash © 1957 House of Cash, Inc. Copyright renewed. All rights administered by BMG Rights Management (US) LLC. All Rights Reserved. Used by permission.

"City of New Orleans"
Words and music by Steven Goodman © 1970 Sony Music Publishing (US). International Copyright Secured. All Rights Reserved. Used by permission.

"No Earthly Good"
Words and music by Johnny Cash © 1977 Song of Cash Music. Copyright renewed. All rights administered by BMG Rights Management (US) LLC. All Rights Reserved. Used by permission.

"The Gambler"

"What Is Success"

"Blowin' in the Wind"

"Martin"

Many thanks for lyrics reprinted by kind permission of Hal Leonard LLC.

Index

Note: Page numbers in italic refer to photos.

CLEVE FRANCIS is a singer, songwriter, and recording artist as well as a medical doctor with a specialty in cardiology. Born into poverty in rural Jennings, Louisiana, he rose through hard work and resolve to become the successful head of a cardiology practice and one of the few Black performers ever to record country music for a major record label as of the early 1990s. He made three country music albums between 1991 and 1994 for Capitol Records' Liberty imprint, and they included his charting singles "Love Light" and "You Do My Heart Good," among others. Throughout his life, Francis has written, performed, and recorded music—a through-line that intertwines with his education and medical career. The founder and CEO of Mount Vernon Cardiology, Francis is now retired from clinical practice and lives in Alexandria, Virginia, with his wife, Hardeep.

The University of Illinois Press
is a founding member of the
Association of University Presses.

Composed in 10.5/13 Mercury Text
with Caecilia display
by Jim Proefrock
at the University of Illinois Press
Manufactured by Versa Press, Inc.

University of Illinois Press
1325 South Oak Street
Champaign, IL 61820-6903
www.press.uillinois.edu